GEORGE GRANT AND THE THEOLOGY OF THE CROSS

The Christian Foundations of His Thought

George Grant and
the Theology of the Cross

The Christian Foundations of His Thought

HARRIS ATHANASIADIS

UNIVERSITY OF TORONTO PRESS
Toronto Buffalo London

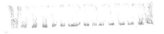

ISBN 0-8020-4875-7

Printed on acid-free paper

Canadian Cataloguing in Publication Data

Athanasiadis, Harris
George Grant and the theology of the cross : the Christian
foundations of his thought

Includes bibliographical references and index.
ISBN 0-8020-4875-7

1. Grant, George, 1918–1988 – Contributions in theology.
2. Philosophical theology.   I. Title.

B995.G74A83 2000   191   C00-932249-3

University of Toronto Press acknowledges the financial assistance to its
publishing program of the Canada Council for the Arts and the Ontario
Arts Council.

This book has been published with the help of a grant from the Humanities
and Social Sciences Federation of Canada, using funds provided by the
Social Sciences and Humanities Research Council of Canada.

University of Toronto Press acknowledges the financial support for its
publishing activities of the Government of Canada through the Book
Publishing Industry Development Program (BPIDP).

To my mother, Anna,
whose emotional and spiritual influence has formed the ground
upon which I stand

my wife, Leanna,
whose nurture, support, and encouragement have become a
daily source of sustenance

and my children, Hannah and Mark,
who both in their uniqueness of being have taught me what it means
to consent to the way of the cross

Contents

Acknowledgments

When one considers the magnitude of the task involved in writing a book, one cannot but acknowledge the miracle of its coming to be. But be that as it may, one must then note those special people who have contributed significantly to its coming to be. I begin with Sheila Grant, whose support of this book as reflecting 'the true George Grant' has given me tremendous confidence and encouragement in persevering to the end. Next in line must come my theological and spiritual mentor, Douglas John Hall, who has taught me everything of significance as a theologian and more, as well as the importance of consenting to the way of the cross as the only legitimate path to the resurrection. He along with his wife, Rhoda, also taught me to love George Grant and to see in him that 'thin tradition' waiting to be unfolded. The focus of this book cannot be separated from my work as a pastor, and in this regard I must acknowledge the support I have received through the research stage of the book by my flock at the Margaret Rodger Memorial Church, Lachute, Quebec, as well as the sustenance received during the final publication stage by my flock at St Mark's Church, Don Mills, Ontario.

In terms of the particulars involved in publishing a book, I cannot imagine a more supportive and helpful editorial staff than that of University of Toronto Press, and I mention especially Ron Schoeffel, Anne Forte, and Ken Lewis. Also to be noted is the gracious counsel of Simon Lapointe of the Humanities and Social Sciences Federation of Canada, as well as the federation itself, which awarded a grant toward the publication of the book.

Finally, I must acknowledge, as an incurable 'Calvinist' whose tradition gets knocked around in this book, the strange designs of divine providence which led me to discover through my struggles with George Grant a path to truth and sanctity which has shaped me decisively. *Soli Deo Gloria!*

GEORGE GRANT AND
THE THEOLOGY OF THE CROSS

Introduction

Who was George Grant? Some say he was the foremost indigenous philosopher Canada has produced, a thinker of popular appeal but also of deep wisdom and originality. He was a critic of modern techno- logical civilization who perceived early on its destructive possibilities for society as a whole as well as for the individual soul. He was con- cerned that the process of globalization made possible by technology was progressively reducing and, ultimately, undermining all distinc- tive nationalities and cultures. He was alarmed by the violence of tech- nological necessity which imposed itself over all aspects of human existence thereby negating authentic expressions of human freedom. Finally, Grant was dismayed at how technological priorities and the thinking accompanying them were displacing alternative sources of meaning and purpose rooted in pre-modern and pre-technological ways of thinking and existing. Technological development threatened to bring about a tyranny greater than any previous in history, for it was progressively eliminating any opposition to its vision of life in the most subtle and, hence, most complete manner.

While some have taken stock of Grant's criticism of technological civilization, others have dismissed him as little more than a paranoid pessimist. His 'lament' over the growth of global technology was rooted in the loss of his ancestral traditions, and an incapacity to open himself to the positive benefits of technology or adjust himself to the world 'as it is.' Grant, they claim, was so locked into his negative 'dirge' that he could not find happiness in the world and love it in spite of its imperfections. A minority, however, have seen behind Grant's criticism a positive love of the world, a love rooted in a commitment to the truth about the way things are along with a vision of how they ought to be. In order to be 'opened' to such a vision, however, one had to be brought to the truth. This required the tearing down of all the illusions and the pointing out of all the inadequacies about the way things are in the world. Only out of such a process of moving toward the truth and being stripped of all illusion and ignorance, was there hope of developing a genuine openness to the 'beauty' of the world in spite of the ugliness within it.

But how could Grant arrive at a vision of the beauty of the world if he was so preoccupied with its ugliness as heightened by technological globalization? Did he do it through political criticism? His writing and commentary on Canadian politics and history could very well suggest this. Did he do it through philosophical reflection? He referred to himself as a political philosopher who preferred ancient to modern philosophy and especially the philosophy of Plato. Did he do it through religion? He did claim his thought to be an attempt to understand his faith, the experience of which was a primal for him. Finally, did he do it through activism? His involvement in the abortion and euthanasia debates, as well as his continuing commentary on Canadian nationalism and national unity, could very well suggest this also.

But was there a centre to Grant's thought? Was there an idea or a set of ideas which governed his approach and response to the wide range of themes and issues he addressed? Was there a source of inspiration that opened him up to a vision of the beauty of the world in spite of all the ugliness within it? The intent of this book is to argue just that. There is a centre to Grant's thought and this centre can be named a 'theology of the cross.' Moreover, we will argue that this theological orientation is the inspiration behind Grant's love for the world even though the vast majority of his thought is taken up with pointing out everything that is wrong with the world as it moves into a technological future.

The phrase 'theology of the cross' was coined by Martin Luther, and Grant clearly had Luther in mind when he used it. Grant did not read much of Luther, however, and this phrase is used more in the spirit of Luther – or, better perhaps, more as a symbol – than as a result of a concrete engagement with Luther's thought. In fact, Grant's use of this phrase and the terminology surrounding it was developed in dialogue with other thinkers. Indeed, we shall argue that even though this phrase as symbol provides the structure and orientation of Grant's engagement of the issues that concerned him throughout his writing, the content is filled in by a number of voices the most important of whom is Simone Weil. What is critical is that Grant understood the implications of this phrase as Luther intended it, and this meaning shaped Grant's response to the issues about which he thought and the thinkers with whose thought he struggled. The language and concepts Grant used to express himself, however, were those of Weil along with other voices who helped him understand the essence of the modern world to which this theology was a response.

This book will be an attempt to unfold how Grant came across the theology of the cross, why it became so central for him, how it developed over the years in his mind as he struggled to understand the modern world as it was, and how it helped him formulate positively a basis for thinking and existing within such a world. The theology of the cross shaped Grant's response to the thinkers whose thought he engaged. It provided the focus of his analysis and criticism of the modern world. It opened him up to a way in which he could love the world in thought and practice in spite of the evil and suffering so prevalent in it.

Even before his untimely death in 1988, there was a considerable amount of writing devoted to Grant and this has intensified since his death. Current plans toward the publication of his collected works will only encourage this intensification. In the last ten years there have been articles, books, and a major biography devoted to his life and thought. Nowhere, however, has the focus of the present writing – namely, the theology of the cross as the centre of Grant's thought – been the subject of a comprehensive study. This fact can be attributed largely to Grant himself. Neither the theology of the cross nor, in a broader sense, Christianity was ever the topic of extended discussion or writing by him. Moreover, the references he does make to Christianity or to this theological tradition do not spell out in any detail how this tradition is related to his faith, or how his faith influences his thought. At the same time, however, Grant offers important clues and affirmations that clearly suggest these connections, and it is the burden of this book to unfold and develop them.

The Structure of Grant's Thought

Grant was not a systematic or analytic-type thinker. He approached issues through the combination of poetic imagination and a set of interpretive principles. The argument of this book is that these principles are rooted in the theological orientation/tradition named a theology of the cross. In chapter 1 we will consider Grant's formation from his earliest years up to the point when he discovers this tradition and its defining impact for his thought thereafter. In chapter 2 we will consider the definition and content of this tradition as developed by Martin Luther in the sixteenth century and why it became so significant for Grant in the twentieth. In chapters 3, 4, and 5 we will consider Grant's thought and demonstrate how the theology of the cross is the interpretive key for understanding and explicating it. It is important to recognize that Grant, like any profound thinker, went through a process of development and maturing. The theology of the cross remained central throughout this development, but his understanding of the modern world, humanity, and God, or the good, deepened over the years. Chapter 3 focuses on Grant's thought in the 1950s, culminating in his book *Philosophy in the Mass Age*. Chapter 4 focuses on the deepening of his thought in the 1960s, culminating in the first and last essays in *Technology and Empire*. Chapter 5 focuses on Grant's thought at its most mature stage in the 1970s and '80s, reaching its height in the essay 'Faith and the Multiversity.' In each stage or period of development, the theology of the cross offers the interpretive key. It operates in a dialectic between two poles – one critical and the other constructive or positive. The critical task of thought requires naming reality or the world as it is. This involves both an analysis of the modern world – how it came to be and where it is headed – and a criticism of all forms or systems of thought which obscure reality by making it appear better than it is. In this task, Grant will be supported by a number of thinkers and movements of thought. The critical task has its completion in the positive task for thought: the opening up of mind and heart to the good or God. In order to do this effectively, however, the thinker must come to the recognition of the limits of human abilities in thought and action in the face of reality. The recognition of human limits is the goal of the critical task of thought. Only then is there room for the birth of a genuine humility and openness to a greater reality above the human which can illumine and transform human thought and action in the world. This dialectic – the back and forth from critical to constructive/positive poles – is repeated at every new stage of Grant's development, beginning in the 1950s, continuing in the 1960s, and attaining maturity in the 1970s and '80s. At the conclusion of chapter 2, we consider in greater detail how the dialectic works within each stage of Grant's thought.

Chapter One

The Great Discovery

How did George Grant come across the theology of the cross? What did it mean for him? Why did it take on such a central place in his thought about the whole? To begin to answer these questions we must begin at the beginning. We must begin with the earliest influences on Grant's intellectual formation as well as some primal experiences which shaped his response to that formation and defined the orientation of his thought thereafter.

1.1. Grant's Roots and Formative Years

Although Grant had little positive to say about his early years or his roots, there is no question that many of the most basic ideas he either embraced or rejected can be traced back to the thought and activity of his progenitors. The three key figures in this regard are George Parkin, George Monro Grant, and William Grant. All three were Protestant educators, believers in historical progress, and promoters of imperial federation. All three were also believers in their divine vocation to work in cooperation with divine providence toward the realization of universal freedom and justice (the kingdom of God) in the world.

George Parkin was Grant's maternal grandfather and when he died in 1922, Grant was only three years old. Yet his influence on Grant was cultivated (one could even say imposed) by his mother and grandmother. Grant felt overwhelmed by the memory of his grandfather, and he spoke of his mother's dream that he was destined to follow in his grandfather's footsteps.[1] Parkin's rise to prominence was impressive. Brought up in a small Atlantic farming community, he went from a career as teacher and administrator to that of international promoter of imperial federation or, as he referred to himself, 'a wandering evangelist of empire.'[2] Parkin's dream was that of Canada, along with the other dominions, joining Britain in the administration of a worldwide empire based on peace and justice.

George Monro Grant also shared this dream. He was Grant's paternal grandfather and although he died in 1902, well before Grant was born, he also exercised a strong influence on the young Grant through his son, Grant's father, William. G.M. Grant's rise to prominence was as impressive as Parkin's. Also brought up in a small farming community, he emerged to become a leading educator and social force in Canadian society. As principal of Queen's University, he transformed it from a small Presbyterian college into a large research university.[3]

Against those who argued that Canadian independence was hindered rather than encouraged by ties with Britain, imperialists argued that without the British connection Canada would be swallowed up by the republic to the south. The American revolutionary belief in manifest destiny was based on a vision of a united North America ruled from Washington. Although some would have found this no worse than being ruled from London, imperialists believed that there was a significant difference between these two fates. The ultimate goal of British imperialism was to enable each dominion to achieve independence and liberty. In order for this to be possible, Britain would help establish order and democracy in the younger nations until such time as they were ready to assume this responsibility for themselves. The American republic, by contrast, was interested primarily in extending its empire by dominating other peoples.

On a deeper level, the imperialists also believed in the moral superiority of British principles and traditions over American ideals. American society was unstable and chaotic, committed to individualism at the expense of the common good, and freedom at the expense of social order. Moreover, its brand of democratic equality discouraged hierarchic order, which included respect of the young for their elders and of the masses for those gifted and destined to rule. In some ways, these developments were inevitable, imperialists argued, given the fact that America was established as an independent nation through an act of violence and lawlessness. This also meant that a contempt for law, order, and discipline would arise. In contrast, Canada with its British connection valued law, order, and social stability. Human nature was such that social restraints on individual freedom were necessary in order to prevent chaos and violence. Democracy in and of itself would not produce enlightened and educated leaders who could hold in check the extravagances and excesses of popular rule, nor would it give the state a unified direction. In addition, imperialists spoke of an inherited Puritan morality which combined with the northern climate to produce straight thinking, toughness, and self-discipline. American society, moreover, was very materialistic. People were differentiated according to their wealth, and money-making was the chief measure of success. Such an emphasis was also associated with the growing industrial civilization, which, along with the businessman, was a frequent target of imperialist criticism. In Canadian society, however, materialism was mitigated by traditions which valued character and honour, along with loyalty to the nation and to the common good.

Of all the imperialists, G.M. Grant held what was perhaps the most mediating position on the place of Canada in relation to Britain and America. Canada was called to a 'divine mission' of serving as a living link between the two nations and, in so doing, unifying the English-speaking peoples divided since 1776. Canada was best situated for such a mission since it

> was American because the atmosphere, climate and other physical conditions under which people grew up, determined to a great extent their character and place in history. But it was British, because we have inherited from Britain not merely that which the United States has inherited, language, literature, laws and blood, and the fundamental principles of civil and religious life, but also continuity of national life.[4]

G.M. Grant looked forward to 'a moral reunion of the english-speaking race, commercial union based on free trade, a common tribunal and a common citizenship, if not more.'

Nonetheless, both he and Parkin were conservative (Tory) reformers. They were critics of unfettered capitalism and industrial civilization, preferring instead the more traditional closely knit agricultural society in which they grew up. Inherent in such a view was the conservative concept of an ideal society composed of functionally and organically linked communities. Such communities were knit together through mutual obligation and historical loyalties, and were supported by a strong central government with a distinct vision of nationality inspired by institutions committed to uphold it. Such a vision stood squarely against the more liberal vision to the south with its worship of individual freedom and materialism.

At the same time, these conservatives were also strong proponents of social reform. G.M. Grant was influenced by the 'muscular' Christianity of Britain and the 'Social Gospel' movement in North America.[5] Both were sensitive to the growing poverty and rootlessness caused by the migration of people from small towns to the expanding and impersonal cities created through industrialization.

Thus, while both Parkin and G.M. Grant believed, like most in their generation, in historical progress, the vision of progress they were working for was quite different than the more liberal vision represented in the United States. Liberal believers, nevertheless, they were. Even though their conservative vision of human nature necessitated a greater role for social restraint and order, they were optimistic about the capacity of human beings to overcome their lawless and sinful nature through education and nurture. They also believed that certain individuals and nations were called to take a leading role in this education. Such progressive optimism was further associated with a social vision inspired by Darwin's evolutionary theory, popular in the late nineteenth and early twentieth centuries, which attached natural inevitability to historical progress. Whether it was through the British Empire or the 'universal and homogeneous state,'[6] human civilization was destined to achieve freedom, justice, and harmony throughout the world.

Finally, for Parkin and G.M. Grant, such a vision was in the deepest sense a religious one, and it is here, perhaps, that the greatest confusion is to be found. Evolution, history, and progress were linked to divine providence. And because of an optimism about human nature, there was a belief in human cooperation with God, as well as the cooperation of science and technology with the church, in the achievement of this destiny. The British Empire was not only the greatest secular instrument for progress in the world, but also a divine providential means to it. As G.M. Grant put it: 'We have a mission on earth ... Our mission is to make this world the home of freedom, of justice, and of peace, and to secure these ends the British Empire is the highest secular instrument the world has ever known.'[7]

Grant spoke little about Parkin in particular, but he did speak about G.M. Grant. He identified him as a liberal Protestant who lived at the high point of nineteenth-century Canada, 'when Protestantism and liberalism were identified, and people could really believe in them together ... and they were really confident that their kind of liberal Protestantism would rule the world.'[8] In an early essay, Grant wrote about G.M. Grant's decision to sever Queen's University's religious affiliation with the Presbyterian Church. In order to expand the teaching of science and technology, Queen's needed money. While the Presbyterian Church was unwilling and unable to provide the funds required, the government could and would so long as the university was willing to function independently of the church. For G.M. Grant this was not a question of putting science and technology before the church because at that time scientific expansion and Christianity, liberal humanism and faith, did not appear to contradict each other. Rather, he believed that truth and goodness would naturally come with this development, and the good life with an expanded means of education.[9]

Now, even though Grant finds fault with his grandfather's naïve and optimistic faith, he is not prepared to be too harsh in his judgment of him. In the same essay, he adds that the only reason he and others are more aware of the distance between modernity and Christianity is 'the horror that God revealed to us at Buchenwald and Moscow, Peking and Detroit.'[10] Grant had the advantage of having seen the effects of such a faith in his generation's experience of the war, an experience which would leave an indelible and decisive mark in his thought. In spite of this fundamental rejection of the faith of his forebears, however, many of their ideas were incorporated into his thought whether as principles to be upheld or visions to be wrestled with.

Unlike the elders Grant and Parkin, William Grant had a more direct influence on his son. Although Grant grouped his father in the same camp with his grandfathers (as far as the synthesizing of liberalism and Christianity in the face of growing secularism was concerned), he also held a deep respect for his father's work as an educator and historian. And more, he respected his father's ideas. William Christian argues that Grant never realized just how deeply, in fact, he was influenced by his father.[11] William fought in the First World War, and Grant often spoke about how that war ruined his father's health. On his return, he decided to let go his teaching position as a historian at Queen's in order to become principal at Upper Canada College. Through this work, he believed, he was better placed to influence the direction education would take in the province as a whole.[12]

The war did not destroy William's optimism in educational and social reform, but his firsthand experience of its destructive consequences turned him into a pacifist and a staunch supporter of the League of Nations. Grant inherited his father's passion for pacifism and international issues. According to Christian, he also inherited a passion for religion.[13] Even though Grant never admitted this to be the case, it is already apparent in his school days at Upper Canada College. His pacifism was related explicitly to Christian principles, and he was actively involved with a group linked to the Student Christian Movement. They studied the religions of the world as well as issues of war and peace, and worked toward an understanding of Jesus based on the gospels.[14]

Grant maintained his pacifism as he went on to study at Queen's. In a letter he wrote to his mother, the relationship of his pacifism to his Christian faith is clearly evident. His argument centres on the teaching, example, and person of Christ. The context of this letter is Grant's growing anxiety and concern over the escalating tensions in Europe in the late 1930s and how one ought to respond. Grant, like his father, realizes the futility of war as 'force is being used on every side and everyone is hopelessly lost.' But, as a Christian, one must never fight. Christ could have called the angels to bring down the temporal powers set against him, but he did not. His example of passive resistance represents a protest and victory far more effective than physical force could ever be. The whole argument, for Grant, hinges on Christ's divinity. If Christ is divine, as Grant believes, then one is 'breaking divine law if one fights, however just one's cause is.' Of course, adds Grant, this does not mean one is prevented from fighting in many peaceful ways through protest and resistance. He ends the letter with an earnest expression of desire to be at the centre of the crisis.[15] He knew that beliefs were easily held from the sidelines and needed to be tested in order to be authentic.

Grant's pacifism was not only principled, it was held in full cognizance of the complexity of the issues. In one book review, written at the time, he recognizes that in some cases pacifists may be forced to consent to war when the aggression of a state such as Germany threatens the greater peace.[16] In another review, he expresses deep admiration for those who maintain principles of justice and truth above ambition, desire, and class or national interest.[17] Moreover, Grant showed an early awareness of other profound factors that affect the ability of people to make clear, principled, rational judgments. In one book review, he comments about the author's concern over the shift in education from teaching students to think, to teaching them techniques in order to get a job. The author associates this shift with a growing American influence which encourages the worship of business and wealth at the expense of contemplation, and the lowering of the quality of education in order to meet the individual tastes of the public.[18] In an essay entitled 'Art and Propaganda,' Grant decries the loss of good art which inspires a sound conscience. This loss is the result of the growing use of art as propaganda by powerful economic and political interests. Untrained minds are manipulated and drugged into accepting the views powerful leaders want them to hold. Such action, writes Grant, which is 'far more effective and far more insidious than physical force, becomes the means whereby civilization may lose its finer instinct and political freedom may become the despised product of a past age.'[19] In another letter to his mother, Grant attacks popular views. Both complacent optimists and arrogant militants are criticized. Grant also expresses a certain helplessness and pessimism about the future as 'Europe is going up in smoke.'[20]

In spite of the ominous signs of the late 1930s and his critical education, Grant still did not distinguish clearly Christian faith and divine providence, on the one hand, and liberal humanism and the progress of history, on the other. He was part of a class and age in which the perfectibility of human nature and civilization was still affirmed as an article of faith even though events in the twentieth century had challenged this doctrine significantly. It is also true, however, that this affirmation was progressively crumbling in Grant's mind and soul as the world was moving ever more quickly into the chaos of war.

1.2. War and 'Conversion'

Without a doubt, the Second World War was a primal event which would shape fundamentally the direction of Grant's thought. As he admitted later, the war was the 'great experience for me,' and the liberalism of his youth 'could not come to terms with it.'[21] Grant also admitted that he was 'ashamed' of his pacifism. There was great pressure morally and practically to make a contribution to the war effort.

When he graduated from Queen's, Grant received the high honour of a Rhodes Scholarship, which took him to Oxford. There he studied law, which, to his mother's great pleasure, would serve him well in public life back in Canada. Even though Grant was a pacifist with Christian principles, his experience at Oxford only revealed to him how much of 'an ambitious little pragmatist'[22] he really was. He met a group of pacifists there who took their Christianity very seriously. It was a Christianity rooted in the gospels, Plato, and poetry. What seemed to distinguish this Christianity from the one he had known was how completely devoid it was of any of the progressive liberalism so prevalent in North America. Moreover, Grant's Christianity was mixed with a need for social and political success. In these people, he witnessed a purity of commitment to principle which was willing to pay the price of social rejection, persecution, and even death in obedience to Christ.[23] Later, Grant would consider this brand of Christianity to have been an inheritance from before the 'age of progress.' Such a tradition was non-existent in North America.

At the same time that Grant was being exposed to this profound brand of Christianity, the war in Europe was intensifying and he, like many individuals, was experiencing great pressure and anguish. First, his pacifism was being tested severely. He felt a deep sense of guilt for studying in comfort while other youth were being killed. He also knew that he could not speak credibly about his pacifist views if he had not tasted firsthand the evils of war. He could not speak about the forgiveness of enemies when he had not been attacked himself.[24] While he was being haunted by such internal doubts, everyone around him was getting involved in the war effort.

Second, Grant's proximity to the conflict revealed to him even more deeply the destructiveness, futility, and waste of war. There was little tolerance for talk of finding a peaceful compromise, for not seeing the issues as black or white, or not seeing one's own side as completely righteous and the other side as totally evil. For a sensitive soul like Grant, such a tense and hostile atmosphere was stifling. Besides keeping all of this to himself (except what he told his mother in letters), he was being enveloped in the sense of meaninglessness around him as all attention and effort became focused on the war.

Grant finally found a way of releasing some of the pressure. Along with his pacifist friends, he trained as a volunteer in an ambulance unit. This was a way to participate in the war without compromising his beliefs. Through training and fellowship with his friends, his pacifism became more deeply religious.[25] Upon completion of training as an Air Raid Precautions Warden, he was sent to a working-class district of London called Bermondsey. His responsibilities were to ensure blackouts were observed, to summon appropriate emergency services when air raids were in progress, to rescue those trapped in the rubble, provide first aid, investigate unexploded bombs, and inform the families of those killed. Besides exhausting him physically, this work wore down his spirit. He was constantly surrounded by suffering and despair. But the worst point came when the shelter was bombed where most of the people of his district, including close friends, were taking cover. The casualties were overwhelming. Grant was totally devastated and broken.[26] Even though nothing this terrible happened to him again, there were still lesser tragedies that ate away his spirit.

His letters to his mother at this time reveal the depth of anguish he was suffering. Any hope or optimism within him was progressively disintegrating, and he was becoming quite cynical with regard to any justification of the war, or the supposed virtue of any of the parties. He was confronted by the selfishness and resentment within himself and in everyone around him. The war produced many heroes, but also destroyed any sense of moral innocence and purity. At the same time, he became forever sensitized to the destructive potentialities made possible by modern science and technology. In one letter, he writes of his wonder at the way in which

> ... a bomb can descend &, in the space of a second, destroy even the most intricate, delicately balanced human personality. Not only is the beautiful mechanism of the body torn, ripped, masticated by the tiger-like violence of the high explosive, but the existence of the person knitted with his thoughts, passions, ambitions, inhibitions is destroyed. For a long while the one possibility about the war I could not envisage was the destruction of my own self. It came from a belief that God just wouldn't have the nerve to let my personality suffer ... Yet, now I feel much more objective.[27]

Here, one can detect the beginning of Grant's realization of the irreparable harm technology can bring about, not only externally but internally, in the human soul. The war forever destroyed in him any idea of the inevitable progress of civilization or optimism about the perfectibility of human nature. But this, in his mind, was not pessimism. Between an easy, blind optimism and a defeated pessimism lay 'cynicism and doubt and disbelief' which are able to face reality, in all its horror, without being cut off from its anguish and pain.[28]

But things became worse for Grant before they became better. The threat from air raids passed when Hitler decided to attempt an invasion of Russia. While this meant greater peace for the British, Grant was not at peace within:

> The mess the world is in is difficult to understand – given a glorious world – of sun and green and ourselves – we have corrupted ourselves

and our fellows. We have not controlled our progenitive instincts with the result that the world is too well populated – we have not controlled our acquisitive instinct with the result that the wealth of the world is not well divided. We have not controlled our pride so that we always want to put something over on somebody else. We have not controlled our frustration so that though we think we are the best in the world, we are always dissatisfied. Then suddenly this cauldron of folly and stupidity, pride and selfishness boils over and results in a welter of hate – and both sides proclaiming that they are fighting for the noblest of motives. To anyone with sensitivity the logic of suicide seems impenetrable. Thank God one isn't too sensitive ...[29]

Grant was more sensitive than he thought. With pressure mounting once again to participate in the war effort now that his job as an Air Raid Precautions Warden was over, he decided to join the Merchant Navy Marine, albeit admitting this to be a rather useless and demeaning act. But it would at least satisfy those who kept putting pressure on him to fulfil his duty to 'King and Country.' Upon a medical examination, however, he was further humiliated when he was found to be tubercular in one lung and, hence, unfit for duty. Grant panicked and ran away. Relatives and friends lost track of him for a while. William Christian suggests that Grant believed that he was going to die.[30] Others suggest that he probably suffered a nervous breakdown.[31] After wandering for a while, Grant found work as a farm labourer in the countryside. Soon after, he learned about the bombing of Pearl Harbor. This meant many more millions of people would be joining the destruction and chaos of the war. For the next three days, he hovered on the brink of suicide, feeling deep anguish, impotence, and despair. Then, one morning as he rode his bicycle to the farm, he entered through the gate and it suddenly came to him: 'God is.'[32]

Grant explained the meaning of this experience later in his life. It was a belief that all was finally well, that 'beyond time and space there is order,' that 'ultimately the world is not a maniacal chaos.' It was the realization that 'I am not my own' but belong to an 'Other.'[33] At the time he wrote to his mother about being 'born again,' of 'unpredictable tremendous forces – mysterious forces within man that are beyond man's understanding driving him – taking him along courses and [over] which he has no or little control.'[34] However this experience is to be explained, Grant claims that it was the defining experience of his life and sustained him throughout. The rest of his life would be devoted to understanding its meaning – *credo ut intelligam*.

This experience had the immediate effect of rejuvenating Grant's spirit, but not at the expense of mitigating the brutality and horror of the war within him. The war only accentuated his own sense of moral inadequacy and the evil in the world. War destroyed people and separated them further from God and from each other. In the insane pursuit of conquest, 'we have created God in the image of our own wills. As some great man said, "We have made him a tame confederate of our petty adventurings."'[35] Unlike the view of his mother and many North Americans who were hoping for greater American intervention, Grant believed any escalation of the war would only serve to further our alienation from God and the destruction of many more people and relationships. At this time, Grant, like most others, was not aware of what was happening to Jews and others in the Nazi death camps. But would this have changed his views on the evil of escalation in war? Grant was not only concerned with the external destruction (in human lives and communities), but also with the internal corruption and brutalization of the soul engaged in war. While the external evil could somehow be mitigated by the fact that the Nazis had to be stopped, it would not prevent the corruption of those having to stop them by brutal force.

Through the help of relatives, Grant was sent back to Canada to recover from his breakdown. His reflections during this period reveal even further his renewed faith in God along with a deep sense of the helplessness and tragedy of life in the world. He writes of hearing the news of a working-class woman he knew in Bermondsey who, along with her son, was caught stealing. This woman had cared for Grant when he was ill. His anger boils over with people who criticize someone like her from their self-righteous comfort, not realizing how deeply the war had 'smashed' her. Yet Grant also speaks of experiencing a peace and calm beyond the gloom and frustration. He is conscious of his weakness of character and his lingering bitterness with those who have let him down. But at the same time he feels gratitude toward people like the woman caught stealing who have supported him as well as admiration for others, like his mother, who have suffered severe grief in life without allowing it to fester within them.[36]

This period also reveals some of Grant's early reflection on his faith in God and the nature of modern civilization. In London he witnessed how little the empire had done for the average person, how much industrialism was severing the connection between the lives of workers and their work, and how capitalism was eroding community and agricultural life in favour of the impersonality of large cities.[37] Later, in Canada, he writes to his sister about his fears of the vast changes industrialism is bringing about: 'urbanism, new forms of work, leisure, tremendous power over nature ...' Nor does he see much hope that something transcendent in humanity will prove victorious since 'this colossal, material change of industrialism has been too much for our great tradition (really a remarkably thin veneer) of personal responsibility, the dignity of the individual.'[38]

Along with his growing doubts about the progress of civilization and the perfectibility of human nature, Grant's conception of God begins to shift as well. Divine providence is no longer conceived of as God intervening in human history or cooperating with human nature, but of God 'waiting':

> God sees the truth but waits. Personally, it is a great emotional discovery – the discovery of God – the first glimpse of that reality – not amateurish or kind – not sentimental or moral, but so beyond our comprehension that the mere glimpse is more than we can bear. God, not as an optimist – nor as the non-mover, but, God, who sees the truth but waits. God waited through the selfish nationalism and ignorant self-seeking of the nineteenth century. God waited through the struggle of the first war, & through the continuance of our sloth and greed & our ignorance from 1918–1939, he saw the truth – he saw what the policies that we were following would mean. He saw that each individual sin multiplied in countries & continents would bring us down to this – yet he did not intervene, he waited.[39]

God's standing apart and waiting is, of course, an act of divine mercy and forbearance. But at the same time there is a natural law of justice and equilibrium in the world that serves God's judgment. In the words of the Bible, 'as you sow, so shall you reap,' or in a Spanish proverb, 'Take what you want said God – take it and pay for it':

> What a tremendous truth for men and societies – with the individual he or she can choose to be cruel – to want power – to be oversensual – to be decadent – to be (like myself) slothful – he can take any and all of these things. He can take them, but will pay for them. Also with nations – they can take empire – or power or wealth – or on the other side isolation and

irresponsibility – they can take them but will pay for them ... As you sow, so shall you reap is the terrible & furious pronouncement of the law of human life ... Right now we are paying for the greed, selfishness, slothfulness & irresponsibility of the past years ... We never faced up to the issue, but gave over to the arbitrament of force without thinking, therefore, after the war we will pay for this.[40]

Grant begins to see human history, not as a progression toward heaven, but a descent into hell. At the same time, he begins to conceive of God not only as judge whose hidden law is the law of natural justice in the world, but as an infinitely patient and merciful God, painfully waiting through, perhaps even hiding behind, the cruel events of human history, waiting for those individuals and societies ready to repent and return to God.

1.3. Post-war Writings

Toward the end of the war, Grant was given an opportunity to work as an adult educator, and after further studies at Oxford, he was offered a teaching job at Dalhousie University. His writings during this period reveal the influence of his progenitors, on the one hand, and his experience of war and conversion, on the other.

In the mid-1940s he was commissioned to write several pamphlets on Canadian nationalism.[41] His perspective is almost identical to that of his progenitors, except that he also incorporates the consequences of the Second World War. He too argues that Canadian nationalism is best safeguarded and maintained by Canada's continued membership within the British federation. He too argues that the real enemy to national identity and independence is to the south. In the emerging 'cold war' world, the British Commonwealth offers a third alternative and a much needed balance to the more aggressive empires of Russia and the United States. Moreover, through its spread of 'Hollywood culture' and materialism, and the assertion of individual freedom, American imperialism is of a more insidious form, progressively infiltrating the entire globe. But what about Canada's participation in the war, a participation brought on because of its link to the Commonwealth? Grant tries to defend this participation without softening the horror of the war:

In 1933 the dream of liberal mankind that we were on the edge of Utopia was rudely shattered by the rise of sadism and perverted Tyranny in the very centre of our western world. Signs of the evil in the heart of man had been appearing with alarming frequency, but here was the final outcrop of it in organized form to tear our footling optimism into shreds. For this was a state that not only acted with barbarism but preached that barbarism was the true way of life, that all our Christian virtues of love and co-operation were a mockery ...

The second date that must be remembered is 1940. For in this year barbarism was first checked – not by vague hopes of the idealists, but by the organized strength of the free nations of the British Commonwealth. The last five years have been cruel. Millions of people's hopes have been smashed by war. But let us learn from this waste. Whatever our illusions before the war may have been, we cannot hold on to them now.[42]

In spite of his growing disillusionment about global progress because of the war, Grant was still deeply conditioned at this time by the liberal optimism of his progenitors rooted in British imperialism.

In the mid-1940s, Grant was also writing a regular column on public education for the Canadian Association for Adult Education, through which he sought to foster people's involvement and participation in building up the nation at the grass-roots level. He encouraged them not to lose all optimism when it seemed that war is an ever present reality in the world. Rather, through involvement in local League of Nations societies, along with churches and other community groups, people could do their part in building a world where war could be eliminated forever.[43]

During this period, Grant also wrote several book reviews in which a number of themes important to his thought are taken up. In one review, he remarks on the author's lament over the loss of moral, intellectual, and artistic emphases in education in favour of an emphasis on technical skills. This shift is the result of growing materialism and individualism, as well as a growing Hollywood culture combined with an expanding scientific, industrial civilization. With the increase in technical training and the decline of art and philosophy also comes the loss of the only means to those transcendent values out of which civilization is born.[44] The theme of education is taken up by Grant in another book review, only this time the author has given up on the value of education altogether. He divides society essentially into two groups: a small minority of energetic rulers and the large majority of the dull and lazy masses, fit only to be ruled. 'All they want is bread to fill their stomachs and circuses to fill their minds.' According to Grant, however, this is totally contrary to the vision of the adult educator who believes human beings are capable of developing, and there is great value in democracy and working with people. The view proposed by this author is 'symptomatic of our world of wars and depressions.' Such individuals have not had the courage to maintain faith in 'human dignity and progress.' They have caved in to an 'all too easy pessimism that said most men were selfish fools or ignorant knaves.' Such people ought to be pitied.[45]

In a review of a book on Francis Bacon by the philosopher Fulton Anderson – a review which would cause Grant trouble later in his career – Grant begins by praising the author's thorough presentation of Bacon's thought. Nonetheless, he fails to relate how Bacon's exaltation of natural science over against religion has brought civilization to its present barrenness, and how 'such an exaltation, coupled with man's original sin, leads straight to the grinning mask of scientific humanism at Hiroshima.'[46]

Finally, Grant reviews a published collection of letters written by Frank Pickersgill, 'a young Canadian who in the war of 1939–1945 worked gallantly for the French underground and was found at the end of the war beaten and tortured on a butcher's hook at Buchenwald.' The letters show Pickersgill's progression from the 'easy hopeful years in the 1930's' to his 'prodigious courage before the evil and horror of the war of the 1940's.' He obeyed his conscience even though it would lead him into a 'terrible agony.' The only virtue greater than Pickersgill's moral courage is charity. But this he also had. 'It is the final condemnation of our epoch that he was forced to employ those virtues in the viciousness of war.'[47]

Through his writing of essays, reviews, and letters, we can see Grant struggling with a number of issues. While he values deeply the moral and spiritual traditions of his progenitors, the experience of war and conversion distances him from them as well. In their naïve optimism, they failed to see how modern scientific, technological civilization undermined their traditions. The war, according to Grant, is the inevitable outcome of progress as conceived by liberal humanism. It reflects individualism and freedom without limitations and restraints, with powerful scientific knowledge and techniques unchecked by an awareness of human sinfulness. Grant struggles between a sense of futility over changing the course of history, and an obligation to try to change it and to restore humanity's faith in God and itself. Even though he still retains the language of optimistic liberalism in much of his writing after the war, one cannot help feeling that he may be speaking this way more out of duty than out of conviction. It is true, however, that he attempts to steer a middle course between a pessimism and despair which prevent belief in human improvement, and a naïve optimism which avoids a confrontation with the harsh realities of the modern world. Even though his faith in God is moving away from a supposed link between divine providence and the course of human history, he still confuses faith in God with faith in humanity. The war reveals to him the distance between humanity and God, human history and divine providence, yet he can still believe that human beings can build a bridge to God.

1.4. Grant's Study of Theology and Philosophy

In 1945 Grant decided to go back to Oxford, only this time he would take up the study of theology and philosophy. The war had changed his preoccupations, and he was now interested in making some sense of his conversion experience, of seeking to understand what he had come to believe. Upon discussion with supervisors, Grant decided to pursue the difficult D.Phil. degree, which would allow him to 'explore the universe'[48] while undertaking research toward a thesis. It was during these explorations that Grant encountered Luther. Although at this time he thought Calvin the greater thinker and Erasmus one he could agree with more, 'that peasant with his feet set on the ground seeking with all his heart and soul and need a gracious God, and at last out of great rough tribulation finding him, is the noblest of the lot. Every charge can be levelled against him except that of being an honest man in great need of peace.'[49] Luther gave Grant the language to name his own inner struggles. Grant makes reference to his own search for a gracious God, 'even though he escapes and escapes because one is not willing to search.' Moreover, he states elsewhere, 'I do not search for God because I am disciplined, charitable and calm, but because I am undisciplined, uncharitable and deep rooted in sin.' Then he adds, paraphrasing Luther, 'I can do no other and anything else would be to my destruction.'[50]

Luther, along with others such as the novelist Henry James, helped Grant begin the process of discovering grounds for faith and hope in life without having to obscure the misery of his own life or that of the world.[51] He refers to himself as being 'enough of a Puritan to know that the very shape of the universe is grief,' and of being humbled, if not despairing, about his own inability to improve himself morally and spiritually. He speaks of having thought that when one was 'born again' it happened quickly and there were only certain levels of despair. But after his conversion, he experienced deeper forms of depression and despair to the point where 'the richness and intensity of life was gradually filtered away.' Because sin turns one inward, it destroys the capacity to transcend oneself and to contemplate the beauty of the world.[52]

Yet at the same time, Grant speaks of the necessity for people like him who 'believed our dreams should come true' to 'go down to the depths of pessimism,' but after having reached this point to rediscover meaning and purpose in the goodness of life. The only thing worse than a complacent pessimism, according to Grant, is a 'snivelling optimism of the Rotarian sort.'[53] Grant even experiences many moments of joy and vitality, of being energized by his studies; although he also realizes that authentic theology 'must be a study where one is surrounded by the dark.'[54]

While Grant's spirit was being challenged through his reading of Luther, James, and others, his mind was also stimulated. He was introduced to two theological poles: rational theology, on the one hand, and neo-orthodoxy, on the other. Like most forms of Protestant theology, these movements were a response, in one form or another, to the philosophy of Kant. Against the Enlightenment, which claimed too much for human reason, and Protestant orthodoxy, which claimed too much for metaphysical rationalism, Kant established clear principles and limits for human reason. In so doing, he demolished the idea that metaphysical concepts such as God, freedom, and immortality could be established by rational arguments, or that human reason is unlimited and can know all mysteries. Kant drove a clear wedge between the finite and the infinite. The finite mind is unable to reach the infinite. This, of course, was an attack on all forms of natural theology which attempt to build bridges to the infinite through human rationality.[55]

Kant did try to establish, however, a way in which metaphysical knowledge could be received by finite mind. As opposed to a rational knowledge based on facts, he argued for a type of moral knowledge based on experience or faith. Such knowledge was rooted in the concepts of the 'Good Will,' the 'categorical imperative,' and the 'autonomous will' with which one consented to obey transcendent, moral, 'categorical' imperatives revealed in the structure of reality. Kant's attempt at establishing a ground for faith was rather bare, no doubt. His primary concern had always been to maintain a certain agnosticism about the infinite, and a distance between the finite and the infinite, in order to safeguard the integrity of rational thought and a place for faith, however small. Nonetheless, he did lay a rational basis for the idea of a final mystery in the infinite, and he argued that any metaphysical knowledge must originate in the infinite (revelation or grace, in theological terms) rather than in human speculation.[56]

The inadequacy of Kant's attempt at establishing a basis for faith and metaphysics, however, led much of the Protestant theology that came after him into searching for credible grounds for metaphysical knowledge and experience. Whether it was through a Hegelian understanding of rationality or a Schleiermachian understanding of feeling or intuition, or some combination or variation of the two, liberal Protestant theology of the nineteenth century attempted to establish these grounds in some aspect of the human personality or will.[57] After the experience of the war in the early part of the twentieth century, however, the neo-orthodox movement reasserted the distance between the finite and the infinite. With the war, hopes in historical progress and human goodness were destroyed for many Europeans. Any faith in God that was too closely linked with faith in the human intellect or will, was also discredited. In order to be credible, faith had to be established on a completely different basis. From the renewed conception of the moral distance between God and humanity, theologians like Karl Barth asserted an absolute distance between reason and revelation.[58] They also rejected any primary place for human rationality or feeling in favour of a complete dependence on divine revelation as the basis for faith and the source of metaphysical truth. While at Oxford, Grant read Barth and Brunner, as well as books by the Scottish theologians John and Donald Baillie. They taught a mediating form of neo-orthodoxy to a whole generation of British students.[59]

Then there were theologians like Austin Farrer, who was teaching at Oxford during Grant's studies. Farrer sought to respond to Kant by re-establishing a basis for natural or rational theology. In his book *The Finite and the Infinite*, written in 1943, he proceeds to argue, by analogy from creation, for a link between the finite and infinite, following Aquinas. The key for him lies in the Aristotelian conception of substance and the importance of the human will.[60] Grant was fascinated by Farrer, albeit not so much by his theology as by his ability to explicate such thinkers as Descartes and Kant with great lucidity and depth. It was through Farrer that Grant first began to study Kant seriously, and this study continued throughout his life.[61]

Also, at this time, Grant bought a complete collection of the works of Saint Augustine.[62] Besides the great theological and spiritual depth Augustine offered Grant, his approach to theological truth appealed to Grant above that of either rational theology or neo-orthodoxy. Augustine's approach was expressed in language already dear to Grant – *credo ut intelligam*. For Augustine, God's being was enveloped in mystery and transcendence. Through God's revelation as Trinity and through divine grace, however, faith was made possible, and it was such faith that formed the basis of union with God. Augustine was also positively inclined toward philosophy and believed in the ability of human reason, rooted in the divine reason, to help the believer understand what had been granted to be believed in faith.[63]

One book which helped Grant understand Saint Augustine was Charles Cochrane's *Christianity and Classical Culture*.[64] What fascinated Grant about the book was not only how clearly and profoundly Cochrane presented the vision of classical culture and that of Christianity as represented most fully in Augustine, but how he related his study to the twentieth-century context. While classical culture attempted to create a perfect civilization through a conception of political order in the state, Christianity saw the state as a remedy for sin at best, and a source of brutal oppression at worst. The Christian vision was rooted in divine grace rather than the human will, and in divine revelation rather than human speculations about goodness, order, and felicity. At the same time, Augustine found in philosophy, and particularly in Plato, a dialogue partner in his attempt to understand and speak the faith in rational terms. Plato's understanding of rationality was much more mystical than that of Aristotle. Human reason participates in divine reason but cannot fully comprehend its mystery and transcendence.

Grant's admiration for Plato also began during his Oxford years. He found *The Republic* to be a 'superb book,' and 'when one has read such pure, clear nobility as Plato's *Republic*, one can have little doubt that really true thought is worth thinking.'[65] Although Kant, Augustine, and Plato would serve as the core sources of Grant's thought, Plato would eventually surpass all others.

In addition to this scholarly reading, Grant was reading the Bible. Indeed, he held the Bible in special reverence as a source of divine revelation. For all the wisdom and knowledge about God to be gained through books, one thing they could never offer was the 'living God.' But the Bible came the closest. 'Whenever I am sad,' he writes, 'I read the last twenty or so verses of 1st Corinthians, chapter 15.'[66] Grant never simply equated the Bible with divine revelation itself. Rather, it was the unique record of divine revelation. And nowhere was this revelation more divine than in the gospel accounts of Jesus, and particularly, the accounts of Gethsemane and Golgotha. In the suffering and death of Christ, supreme truth is to be found about who we are and who we are called to be. Yet because of our sin and the limits of our intellectual and experiential capacities, we can only grasp this truth as a profound mystery, a mystery we can never fully comprehend.

All this reading and study served as necessary background for Grant's thesis. The topic he chose to focus on was 'The Concept of Nature and Supernature in the Theology of John Oman.' Oman was a Scottish-born and -educated theologian whose book *The Natural and the Supernatural*[67] is an attempt to express Christian faith in philosophical language. Like Schleiermacher before him (whose book Oman had translated into English), his purpose is to persuade the 'cultured despisers' of religion in his own day. What Oman did for Grant, however, was to introduce him in a decisive way to the theology of the cross. Grant's interest in Oman's book is to show how it 'should be read within the context of his "*theologia crucis*," which is given in his earlier theological writings.' Although Grant does not explain the origin of this term, it is clearly connected to Luther. The central question for Oman was 'how men shall find a gracious God,' and 'to preempt Luther's great phrases, Oman emphasizes the "*theologia crucis*" while insisting on the dangers of the "*theologia gloriae*."'[68] The theology of the cross must have been sufficiently familiar in the British theological context in which Grant was studying that he did not need to explain the origin and content of the term. By failing to provide more detailed references, Grant must have assumed this to be the case and his supervisors did not indicate otherwise. Books like Baillie's *Our Knowledge of God* quote theses 19–21 of the Heidelberg disputation and present Luther's antagonism to natural theology or '*theologia gloriae*.'[69]

Grant does explain, however, what the theology of the cross means to Oman. 'Oman's faith is that our Lord on the Cross reveals the Father as Love, Who demands from men that they take up their crosses in forgiveness.'[70] Nor is such forgiveness any easy possibility. Christ's forgiving love is directed to those who have degraded and tortured him. The cross reveals God's forgiving love to sinners; a love that refuses to be overcome by the evil in human life and the world. But Oman goes further. The cross reveals the Father's will. It reveals how all the circumstances and events of life serve God's providence and our redemption. Does this mean that God is the author of evil? Certainly not. But it does mean the affirmation (expressed paradoxically in Luther and others) that even the evil things of this life must serve the divine purposes for human beings and the world. In order to safeguard this truth without asserting that 'evil is good and good evil,' Oman, who is an Augustinian and a Platonist, retains a certain mystery and hiddenness about God's purposes in the world. This means that the Christian lives by faith and not by sight. Even though as a Presbyterian Oman admired Calvin, unlike Luther and Paul 'Calvin found mystery in life but not in God's ordinances.' Hence, 'his map of God's scheme of salvation tended to become a law and ceases to be a Gospel. He therefore missed St. Paul's understanding of the mystery of God's purposes for men, even after Jesus Christ, which makes all faith a half-seen vision.'[71]

Grant then asks Oman about the fate of those who do not have faith. Are they excluded from God's redeeming purposes for human life? Here Grant parts ways with Oman. While Oman criticizes Kant for having no doctrine of grace, Grant finds Oman wanting in relation to those who are sceptical and defeated. Even though Oman accuses Kant of Pelagianism, Oman places considerable belief in human freedom's ability to respond adequately to divine forgiveness. Moreover, he offers no solid doctrine of original sin, and, therefore, his whole emphasis on the necessity of a divine redemption is brought into question. Grant attributes this deficiency in Oman to the fact that he grew up in the strong religious environment of the Orkney Islands of Scotland, where he was far removed from the growing scepticism and secularization in the rest of Europe.[72] In the deepest sense, however, Oman's failure to appreciate sufficiently the limits of human freedom and the necessity and mystery of divine grace, is rooted in his understanding of the theology of the cross itself. For Grant, the cry of the sceptic and the defeated is revealed in Jesus' own agony at Gethsemane and Golgotha. The choice to believe in the sovereignty of divine love, and to consent to the forgiveness of all, is much more hidden in the mystery of divine grace Oman is prepared to admit. The failure to recognize the difficulty of faith is, finally, a failure to comprehend the evil in the world with sufficient depth. The evil in the world, revealed on the cross, so hides God that only divine grace can reveal God and enable one to have faith and obey the call of forgiveness.

The failure to recognize the depths of evil which hide God and the divine purposes in the world, is also revealed in Oman's understanding of divine providence. Here the contradiction between Oman's theology of the cross and his liberal optimism about historical progress and human freedom becomes more evident. While in terms of faith Oman speaks of the mystery and hiddenness of divine providence in an evil world, he also speaks of the progressive moralization of humanity and the progress of the human race. Oman has confused the Christian doctrine of providence with the secular doctrine of progress, which is part of the larger movement of secularization of which he appears insufficiently aware.[73] In the process, he is also trivializing the evil in the world and making divine providence too 'scrutable' to human thought and too closely linked to the 'progress' of the human race.

The dangers of this contradiction in Oman are revealed, finally, in his practical ethics. Before the question of whether the Christian should fight in the First World War, Oman supports Britain's participation in the war.[74] Before an Augustinian and Lutheran caution about changing the world through human activity, Oman prefers a Puritan Calvinist ethic of transforming the social order. Even though he rejects the scientific, technological approach to the natural order (which strives to manipulate and control nature) in preference for an approach of reverence for nature as a reflection of divine beauty,[75] he does not perceive how the course of historical change is moving toward the exclusive domination of the scientific, technological world-view over all others.

Despite these fundamental criticisms of Oman's theology, Grant also has much in common with him. Oman's method is clearly informed by the Augustinian, Anselmian formula *Credo ut intelligam*. This is in contrast to all rational or 'natural' theologies, which do not recognize sufficiently the primacy of revelation and faith. It is also in contrast to the neo-orthodox approach, which has no use for philosophy or a need to communicate the faith intelligibly to the 'cultured despisers' of the day. Grant also appreciates the tradition of 'egalitarianism' and the primacy of charity which Oman inherited from his Presbyterian roots. This makes Christianity accessible to everyone as opposed to philosophy, which has stressed contemplation above charity and, therefore, encouraged an elitism of the intelligent. Moreover, even though Grant takes the theology of the cross further than Oman by recognizing Jesus' agony before the hiddenness of God, he believes Oman would have agreed that the accounts of Gethsemane and Golgotha are superior to the dialogues about the last days of Socrates, and the ethics of the Sermon on the Mount to those of *The Republic*.[76] Even though Oman did not comprehend the full significance of the theology of the cross, it was through him that Grant discovered it. This discovery would serve as the foundation upon which Grant's thought would be built.

The fundamental issues and struggles within Grant's thought can already be discerned from his earliest influences and experiences. The influence of his progenitors shaped his thinking in fundamental ways, and even after the war this influence continued to be present. Where he parted ways with them was not in their principles, but with respect to their naïve incorporation of these principles into the larger modern liberal humanism which was the child of the Enlightenment and the intellectual handmaid of the scientific, technological revolution. Indeed, their principles mitigated a more total espousal of modernity than would be found in liberal expressions of faith in America. The whole idea of restraint on individual freedom and the emphasis on law and order arose from a deeper suspicion of human nature and an awareness of the reality of sin and evil. The idea of communal interdependence and national loyalty arose from a deeper knowledge of the limits of human independence and self-sufficiency. Yet for men like George Parkin, G.M. Grant, and W. Grant, such ideas were weakened and compromised by a profound optimism and belief in the future progress of the human race, a future which, in cooperation with God, they had a special calling to fulfil.

Clearly, the war broke the back of Grant's earlier faith. Not only did it reveal to him the dark potentialities for evil in humanity, but it also showed him how these potentialities were fuelled and enabled by the modern view of human freedom and destiny to make the world. This view, combined with the potentialities made possible by the scientific, technological revolution, brought the world to the disastrous state it found itself in the twentieth century. Moreover, the war revealed to Grant how its brutality could crush the soul as well as the body. Through his own experiences and through what he witnessed around him, he saw the affliction and defeat of many souls. Optimistic theories of progress, and even reformist theories of repentance and renewal, could not account or atone for the depths of such destruction.

In terms of thinking, Grant began to make connections between the ideas of human freedom in the modern faith, how this led to the destruction of restraints and loyalties and, hence, to war, and how, finally, this movement influenced the coming to be of modern industrial and technological society. While his progenitors were suspicious of this development, they failed to see how the very ideas of human progress they held encouraged this to take place and, indeed, precipitated the destruction of any forms of faith and thought from before the age of progress.

Grant was saved from the alternative of pessimism by his 'conversion.' As far as he was concerned, the Christianity he had held before this experience was not the real article. It was a faith that was too rooted in himself to be rooted in God alone. But with his continuing descent into the hell of the war and the affliction he witnessed within and around him, the faith he was granted as he walked through the gate was something beyond his possibilities. Thus, it was a faith that 'I am not my own' but belong to an 'Other,' that there is a changeless order above us according to which everything we are and do is measured and defined. His conception of God began to take shape accordingly. While he experienced, perhaps, a God who was absent or hidden in the afflictions of the war, after his conversion he also experienced a God who refrains from intervening in the affairs of human beings, a God who waits. Far from being an act of indifference, this revealed a God who was infinitely merciful and patient with the tragic and stubborn refusal of human beings to repent and return to God. Furthermore, the concept of a waiting, non-interventionist God was totally opposed to the liberal idea of a God who interfered in history and whose purposes were closely aligned to those of human beings at their loftiest.

At the same time as God was one who waited, God was also manifested indirectly in the law of nature and history. The law serves as a judgment on human thought and activity. As one sows, so shall one reap; as one takes, one will pay. Grant was not suggesting here that insofar as such a law humbles human beings it also serves a redemptive purpose (albeit he recognized the paradox that maturity did often arise after suffering). He was merely suggesting this to be the truth about the way things were in the world.

It is also true, however, that Grant still retained some measure of belief in the value of reform and the possibility of changing the world toward God's purposes. More importantly, he still believed in the moral superiority and goodness of 'Christian man,' who was destined to lead the rest of the world into progress and civilization. It would take years before Grant fully shed the modern world-view from his thinking and conceived of a different way of being and loving in the world.

Clearly, these views were challenged during his studies at Oxford, and particularly as he struggled with the thought of John Oman. Oman introduced Grant to the theology of the cross, although, in the end, Oman failed to understand the deepest implications of this theology. Because he still retained a strong belief in human freedom toward goodness, he failed to see the fragility and limitations of the human will. Oman's faith and thought represented that of Grant's progenitors. It was a liberalism of a more conservative variety with principles that were motivated by Christian charity. Yet it was also a way of thinking that was naïve about the world and about human nature. By being so naïve, it was also insensitive to the ways in which people were mangled in the world. Through his experience of the war and his conversion in the midst of it, Grant saw more deeply the message of the cross to those who were crushed and defeated by life. If God's love was truly sovereign, it had to reach into these depths and cross that distance. At Gethsemane and Golgotha, Jesus revealed the agony of such love, as well as its redemptive power. It was only by the gracious gift of faith that human beings could be opened to that redemptive power, not through their own freedom, abilities, and accomplishments in the world.

Oman, nonetheless, like Augustine, Plato, and even Kant, retained a certain 'agnosticism' and mystery about God. This implied that faith in God did not mean a complete knowledge of God's purposes in the world. Such agnosticism was essential in order that evil was not called good and good evil, or, in other words, so that evil was not trivialized and God was not mistaken for some idol of human making and devotion in the world. Oman could also assert that on the cross God revealed that even evil must serve the divine redemptive purposes for human life. Yet Oman's liberalism in practical matters, anticipated in his faith in human freedom and goodness, eliminated the mystery at the centre of faith. In associating God's purposes too closely with human purposes in history, Oman ended up calling evil good and good evil. If there was a way of asserting, at one and the same time, that all that happened in the world was according to God's will, but also that the world was governed by evil and, hence, at the furthest distance from God, then one could also affirm that for believers 'all things work together for good for those who love God, who are called according to God's purpose.'[77] One could assert these words because in respecting the distance between God's purposes and the events of human history, such purposes were a matter of faith and not of sight. Grant was very sure about the importance of mystery in faith, but at this point he was more hesitant about asserting clearly that even the evil things of this world must serve God's good purposes for human life, whatever these purposes may be. The challenge for Grant was to think the truth of God as experienced in faith in a way that respected the distance between the world and God (a distance reflected by the evil and suffering within the world), yet also in a way that revealed how God's love was real and active in the world and in the human soul living in the world.

The theology of the cross was a great discovery for Grant, a discovery that would shape his thought for the rest of his life. In his struggle with his own formative influences, in his experience of war and conversion, in his studies and his struggle with Oman's theology, we begin to see why the discovery of the theology of the cross became so central to his thought and what it began to mean for him. We need now to consider the origins and meaning of this theology in greater detail, as well as the significance it took on for Grant's thought as a whole.

Chapter Two

The Theology of the Cross: Its Origins, Meaning, and Significance

2.1. The Origins and Meaning of the 'Theology of the Cross'

Although the theology of the cross represents an orientation of thought about God and the world that may be found in a number of thinkers within the Christian tradition and along its fringes beginning in the early church, the phrase itself has its origins in the Protestant reformer Martin Luther. When Grant came upon it in Oman, and when he used it, he clearly had Luther in mind. But what did the theology of the cross mean for Luther? Luther may have coined the phrase 'theology of the cross,' but he found his way to its meaning through his studies of the Psalms, Paul, Augustine, and the German mystics, coupled with his inner struggle to find redemption in his life. Accordingly, the theology of the cross was not only a way of thinking, but a way of existing, and because such existing drove Luther out of the monastery into the wider world, it intensified both his thinking and existing.[1]

If Luther's study and struggle led him toward a theology of the cross, he was also stimulated to define it more precisely in his opposition to what he termed a 'theology of glory.' The theology of glory signified the whole system of scholastic theology which had preceded him and in which he himself was schooled. To find his way to the truth about God, humanity, and the world, Luther felt compelled to stand against what he had received and what was being taught in the universities and churches of his day. The classic expression of his theology of the cross in opposition to the theology of glory is found in the theses he submitted for a theological and philosophical disputation held in Heidelberg, Germany, in 1518. Of particular relevance are theses 19–21:

19: That person does not deserve to be called a theologian who looks upon the invisible things of God as though they were clearly perceptible in those things which have actually happened [Rom. 1:20].

20: He deserves to be called a theologian, however, who comprehends the visible and manifest (*posteriora*) things of God seen through suffering and the cross.

21: A theologian of glory calls evil good and good evil. A theologian of the cross calls the thing what it actually is (*quod res est*).[2]

Let us now consider the meaning of these theses.[3]

1) For a theology of the cross, knowledge about God's being and activity in the world cannot be gained through human wisdom or speculation, but only through God's revelation of this knowledge to human beings.

In order to understand what this means, it must be understood that Luther believed knowledge about God to be intimately related to knowledge about ourselves in relation to God and in relation to the world. But how is such knowledge to be gained? Are we able to look at ourselves honestly or 'objectively'? Are we able to perceive God or our relationships truthfully? Are we able to think clearly about God and ourselves without distorting the picture in our favour or serving our needs for self-congratulation or importance? Clearly, for Luther, the answer is no. Not only are we unable to know who we are, but we mistake who God is and the nature of God's presence in the world.

Our whole problem, according to Luther, is our desire to be God in God's place. We are unable to accept the fragility and limitations of our existence, our 'fallenness' and, thus, our helplessness to save ourselves without God's sovereign working in our lives. We want to think ourselves capable of entering heaven with our thoughts and our deeds, rather than having to face the constant barrage of evidence in our daily living that reveals our finitude and hopeless participation in evil. We are, finally, 'unable to want God to be God'[4] in our lives: to want God to reveal God's self to us in the manner and form in which God chooses; to judge us and forgive us our participation in evil; and to liberate us from such helpless participation, and empower us for genuine good. Because we refuse to let God be God in our lives, we forge our own idea of God in our image and confuse God's will with our own.

It was a theology of glory which fostered such distorted ideas. First, a theology of glory held a false conception of God. The image of God inherited through the dialogue of scholastic theology with Aristotelian philosophy was of one who punished the wicked and rewarded the righteous. God's attitude toward human beings was conditional on the moral quality of human life. Second, a theology of glory held a false conception of human nature. Human beings were believed capable of some measure of movement toward the good (i.e., toward love of God and neighbour with one's whole being) and, hence, toward meriting God's grace. According to theologians such as Gabriel Biel, who had taught Luther, if one did 'what is in him' (i.e., one's best), God would grant God's grace of justification and sanctification. Although, in the deepest sense, one was unable to do one's best without an 'infusion' of divine grace into the human soul, God's attitude and actions toward a human being remained, nonetheless, conditional on what he/she did. The focus was on human beings, not on God. Even though God had arranged the means for redemption, it was up to human beings to effect the process. Even with the assistance of infused grace, the movement toward the good was rooted in human beings, and, thus, redemption was based at some level on merit. As a consequence, God's relationship to humanity could only be conditional and contractual.[5] Moreover, if human beings were capable of some movement toward the good under the assistance of divine grace, then God's working could be perceived clearly in the positive thoughts and actions of human beings in the world. God's will and the human will could come together in the moulding of individual and collective life in history.

Although Luther was reared on such teaching, he was too honest with himself and before God to be satisfied with a system of faith which permitted a place for the human will, however slight, in the process of salvation. Luther was too plagued with a knowledge of his participation in evil, even when he tried to do his best, to be assured that he had done his part to merit God's gracious acceptance. How could he, unrighteous as he was, stand before a holy God perfect in righteousness? Already in his early years as a theologian, then, Luther could not sustain the optimistic view of human nature held by his predecessors and colleagues. He saw himself, and therefore human nature as a whole, as hopelessly bound by spiritual limits, failures, and an impotence of will for anything ultimately but evil. His accompanying conception of God was equally dark. If human beings were hopelessly bound to evil, they were no less responsible for committing it. Hence, they merited nothing but God's fiery wrath and condemnation. Here is how Luther described his situation at the time:

> Though I lived as a monk without reproach, I felt that I was a sinner before God with an extremely disturbed conscience. I could not believe that he was placated by my satisfaction. I did not love, yes, I hated the righteous God who punishes sinners, and secretly, if not blasphemously, certainly murmuring greatly, I was angry with God, and said, 'As if, indeed, it is not enough, that miserable sinners, eternally lost through original sin, are crushed by every kind of calamity by the law of the decalogue, without having God add pain to pain by the gospel and also by the gospel threatening us with his righteousness and wrath!'[6]

At last, feeling all alone before an angry God and reduced to bitter, hopeless despair, the true meaning of the gospel was revealed to him in Paul's words: 'He who through faith is righteous shall live.' Here is how Luther himself explained it:

> There I began to understand that the righteousness of God is that by which the righteous lives by a gift of God, namely by faith. And this is the meaning: the righteousness of God is revealed by the gospel, namely, the passive righteousness with which merciful God justifies us by faith, as it is written, 'He who through faith is righteous shall live.' Here I felt that I was altogether born again and had entered paradise itself through open gates ...[7]

Luther came to see another face of God behind God's wrath: God's gracious mercy. When he was reduced to seeing the futility of any attempt at reaching God through mind and will, experiencing only God's wrath in such failed attempts, he was also opened to the revelation of God's love behind God's wrath. Although the gospel spoke of God's love and about God's justifying forgiveness of the sinner, Luther could not bear such teaching because he felt himself a hopeless sinner constantly breaking God's holy law and, thus, incurring God's growing condemnation. While at first he perceived such a situation to be a great obstacle to his salvation, he came to realize that it was actually the greatest preparation. In being confronted by his own futile attempts at meriting redemption, he was reduced to standing before God with empty hands. If salvation could ever be possible for him, it was God alone who could accomplish it. Faith itself came to be understood as a divine gift making one capable of perceiving and appropriating this free grace of God, and trusting such grace even when life appeared little more than great suffering under divine wrath.[8]

The theology of the cross, then, rejects any attempt at conceiving God that is rooted in human speculation and reasoning. Rather, the proper human stance is that of emptiness and openness to receive God's revelation. The revelation of God's love for us can only be received, however, when we are also shown our hopeless bondage to, and spiritual impotence before, the world's evil, meriting only God's righteous judgment.[9] The theology of glory underestimates the great distance between God and ourselves. In so doing, it also trivializes the depth of evil within us and the world, evil which separates us from God and merits nothing but God's wrath. Finally, the theology of glory minimizes the great distance that needs to be bridged in order to perceive the love of God behind such evil and wrath.

2) The revelation of God's love, as suggested above, is not apparent or visible but 'hidden' from us and in the world.

Luther utilizes several expressions to explain this aspect of the theology of the cross. In the theses for the Heidelberg disputation, he speaks of the hiddenness of God's revelation in the 'suffering and cross' of Christ. The word he uses here is *'posteriora.'*[10] The translation of this word in the American edition of Luther's works as the 'manifest' things of God fails to grasp the proper meaning. A more accurate translation would be the 'rearward' parts of God, indicating Luther's allusion to Exodus 33:23, when God refused to show God's face or 'glory' directly to the people (because of their sinfulness), but chose, rather, to show God's 'backside.' For Luther, this passage became a key pointer for God's whole way of revealing God's being and activity in the world. Another important passage was Isaiah 45:15: 'Truly thou art a God who hidest thyself,' and Luther frequently liked to refer to the crucified and hidden (*absconditus*) God.[11] Finally, Luther thought of God's hiddenness in a very specific way. God was hidden beneath God's opposite, *'abscondita sub contrariis.'*[12] Let us consider the meaning of these expressions more closely.

For Luther, God's hiddenness in the world was not an abstract idea, but something he experienced to his very depths. For the theologian of glory, speculation about God's being and will is a human possibility, and God's presence in the world is visible positively in nature and human history. However, for someone like Luther, who was so deeply struck by the evil and suffering in the world and his own helpless entanglement within it, God could not be further away. Indeed, Luther could experience God's hiddenness so deeply that he could speak of feeling completely forsaken or abandoned by God (like Jesus on the cross). The experience of total abandonment was equivalent to abiding in hell. Hell was nothing other than the total absence of God.[13] God's absence from us was also God's righteous judgment pronounced upon us. This was already visible in the suffering and death that were understood in Luther's time to be a natural consequence of our participation in evil. What was visible was not God's goodness or our own, but God's holy wrath and our evil, hopelessness, and suffering – all consequences of human sinfulness.[14]

Yet even though Luther could at times experience God as so deeply hidden that God seemed altogether absent or wrathful, he came to discover that God was paradoxically most truly present and merciful through this experience of divine absence/wrath. Not only was the experience of God's absence indirectly a knowledge about God: namely, that God was perfect good and could not abide evil, and, therefore, human entanglement in evil merited the divine absence from and judgment on human life. But to say that God was hidden was also to perceive that God was secretly present in the world and in human life. God was most truly present when we were driven to experience God's absence/wrath and our own brokenness before God and in the world. In such experience, any pride in our thinking or doing could not be sustained, and we stood before God with empty hands. It was only in such a situation that there was any room for genuine faith to occur. Only by being reduced to despair in our own powers could we stand empty and open before God. Thus, God's hiddenness was not only a reflection of God's distance from human evil and a righteous judgment upon it, but also the way to divine redemption. Through God's hiddenness, God was seeking to purify us by breaking us and preparing us to be turned to God for grace and salvation.[15]

Luther expressed this meaning most concretely when he spoke of God being hidden beneath God's opposite. God's loving, redeeming will for humanity and the world was hidden beneath the experience of evil.[16] To experience the evil in ourselves and the world was to be forced to face reality in all its horror – our own pathetic situation and the evil and suffering around us. Even though evil in itself was destructive of life and the divine image within us, God could also use it as the means to our purification and preparation to be turned to God. Luther came to express this paradoxical hiddenness/presence of God in various ways. He spoke of God's mercy hidden under God's wrath,

God's forgiveness under God's judgment, God's saving gospel under God's accusing law, and God's 'proper' or 'own' work under God's 'alien' or 'strange' work. He could even speak at times of God hidden beneath the Devil![17] In all these ways, Luther was seeking to express God's loving, redeeming presence secretly working within our lives, bringing us back to God by revealing to us our hopeless condition and need for grace. The strongest expression of the revelation of God under God's 'opposite' was God's presence in the crucified Christ. This is the theme of our next section and the very heart of the theology of the cross.

Before we discuss this theme, however, we need to consider what many scholars have perceived to be a contradiction in Luther's understanding of the hidden God. On the one hand, he speaks of God hidden in the crucified Christ. We encounter this way of speaking, for instance, in the theses for the Heidelberg disputation. On the other hand, Luther also speaks of God hidden apart from God's revelation in Christ. The best known example of this understanding is found in Luther's major work, *The Bondage of the Will*.[18] He appeals to this understanding especially when trying to reconcile God's predestination of people to both salvation and damnation with God's loving, redeeming will for the whole world revealed in the cross of Christ. Some scholars have suggested that these two ways of understanding God are, finally, irreconcilable.[19]

Others have argued that there are mediating elements in Luther's theology which bridge these two understandings of the hidden God. The most significant attempts in this regard are by theologians who have argued that Luther's doctrine of faith combined with his doctrine of God's sovereign working in the world (*monergism*)[20] help mitigate the extremities of his thought in this area. Clearly, his doctrine of God's predestination to both salvation and damnation is a corollary of his more primary doctrine of God's sovereign working in the world. Moreover, his understanding of faith is one totally defined by humble trust in God and open receptivity to whatever God wills. There is no room here for one's active search for God or speculation about aspects of God's being and will not revealed to us. The idea that there may be a part of God not revealed to us, and aspects of God's working in the world hidden from us, is consistent with the humility and trust that are the marks of genuine faith. Such faith does not seek more than what is given and is ready to accept the inscrutability and mystery of God's being and will outside divine revelation in the crucified Christ.[21]

Although such reasoning has not convinced some scholars, it suffices for the purposes of our discussion, focused as it is on Luther's theology of the cross rather than on his theology as a whole.

3) God is both hidden and revealed most fully in the suffering and death of Jesus the Christ.

In the cross of Christ, we see the rearward or back parts of God, God hidden beneath God's most extreme opposite. Perhaps another way of expressing this paradox would be to state that in the cross of Christ, God is completely absent and, yet, most truly present. In order to appreciate the meaning of the paradox, it is essential to recognize that for Luther the cross has as much to do with us as it has to do with God.[22]

First, the cross is the clearest revelation of God's distance from and judgment on the sin and evil in us and the world. This is reflected in the suffering, agony, and death of Jesus. On the cross, Jesus, the beloved son of God, was suffering what we ought to be suffering as a natural consequence of our sinful condition. The cross represents God's decisive condemnation of sin: 'Cursed is everyone who hangs on a tree' (Galatians 3:13). The cross also represents God's distance from evil and sin: 'My God, my God, why have you forsaken me?' (Mark 15:34). While the theologian of glory looks to God's positive working and is filled with self-assurance in his own wisdom and works, the theologian of the cross looks to the crucified Christ and is filled with fear and trembling at his miserable condition, and the suffering and death such a condition deserves. Already in this experience of fear and trembling God is hidden under God's condemnation, humbling human beings into facing the reality of their existence in the world.[23]

Luther was by no means the first to take the cross of Christ seriously as a revelation of God's judgment on sin. The depth of Luther's contemplation of this judgment, however, and the suffering that came with it, was his own. Jesus suffered to the very depths the consequences of our sinful condition. He suffered complete humiliation and abandonment, forsaken by God. He experienced nothing less than a descent into hell – a guilty conscience, the wrath of God on sin, and the absolute distance or absence of the loving God by whom he was sustained in life.[24]

But why was it essential that Jesus' suffering extend to these horrible depths? This leads to the second aspect of the meaning of the cross. The cross which reveals our hopeless, miserable condition before God and, hence, God's righteous condemnation of and absence from our existence, also reveals the means to our redemption in the world. This revelation has two components.

First, the cross reveals God's love for us and the world in the deepest way. It was essential that Jesus suffer the consequences of our fallen condition to the very depths. For only by passing through our misery to its very depths could he be present with us to redeem us from our spiritual bondage and helpless despair.[25] Luther expressed this redemptive meaning of the cross in a number of ways drawn from a combination of earlier theological reflection on the atonement and his own experiences. While some scholars have argued that Luther spoke of the atoning work of God on the cross in very specific terms only, others have shown how widely Luther borrowed imagery and language to express this aspect of the cross's meaning.[26] What is most significant for our purposes, however, is that the loving, redeeming meaning of the cross is not readily visible or perceptible to Luther. On an immediate level, what is visible is a pathetic, weak human being crushed by the forces around him. On a deeper level, through self-reflection and study of scripture (law), one can see God's holy wrath and the damning, horrifying consequences of sin. But to see hidden beneath the cross God's loving, redeeming will for human life was not something one could perceive through any reflection or speculation, but only if and when it was revealed to one by God alone.[27]

This leads to the second component of the redemptive revelation of the cross: our inner preparation to receive it. Here, the battle lines between the theologian of glory and the theologian of the cross are drawn to their sharpest. The theologian of glory flees any exposure to his sin and the condemnation he deserves as a result. He refuses to face the limits of his virtue and the self-serving motives underlying his good works. He refuses to be humbled and reduced to nothing before God. The theologian of the cross, however, values such humbling by God more than his own attempts at pleasing God. He submits to God's work in him rather than to his work for God. He submits completely to his own annihilation and crucifixion in order to be 'conformed' to Christ,[28] sharing his resurrection (justification) by sharing his suffering (self-condemnation before God):

He [the theologian of glory] who does not know Christ does not know

God hidden in suffering. Therefore, he prefers works to suffering, glory to
the cross, strength to weakness, wisdom to folly, and in general, good to
evil ... God can be found only in suffering and the cross ... Therefore the
friends of the cross say that the cross is good and that works are evil, for
through the cross works are dethroned and the old Adam, who is especially edified by works, is crucified. It is impossible for a person not to be
puffed up by his good works unless he has been deflated and destroyed
by suffering and evil until he knows that he is worthless and that his
works are not his but God's.[29]

This divine 'work' of humbling and reducing us to nothing, which
Luther calls God's 'strange' or 'alien' work (as mentioned earlier),
is necessary in order that God can work God's 'proper' or 'own'
work of making us receptive of grace and bearers of genuine spiritual fruit:

And that it is which Isa.28 [21] calls the alien work of God so that he may
do his work (that is, he humbles us thoroughly, making us despair, so that
he may exalt us in his mercy ...). In this way, consequently, the unattractive
works which God does in us, that is, those which are humble and devout,
are really eternal, for humility and fear of God are our entire merit.[30]

The divine work on the cross is consistent with God's creative work
from the beginning of time. God is always creating life out of nothing
(*ex nihilo*). Thus, God must reduce us to nothing in ourselves in order
to create new life in us, or so that God can live within us and through
us, re-creating life in the world.

*4) The revelation of God in the suffering and crucifixion of Christ is a matter
of faith.*

We touched on the place of faith in the theology of the cross earlier,
but now it is necessary to explore this theme more fully. If, as we began
our discussion, the theology of the cross is about relinquishing our
control and will in life in order to allow God to live and work within
us, breaking and moulding us into the image of Christ, then faith has
to do with open trust and 'passive' receptivity of this divine work in
our lives.[31] Luther believed, most certainly, that God is ultimately in
control and God's will is ultimately accomplished in the world
whether one recognizes it or not, or whether one desires it or not. The

reality of faith, however, has to do with our free, open, trusting consent to God's will, and a deep desire and hunger for it, even if and when this includes severe trials and afflictions in which God appears altogether hidden or absent.[32] Suffering in and of itself may be evil and destructive, but God, being all sovereign, uses even evil to accomplish God's goodwill. Evil and suffering can serve our redemption by breaking us and revealing to us our weakness and impotence. Being reduced in this way, we are prepared to receive the grace of God's justifying forgiveness and sanctifying love:

> He permits the godly to become powerless and to be brought low, until everyone supposes their end is near, whereas in these very things he is present to them with all his power, yet so hidden and in secret that even those who suffer the oppression do not feel it but only believe. There is the fullness of God's power and his outstretched arm. For where man's strength ends, God's strength begins, provided faith is present and waits on him. And when the oppression comes to an end, it becomes manifest what great strength was hidden under the weakness. Even so, Christ was powerless on the cross; and yet there he performed his mightiest work and conquered sin, death, world, hell, devil, and all evil.[33]

At times, however, the affliction of body and soul may be so severe and our conscience so troubled, that any faith, if it exists at all, is completely hidden from our consciousness. All we experience is pain and dread before divine wrath, or complete abandonment before the forces of evil. Luther expressed his own experiences in this way:

> I myself 'knew a man' [2 Cor. 12:2] who claimed he had often suffered these punishments [as described by the mystics] ... At such a time God seems terribly angry, and with him the whole creation. At such a time there is no flight, no comfort, within or without, but all things accuse ... In this moment (strange to say) the soul cannot believe that it can ever be redeemed other than that the punishment is not yet completely felt ... All that remains is the stark-naked desire for help and a terrible groaning, but it does not know where to turn for help. In this instance the person is stretched out with Christ so that all his bones may be counted, and every corner of his soul is filled with the greatest bitterness, dread, trembling, and sorrow ...[34]

For those who have experienced the trials and afflictions of life this deeply, faith, whenever it arises in the soul, can only be a divine work.

Yet if one is not reduced to such an extent, there is still room for holding the idea that faith can be a human work. It is already part of faith,
therefore, to see this experience of suffering (as dreadful as it is) as a
divine work, and to trust in the redemptive purposes of suffering even
though such purposes are totally hidden from us. Luther could express
this so forcefully that he spoke of trusting in God even 'against' our
experiences of evil and suffering.[35]

This, as we have already suggested, was no simple human possibility. Luther knew well the fragile nature of faith, especially under
suffering. Indeed, where the possibilities for redemption were the
greatest, the dangers of falling further away from grace were the deepest. Luther even came to define the essence of sin as the opposite of
faith – that is, unbelief. Unbelief is a refusal or incapacity to trust God
in all things. One who cannot or will not trust God holds oneself at the
centre of existence. Unbelief manifests itself in pride which refuses to
be humbled or broken by God. It also manifests itself in despair, when
one is so embittered and self-absorbed in one's suffering that one cannot trust God, endure patiently, and consent to God's work, which is
accomplished most incisively through suffering.[36]

However, while faith stands against experiences of suffering and
divine wrath, it can become the vehicle for the most powerful experiences of grace. At the centre of such experience lies the assurance of
God's gracious, loving acceptance against all doubts, guilt, fear, and
suffering. This experience of divine love could be so powerful that
Luther spoke of faith as

> a living, daring confidence in God's grace, so sure and certain that the
> believer would stake his life on it a thousand times. This knowledge of
> and confidence in God's grace makes men glad and bold and happy in
> dealing with God and with all creatures.[37]

Such positive experiences of faith, combined with the self-negating
experience of God's work in us through suffering, were so potent a
combination that Luther could speak of faith as complete obedience to
God in all things. Such obedience was rooted neither in fear of condemnation nor hope of reward, but in the pure love of God. When that
part of us which resists God has been destroyed and God alone lives
and moves within us, then divine love becomes both the source and
the goal of our lives. Obedience to God moves from being merely a
voluntary act to an inwardly necessary one. The depth of such obedi-

ence can be discerned when the believer is ready to be damned if that be God's will (*resignatio ad infernum*).[38]

Finally, if faith is 'passive' receptivity of divine love and active obedience to that love, then faith is also active love in relation to the neighbour:

> We conclude, therefore, that a Christian lives not in himself, but in Christ and in his neighbour ... He lives in Christ through faith, in his neighbour through love. By faith he is caught up beyond himself into God. By love he descends beneath himself into his neighbour.[39]

Luther could even speak of Christians being Christ to their neighbour and serving Christ in serving their neighbour. The same divine love that has created and redeemed us seeks to flow through us into the neighbour. Such a movement can only be a reality, however, when we have been reduced to nothing in ourselves and God alone lives and moves in and through us.

It follows, then, that the love active through faith is divine rather than human, rooted in God rather than in ourselves. Human love is selfish and must find something lovable in another to exist. The love of God, however, is creative. Just as it takes root in one who has been reduced to nothing and who is then brought to newness of life in God, so it passes through one into others who are enslaved to sin and death, and raises them to new life. Luther expresses this most beautifully in thesis 28 of the Heidelberg disputation: 'The love of God does not find, but creates, that which is pleasing to it. The love of man comes into being through that which is pleasing to it.' Luther explains it thus:

> The first part is clear because the love of God which lives in man loves sinners, evil persons, fools, and weaklings in order to make them righteous, good, wise, and strong. Rather than seeking its own good, the love' of God flows forth and bestows good. Therefore sinners are attractive because they are loved; they are not loved because they are attractive. For this reason the love of man avoids sinners and evil persons ... This is the love of the cross, born of the cross, which turns in the direction where it does not find good which it may enjoy, but where it may confer good on the bad and needy person ... for the intellect cannot by nature comprehend an object which does not exist, that is the poor and needy person, but only a thing that does exist, that is the true and the good. Therefore it judges according to appearances, is a respecter of persons, and judges according to that which can be seen, etc.[40]

Thus, the love of God (love of the cross), which lives in one who has been broken and humbled, is creative rather than selfish, bestowing life on those who are deprived of it because of evil and suffering. This image of divine love was lived most perfectly, according to Luther, by Jesus on the cross. Even under the complete forsakenness and wrath of God, the severe affliction in body and soul, he denied himself so that God's creative love could live in and through him, giving life to a world bound to sin and death.[41]

5) *For the theology of the cross, faith is always in tension with suffering, which includes doubt.*

From what has been stated in the foregoing, this may only be too obvious. But it is essential to explore this idea more fully. Luther understands suffering in a very specific way indicated by his choice of words: in German, *Anfechtung*; in Latin, *tentatio*. While the Latin *tentatio*[42] denotes the common word for temptation, the German *Anfechtung*[43] is given more particular meaning in relation to suffering. Luther distinguished *Anfechtung* from ordinary temptation or suffering by understanding it to be an assault by the devil. This may include the experience of physical pain, a guilty conscience, social condemnation, and divine wrath or hiddenness, all of which could lead to profound self-doubt and terror.

We have already discussed how such suffering was experienced by Luther and how it was experienced through faith. What is important to emphasize at this point is how strongly Luther rejected any idea that one must seek out suffering. Not only was self-chosen or contrived suffering perverse, it was misguided. To seek out one's own suffering is to be in control. Genuine suffering is imposed on one totally against one's wishes and destroys one's best-laid plans.[44] Moreover, Luther rejected the idea that one can develop humility by practising ascetic exercises or a disciplined life, however much these were valuable in and of themselves. Rather, one had to be humbled or humiliated against one's will.[45] One had to be reduced to nothing in one's righteousness, strength, social standing, and comfort. Being reduced is being forced against one's will to face the reality of one's moral and physical finitude in relation to God and the world. Too often it is suffering alone that can reveal such reality to us.

On one level, such humiliation and suffering are evil and, therefore, the work of the devil. On another level, however, an all-sovereign God permits a certain place for evil in order to use it for God's redemptive purposes.[46] While the devil's goal is to destroy us by driving us to complete despair of God and complete bitterness in relation to the life around us, God's goal is to destroy that part of us which says 'I' and prevents the complete indwelling of God in our lives. Suffering endured with openness before God compels us to experience our nothingness. This is necessary in order to experience God's omnipotent, redeeming love, waiting in secret to fill our nothingness with the fullness of divine grace.

While Luther is best known for having framed the basic tenets of the Reformation – through scripture alone; by grace through faith alone; in Christ alone – such tenets cannot be appreciated in any depth unless they are understood within the framework of Luther's theology of the cross. What all of these have in common and what the theology of the cross attempts to describe, is how the salvation of human life in the world must be removed from human hands and given over to God, who alone can accomplish it. Scripture alone must stand against human tradition, grace alone against human rites, faith alone against human works, and Christ alone against human institutions. The process of giving these up and being humbled and broken in one's abilities and accomplishments is never something to which human beings readily submit, nor are the results visibly attractive. Indeed, any confrontation with the stark reality of evil and suffering – our limits – and the numerous ways these mark our lives at every stage, is discouraging, at best, and terrorizing, at worst.

Yet the theology of the cross is about reality rather than illusion. It is concerned with the possibility of genuine salvation in the world rather than human ideas that only serve to provide escape routes from the world. If it posits an absolute belief in God, it does so in full engagement with the darkness that has so crippled earthly life that God can scarcely be imagined, let alone thought, with any clarity. If it thinks God at all, it is a God hidden or wrathful, according to one's experience of evil and suffering in a given situation. To think and experience God as love, and to receive mediations of such love in one's life and in one's earthly relationships, is truly a miracle. Faith, however, is an openness and trust in the midst of the darkness. It is a patient, faithful, waiting even under suffering. The grace to endure, as well as the grace to experience divine love, are equally God's gifts to fragile creatures. Such grace can only be received by one who consents to the 'unbecoming' (*entwerden*)[47] of one's false self and the becoming of one's true self in the image of God.

2.2. The Significance of the Theology of the Cross for Grant

Apart from occasional references to the theology of the cross and to Luther, a quotation of theses 19–21 of the Heidelberg disputation in a footnote, and a number of references to thesis 21 in part or completely, and in Grant's own variation, there is little on the surface to suggest the significance of this theological tradition as informing the substance and focus of Grant's thought. Yet the way in which these references have been made, we shall argue, does suggest that this theology serves to orient, structure, and guide Grant's thought in its critical, as well as constructive, dimensions. The reasons why this theology became so central to Grant's thought can already be perceived well before he discovered it formally in Oman. Grant's personal struggle with his formative influences, his experience of war, his conversion in the midst of it, and his reflections thereafter all prepared him for his encounter with the theology of the cross. In Oman, he discovered the language and meaning of this theology, although his understanding of its significance went beyond Oman's interpretation of it. Where Oman is found wanting in his ability to engage the depth of evil and suffering in the world (i.e., with regard to the sceptic and defeated) or in his optimism about human freedom and historical progress, the theology of the cross is held up as the most profound response to this reality. By having considered what the theology of the cross meant to Luther, who coined the phrase, we can begin to understand more deeply the reasons why this theological tradition became so meaningful to Grant.

Luther, like Grant, also had his period of despair when the older system of faith and meaning in which he was reared and educated did not address the evil and suffering in himself and the world. In the midst of this despair, however, he experienced the love of God, and the gift of this experience – faith – became the foundation for his thought about God, humanity, and the world. Luther, like Grant, recognized the need to think about this experience of faith in relation to God and the world, but also, how limited theology or philosophy was outside this experience. There was no direct way to God outside God's revelation and grace in human life. Human speculation and will could only be humble servants of this movement from above, and could not displace it. Any theology or philosophy that served to obscure the evil and suffer-

ing of the human situation, that could not engage the depths of affliction to which human life was vulnerable, was a theology of glory. Any
theology or philosophy which obscured the distance or absence of God
in a world of evil and suffering by locating absolute good within
human possibility or imagination, was also a theology of glory.

The theologian of the cross recognizes reality as it truly is. The reality
of the world is one of evil, suffering, misery, and affliction. The good
that is experienced is also fragile, dependent on circumstances, and
vulnerable to destruction. God is not immediately visible, but hidden
or absent. Thus, in order to maintain an honesty about reality, it is also
necessary to maintain a certain agnosticism or mystery about God's
presence and working in the world. By maintaining this honesty about
the way the world is, the fragility of human life, and the mystery of
God's providence because of God's hiddenness in the world, one is
then also prepared to experience God, if and when such an experience
is graciously given. Because such an experience was given to Grant, as
to Luther, it was possible to see the world as God's world and to love it
in one's being and acting in the world. For the Christian, the experience of faith and its possibilities is mediated most profoundly through
the suffering and death of Christ. At Gethsemane and Golgotha, the
path of despair and self-denial is exposed in all its agonizing, as well as
redemptive, dimensions. On the cross, the height of divine love is
revealed in all its sovereign power in the midst of the horror and affliction to which all life is vulnerable. It is these basic affirmations which
bring Grant and Luther close together and reveal the meaning of this
theology in Grant's intellect and spirit.

The significance that the theology of the cross begins to have in ori-
enting and guiding Grant's thought is evident from one of his earliest
writings, entitled 'Two Theological Languages.' Here the foundations
for the critical and constructive tasks of thought are laid out clearly.
Grant begins by asserting the importance of theology. Theology like
philosophy proceeds from 'faith seeking understanding.' The danger
for Christianity in North America is a simple reliance on faith while
neglecting theology and philosophy. This leads to superficiality and a
failure to communicate effectively and critically within the modern
context. To begin with, two facts need to be remembered about theological study. First, it is the most difficult of studies because it deals
with 'the ultimate,' and its truth can only be discovered through deep
experience and rigorous thought. Second, theology must be 'rethought
and relived in every generation of the church.' It comes to existence in

the meeting between the infinite and the finite in a particular time and place. It must attempt to relate the truths of faith with the various currents of thought and life.[48]

In order to proceed effectively, however, theology must ask itself a decisive question: what is the relation between the language of traditional rational theology and that of the Bible? Grant then defines what he understands by each of these languages. Rational theology was first expressed by Plato and Aristotle. The two key words used are 'reason' and 'desire.' Man's true desire is one to which he is directed by his own nature. Reason, which may become enslaved to the passions, also provides the idea of the highest good or God, which is the source and goal of human fulfilment. Reason not only gives us the idea of the highest good, but also directs our desire toward it. Grant prefers Plato to Aristotle because of the former's emphasis on the transcendence of God as opposed to the latter's virtual identification of God with our aspirations. Both of them, nevertheless, consider reason as that in human beings which is closest to God. Freedom, according to this language, means the acceptance by human beings, consciously and thoughtfully, of what they most truly are. Freedom is the movement out of ignorance into the light, the gift of truth.

Biblical theology, by contrast, expresses itself in the 'ethical' language of the Bible. It uses words like 'responsibility,' 'guilt,' 'sin,' 'remorse,' 'rebellion,' and 'disobedience.' Responsibility means that we could have done at one time or another what we did not do. Freedom is not the gift of truth inferred by reason, but something given apart from reason. The wicked are as free as the good. Freedom is absolute, irrational or suprarational, and based on experience. It is 'an abyss into which our reasons are swallowed up.'

In the first language, freedom is granted through the intelligence. It is the achievement of self-perfection through our rational nature. In the second language, freedom is irrational, prior to good or evil, and eludes the categories of reason. The first language claims 'intellectual superiority.' The second language claims 'existential depth.' It speaks of 'suffering,' 'abysses,' 'tragedies,' and 'mysteries.' Knowledge of truth depends on experience. 'Wait upon the transcendent,' it says, 'and you will know its infinite qualitative difference from the petty abstractions of traditional metaphysics.' Grant associates this language with neo-orthodox theology and existentialist philosophy. Elsewhere he states that existentialism has become the philosophical framework within which most Protestant theology is expounded in the twentieth century. This is because both make 'a mutual appeal to the authentic freedom of the individual which no rational scheme can encompass.'[49]

Grant criticizes biblical or neo-orthodox theology because it rejects rational theology. Faith grounded in experience does not seek understanding rooted in rationality. However, he asserts that only biblical theology gives an account of freedom by which responsibility is adequately explained. The idea that we could have done something other than we did is a mystery to our reason. Yet without appreciating the truth of this idea and its consequent idea of guilt, 'the essential seriousness of the human condition is lost.' Grant's dilemma is in trying to hold to both his trust in reason and his certainty in what he calls 'primary freedom.' He has not found a theology which has adequately and consistently related the two.

Grant then goes on to elaborate the essential weakness of rational theology. It always seems to 'disregard the problem of evil or to trivialize it.' With the problem of evil, it is good to talk of mysteries and abysses. While rational theology posits a continuity at some level between the finite and the infinite, biblical theology asserts a discontinuity and independence between them. This alone can account for a certain mystery in human responsibility and agnosticism about the problem of evil. Without such agnosticism, Grant claims, one ends up saying that 'good is evil and evil is good – rather than the very different affirmation that the thing is as it is.' While biblical theology tends toward irrationalism, rational theology not only trivializes the reality of sin and evil, but also 'makes God a tame confederate for our petty adventurings.' What, for instance, could rational theology say to the words 'not my will but thine be done'? Or would the cry of dereliction mean that Jesus held an imperfect adherence to the sovereignty of universal rational good? Jesus' cry was not 'God does not exist.' Nor can one claim rational confusion on his part.

The truth is that rational theology needs biblical theology as much as biblical theology needs rational theology. Yet it is no easy feat to bring them together. Any authentic theology today must 'go forward ... theoretically facing the deepest problems of reason, practically facing the dilemmas of contemporary technological society.' This is an incredibly difficult achievement and will require much sweat, agony, cooperative thought, and loneliness. It may even mean its rejection by the church.

In this writing, for the first time, Grant makes explicit reference to the twenty-first thesis of the Heidelberg disputation. Grant's paraphrase, 'the thing is as it is,' is slightly different from a more accurate translation, 'what it actually is,' yet the meaning is the same. A theology of glory – in this case, 'rational theology' – calls good evil and evil good. It trivializes the true nature and depth of evil and suffering in the thing itself (i.e., in humanity and the world in the technological society); and it makes God 'a tame confederate for our petty adventurings' (i.e., it makes God's purposes scrutable and even identifiable with the aims and pursuits of human thought and activity in history). In sharp contrast, a theology of the cross is sensitive to the true depths of evil and experiences the weight of suffering. Consequently, it is unable to relate God easily to human life and the world as it is in the technological society. Rather, God is hidden, distant, or absent in the same way as pure good is absent from profound evil and suffering. Appreciating this distance in experience is agonizing, and the attempt to think God's presence and will in the world impossible to the human intellect. The anguish and suffering of Jesus at Gethsemane and Golgotha is the classic revelation of this truth. Faith in God, then, can only arise as a gift of grace and God's truth as divine revelation.

Even though this line of thinking is basic to the theology, of the cross, Grant is unable to express himself clearly here for two reasons. First, although he begins to make a distinction between Platonic and Aristotelian thinking, he has not as yet separated them. He realizes that Plato asserts the transcendence of God in a way that Aristotle does not. Indeed, Aristotle's virtual identification of God with human aspirations, as noble as they may be, prevents an appreciation of the great distance between the finite and the infinite. Too often, Grant associates Luther's rejection of natural theology, as influenced by Aristotle, with his rejection of philosophy and rationality as a whole. This prevents him from finding a way in which a theology of the cross can be linked to a philosophy of a more Platonic, mystical orientation.

Second, Grant's simplistic characterization of neo-orthodox theology, and his lumping of all Protestant theology more or less in this camp, prevents him from appreciating the serious attempts at rational thought by a number of Protestant theologians. Moreover, in emphasizing the importance of freedom in neo-orthodox theology, he fails to emphasize the equally primary importance of grace, which is, finally, the only hope for human salvation.[50] As he states elsewhere, 'in the language of metaphysics freedom is the acceptance of rational necessity; in the language of religion it is the acceptance of the grace of God.'[51] Such a statement would go far in showing how a rational theology in the Platonic form and a biblical theology of the Augustinian,

Lutheran[52] form could be brought together in a way which adheres to a theology of the cross in faith and thought. Indeed, in later life, Grant criticizes this paper for its faulty understanding of freedom in biblical thought, influenced as it was by the existentialist view. Genuine freedom can never be prior to good and evil, and it finds its fulfilment in obedience to the truth – the truth which is the substance of revelation and the goal of reason.[53] Grant's understanding of freedom in relation to faith and philosophy, revelation and reason, will develop in maturity and clarity over the years.

Regardless of Grant's confusions in this early stage of his thought, the guiding principles for the critical and constructive task for thought, based as they are on a theology of the cross, can already be discerned. The critical task of thought is twofold. First, it involves naming reality as it is – the thing itself. The thing itself in the modern context is scientific, technological civilization as it is developing in North America. In the 1950s, he will think about the expanding mass society (see sections 3.1 and 3.2); in the 1960s, the technological society (4.1 and 4.2); and in the 1970s and '80s, technology as the modern 'ontology' (5.1). The first critical task of thought, then, is to understand and articulate the thing as it is, and all of Grant's writing is a critical dialogue with forms of thought which are measured according to their ability to do so. The standard of this measurement by the mid-1950s is the thought of Simone Weil. Weil was a French mystic whose writing about the modern world as it is, as well as her experience of God in the midst of it, moved Grant as no other writing had ever done or ever would do. Even though he had discovered the theology of the cross through Oman and Luther, the language and concepts he would employ to express it would be those of Weil. But there were other voices, as well. In the 1950s, Grant's praise is for existentialism. In the 1960s, it is for thinkers like Jacques Ellul, Leo Strauss, and Philip Sherrard. In the 1970s and '80s, it is for Friedrich Nietzsche, Martin Heidegger, and Louis-Ferdinand Céline. These thinkers and movements of thought helped Grant understand the thing as it is, as well as the consequences and effects of modern technological society on human life.

The second critical task of thought involves criticism of all forms of thought which obscure the thing as it is by calling good evil and evil good. These forms of thought function as theologies of glory. They fail to recognize the distance between the world and God. In so doing, they trivialize the evil and suffering in the world, on the one hand, and/or mistake God for some idol of human imagination or possibility within the world, on the other. In this group, Grant places modern liberalism in its various positivist, humanist, and Marxist European forms, as well as its more superficial incarnations in North America (3.3, 4.3, 5.2). In later years, Grant will see an even greater threat in the growing historicist nihilism he perceived to be emerging in North America and displacing the kindler, gentler liberalism which gave it birth.

The vast majority of Grant's writing is focused on the critical (negative) task of thought as defined by a theology of the cross. By being forced to face reality for what it was, people would also be brought to realize the inadequacy of any human attempts, in intellect and will, to redeem human life and the world. People would be brought to the foot of the cross, to a space in which, perhaps, there could be an opening for the activation of the divine presence and possibilities hidden beneath the evil and suffering (the cross) in the world as it is. But Grant also gives important clues and glimpses toward the constructive task for thought inspired by faith (3.4, 4.4). And as the years progress, he becomes more explicit about the positive implications of faith for thinking about and existing positively in the world (5.3). Again, the influence of Simone Weil is central in providing Grant a language for a positive vision faithful to the theology of the cross.

Let us now consider the critical and constructive tasks of philosophy for Grant as it is informed by a theology of the cross.

Chapter Three

Philosophy in the Mass Age

Following his being awarded a D.Phil. degree by Oxford in 1950, Grant returned to Dalhousie University, and during the next ten years he began to formulate the fundamental questions for which he would seek answers throughout the remainder of his life. His thinking during this period is shaped, on the one hand, by the influences and experiences of his earlier years, and how these are worked through during his studies at Oxford and the writing of his thesis on John Oman; and, on the other hand, by his continuing study of thinkers and movements in the context of the expanding mass society. Under the guidance of the theology of the cross, he attempts the critical and constructive task of philosophy – that is, analysing society and the human situation as they are, as well as opening up spaces for a divine answer to these realities. Of particular importance during this period is Grant's initial encounter with the thought of Simone Weil and his ambivalence over modern liberalism as represented at its best in the thought of Hegel.

3.1. The Mass Society: What It Is and How It Came to Be

What is the mass society? How did it come to be? These are primary questions for any philosophical enquiry seeking to be contextual and concrete. In a letter to his mother, Grant stresses the necessity for such an enquiry for one who is a philosopher: 'It is my job as a philosopher to try and see the industrial society as it is with all its virtues and its failures or else my philosophy will just be a barren intellectual game ...'[1] Even though some liberals would tell Grant to settle with becoming a 'happy agnostic,' Grant believes the point of life is to see what is, more and more deeply, even as one is 'surrounded by darkness and uncertainty.' In spite of the darkness, however, Grant is kept from being a pessimist, 'for I know that the highest virtue is charity, but the second highest is joy, and I never give up the effort to try and see the world as God's world.'

Nonetheless, the task of seeing the world 'as it is,' and yet as God's world, was to prove a great struggle for Grant. In an unpublished speech given to participants in a United Way campaign, Grant describes the modern world as dominated by scientific technology. The unbelievable change in humanity's relationship to nature is taken for granted. This change, however, is responsible for the greatest disruptions in human existence and community. The calamities we have lived, and will continue to live through, during this century, are the result of human inability to come to grips with and understand the nature of this change. The tragedy of the economic depression of the 1930s has revealed how little the mass industrial economy is under human control. The tragedy of modern wars has revealed the evil in human hearts magnified by the mass means at their disposal.[2]

It is true that there is a good side to the mass society. There is unprecedented surplus wealth, which has led to an ease in earning a living for more people than ever before. This is in contrast to the back-breaking labour that has marked previous centuries. With this ease comes greater leisure time. But have human beings cultivated the knowledge of what is worth doing with their leisure time? Not really. The growth in cheap and vulgar sensuality is also a sign of the times.

Moreover, there is a price to be paid for a mass society in terms of community. The old rural, agricultural, and commercial communities have been swept away by the growth of cities. With large cities come alienation, loneliness, and frustration for the masses. With migration to cities also comes uprootedness and the formation of new communities with no past. This leads to a withering of spirit. Furthermore, new forms of industrial labour require little skill or thought by workers, who are like cogs in a large mechanism. With uncreative and meaningless work also comes a withering of the spirit.

In another paper, Grant addresses the popular assumption in North America that once the world overcomes external menaces like war and becomes 'one big, prosperous, suburb like Toronto or Detroit,' all will be well.[3] Implicit in this assumption is the view that the West holds the key to global progress and that this progress is associated with unlimited economic expansion. Economic expansion through the control and domination of nature by science is held up as the highest goal of human individual and collective life. It is the God that is worshipped and the purpose to which all else is subordinated. It is true that the mass society has brought good things such as leisure and medicine. Yet it has also turned human beings away from their true purpose. The purpose of human existence must be defined in terms of freedom. Freedom means that we are able to stand apart from society and are not enslaved by it. It means that we can see the world as God sees it and judge ourselves and our society accordingly.

The truth is that whatever benefits the mass society may provide for us, we must always treat these only as means to the true richness of life for the individual and society. Such a richness is spiritual rather than material. The expanding economy, however, has become the end for us. Our philosophy is one of bigger and better. Our motto is 'seek ye first the kingdom of the boom and all shall be added unto you.' If we seek economic expansion first, we believe, we will also receive truth and beauty. What we have received is a nice blend of sentimentality and culture unable to offer us a critical vision of the world we live in.

Elsewhere Grant focuses his critique on the capitalistic nature of modern mass society. This society expresses itself through the control and domination of nature by means of science and technology, whereby a greater level of comfort and leisure has been achieved than ever before in history. But it also expresses itself in the domination of some human beings over others. The structure and organization by which this has been made possible Grant calls 'late state capitalism,' a term he borrows from social analysis. Society is capitalist in that leadership in economic affairs, and increasingly in all affairs, is in the hands of privately owned and controlled corporations. It is 'late' in that it is vastly different from earlier forms of capitalism, centred in smaller industries, businesses, and farms. Social and economic priorities are now determined by fewer and fewer people, who direct society according to their own self-interest and greed. It is 'state' in that the government still plays a large role in the management of society. The reality, however, is that the growth and power of corporations far exceeds any balancing power maintained by government or organized labour.[4]

Indeed, the structure is growing so rapidly that even those in power can no longer control it. The capitalist system, believed by many to be the source of the greatest economic and democratic liberation in society, is actually leading society into greater bondage. The ends which this system serves constitute a straightjacket within which everyone is bound. Individual consumption and the acquisition of goods and services for the means of satisfying a variety of human needs and appetites have become the unquestioned goals and purposes of existence. While it is true that, in terms of prosperity and leisure, capitalism has brought unprecedented gains, in terms of spiritual fulfilment and freedom it has brought new kinds of enslavement. Expansion and growth in production are peddled as unquestioned goods. Production of goods for private profit is put forth as the final goal of the economy. The benefits for the masses are prosperity and comfort. The goal of marketing is to stimulate desires and fuel the appetites. But is this good for society or the individual?

It is important for critics of capitalism to hold a clear conception of what is good for society, as many of the most pressing problems involve not only quantitative but qualitative distinctions. If people are hungry, exhausted from overwork, or ill, the solutions are very clear: more food, less work, and greater medical attention. But as technological mastery becomes an increasingly all-pervasive force, it must be asked which activities encourage and which hinder the flourishing of the human spirit. Which activities build community and which destroy it? We have already seen how critical Grant is about the expansion of industrialization and cities, and how such expansion destroys any sense of community among people. Moreover, self-interest and individual consumption and greed do not encourage the cultivation of the spirit of charity or mutual care among people. The new ideal heroes are the slick managers and the shrewd businessmen whose pursuit of profit has become the standard of success and progress.

In order to understand the mass society as it is in greater depth, Grant also attempts to understand how it came to have such predominance in North America. He finds the clue in the importance that is attached to the word 'freedom,'[5] and the unique meaning this word has been given in North America. Understanding the meaning of freedom in modern North American society, however, is complicated by several factors. The pioneering spirit, which was instrumental in taming and cultivating the New World, also led to the practical achievements of modern mass industrial, technological society on this continent. The focus on the practical prevented a focus on thought. The necessity of and success in their practical achievements gave our ancestors a strong sense of optimism in the future, but little motivation to think seriously about the implications and consequences of their achievements. In such a climate, freedom came to be associated with change and manipulation of the external environment toward greater comfort, security, and control. Techniques were valued more than the humanities and arts. Secularization offered greater freedom from the restrictions of 'metaphysical' standards imposed from without. Freedom came to mean the opportunities afforded for attaining an increasing number of objective desirables, including prosperity, technological instruments providing more comfort and pleasure, less strenuous work, and social equality in terms of accessibility. Freedom now meant the ability to get what one wants, when one wants it. So foundational did this meaning become to North American existence that Grant calls it the modern 'faith.'

Although practical achievements led to this faith, there were also theoretical movements which had a primary bearing on its development. These movements were centred in the pervading influence of Puritan Protestantism on North American life. In attempting to understand Puritanism, Grant was helped by two books in particular: A.S.P. Woodhouse's *Puritanism and Liberty* and M. Weber's *The Protestant Ethic and the Spirit of Capitalism*. Woodhouse isolates the two most significant issues in Puritan political thought: a break with the past – old religious and political forms – and an emphasis on democracy – reform of the constitution in the direction of liberty and equality. Although there was an immense variety of thinking within Puritanism, its common seedbed was Calvinist Protestantism. Puritans understood their destiny as a divine calling to establish their standards of holiness in the world and thereby transform the world toward greater conformity to the kingdom of God. Puritan thought was shaped by the study of the Bible to the exclusion of other forms of thought. A zeal for active reform led to an aversion for contemplation, whether of rational or mystical form. A passion for the reform of personal and social life was a response to an inner need to find assurance of salvation. A belief in the eternal, inscrutable predestination of souls by God left little room for finding assurance directly through prayer and adoration. Practical works, though not a means to salvation, were to become the unmistakable sign of one's election by God. The focus on the external and practical in the world also led Puritans into seeking out signs of God's working in the world. They came to believe in particular providence and God's intervention in history. Consequently, they also came to associate divine providence with their own reforming aims.

Puritans also held staunchly to the doctrines of liberty and equality. Initially, they called for liberty of conscience against religious oppression. This was also associated with an individualism in terms of one's faith and conscience before God. When having to draft a constitution, liberty was entrenched in the ordering of society in the form of equality. Democracy in political form guaranteed that tyranny and oppression would be eliminated and all citizens would have a voice in the political process. While there continued to be vast differences in emphasis among Puritans, there was a clear sense that divine providence was working itself out in history through their reforming work.[6]

Weber, on his part, also emphasizes the Puritan Calvinist desire to find assurance of salvation. God's eternal decrees were hidden in a dark mystery impossible to pierce and presumptuous to question. Yet the fate of every individual, and the regulation of even the tiniest detail in the world, were established from eternity. The combination of the absolute transcendence of God with a sense of inner anguish and loneliness before such a God, also led Puritans to an intense search for signs of their election as individuals. Because of an equally intense belief in the depravity of the flesh, any release in the sensual and emotional side of life was proscribed. Puritans found their release in practical work in the world for the glory of God. This work took the form of free enterprise and small-scale capitalism. Because of a rejection of the flesh, profit was accumulated rather than used in the indulging of the appetites. Weber identifies this form of self-disciplined capitalism as 'worldly asceticism.'[7] Capitalism allowed the individual to work out assurance of salvation through hard work and financial gain. Prosperity became a sign of God's favour and blessing. Hard work became the antidote for the temptations of the flesh, and laziness was considered a cardinal sin.

One can see clearly how Puritan Calvinism has shaped North American life. Emphasis on liberty, equality, democracy, and individualism, combined with a focus on small, individually based business enterprise and the making of profit, became the founding principles of this continent, especially in America. But why, Grant asks, has the very foundation of and incentive for these principles – Puritan Protestant faith in and obedience to God – been replaced by secularism in thought and greed in practice? The reason, he argues, can be found in Protestantism itself. A simplistic dependence on the Bible for moral theory and a self-disciplined drive for profit-making were unable to hold the minds of either intellectuals or industrial workers. This goes back to Luther's rejection of Aristotelian scholasticism, which, albeit necessary, also led to an unfortunate denigration of reason as a whole, leaving

Protestantism with no critical theory in relation to the 'vicissitudes of history.'[8]

The emphasis on the practical and the denigration of rational contemplation can also be traced to biblical ideas. Biblical faith manifests a God who acts in history (meaning history as a series of unique, meaningful events). Human beings are called upon to act in history in order to shape it to God's purposes. While the Greek emphasis is on thought, the biblical is on reformist action. We have already encountered Grant's problematic conception of the relationship between Greek and biblical modes of thought in 'Two Theological Languages.' Grant will deepen in this aspect of his thought over the years. What is important to emphasize at this point, however, is that the Calvinist, Puritan heritage, which is uniquely dominant in North America and has its roots in a particular reading of the Bible, is also the source of the thinking which undergirds the modern mass technological society and gives it its practical focus and libertarian emphasis.

3.2. The Consequences of the Mass Society on Human Life: Simone Weil and Existentialism

Once Grant has described the context of modern North American society as one of mass technological expansion, he then enquires about its consequences and effects on human life. As we have already seen in 'Two Theological Languages' and in his reflection on how mass technological society has come to be in North America, the word 'freedom' is a key means to understanding this society as it is.

3.2.1. Simone Weil's Analysis of Force and Affliction

In the early 1950s, Grant was asked to review a book by a recently discovered French mystic named Simone Weil. What Grant encountered in her writing was life-changing for him. In Weil he found the thinking and language that could express the depths of the thing as it is, as well as the heights of a divine answer to this situation. By the late 1950s, Grant was reading Weil with great intensity, and he was convinced that she understood reality as no one else did. Weil spoke the truth about the human condition with incomparable depth. Her analysis of the human condition was rooted in the concepts of force and affliction. Force determines the relationship of human beings with each other and with nature. Affliction is the effect of force on those who are subjected to it. According to Weil, human beings are born into a world which is governed by force. In nature this force takes the form of necessity and chance. Necessity is 'a mathematical progression of causes and effects.'[9] It is absolutely indifferent to human desire and 'from time to time makes of us a sort of formless jelly.' It is chance which determines whether nature brutalizes some or spares others, not human interest or welfare. In this vast universe, human beings are insignificant, vulnerable, and powerless, enslaved to forces beyond them.

And yet, human beings cannot help believing that they are born for something quite different:

> Nothing on earth can stop man from feeling himself born for liberty. Never, whatever may happen, can he accept servitude; for he is a thinking creature. He has never ceased to dream of a boundless liberty, whether as a past state of happiness of which a punishment has deprived him, or as a future state of happiness that is due him by reason of a sort of pact with some mysterious providence.[10]

Such a dream of freedom appeared to be a possibility with the advent of the scientific, technological revolution in the modern world. Now human beings were able to dominate and control nature, mitigating its brutalizing effects. Nonetheless, the spirit of domination inherent in nature – namely, 'force' – could not be overcome. Force now took on a predominantly human face: oppression. This oppression revealed itself in varying forms, such as capitalism and communism. Whether it was through society, the market, or institutions, human beings were enslaved and oppressed by the same forces they hoped to harness in the service of freedom. In fact, the more universal technological forces became, the more enslaved and oppressed people would become.[11]

In her early years, Weil looked to Marxist socialism as the best solution to the problem of oppression but was soon disillusioned. Marx was right in perceiving that oppression in the modern industrialized world was the result of economic rather than military power. But he was wrong in thinking that a shift in economic power would eliminate oppression. Somehow, Marx believed, social forces would naturally serve the good in history, or they could be managed to do so. He failed to see how force was by nature indifferent to good, if not opposed to it. Such a belief proves that Marx failed to understand force and how it dominates everyone who comes into contact with it. Weil even went so far as to state that 'it is not religion but revolution which is the opium of the people.' It obscured the truth about human relations:

> The constant illusion of Revolution consists in believing that the victims of force, being innocent of the outrages that are committed, will use force justly if it is put into their hands. But except for souls which are fairly near saintliness, the victims are defiled by force just as their tormentors are. The evil which is in the handle of the sword is transmitted to its point. So the victims thus put in power and intoxicated by the change do as much harm or more, and soon sink back to where they were before.[12]

Weil's most inspired analysis of force, or as it is sometimes translated, 'might,' is found in an essay she wrote on Homer's epic poem *The Iliad*.[13] According to her, this work deeply expresses the dynamics of force and its effects on human life. She states that the essential subject matter, and true hero, of *The Iliad* is force. Force is 'that which makes a thing of anybody who comes under its sway. When exercised to the full, it makes a thing of a man in the most literal sense, for it makes him a corpse.' Human dignity in the world is identified with freedom to 'consent' to or 'refuse' whatever happens to us or whatever we are drawn into. When this freedom is taken away by force, we are no different than a piece of matter pushed and pulled wherever the force of necessity and chance takes us. *The Iliad* depicts, most poignantly, how human beings become enslaved to force and lose their freedom and dignity in the process. This applies to both oppressors and oppressed. Those with power depend slavishly on force to maintain it, while those who have no power admire it even as they are brutalized by it. Either way, both oppressor and oppressed are slaves to force. Any sense of moderation or responsibility is wiped out by the intoxicating power of force as is any dignity in those who are crushed by it.

Furthermore, force is something external to human beings and, therefore, can be lost. Those in power are too intoxicated to realize this:

> They conclude from this that destiny has given all licence to them and none to their inferiors. Henceforth they go beyond the measure of their strength, and inevitably so, because they do not know its limit. Thus they are delivered up helpless before chance, and things no longer obey them. Sometimes chance serves them, at other times it hinders, and here they are, exposed, naked before misfortune without the armour of might

which protected their souls, without anything anymore to separate them from tears.[14]

In *The Iliad*, the victors one day are the vanquished the next. Everyone is a slave to force, and thus they are reduced to 'things.' People become things by losing their souls – either their human dignity or their sense of moderation and responsibility – and they become things in the physical sense when they are brutalized and killed. When caught in the vicious cycle of force there are no heroes ultimately, and those in power are upheld by circumstances external to them, which can shift at any time. But most inoculate themselves by

disguising the rigours of destiny in their own eyes, by the help of illusion, of intoxication, or of fanaticism. Unless protected by an armour of lies, man cannot endure might without suffering a blow in the depth of his soul.[15]

This 'blow in the depths of his soul' is what Weil names 'affliction,' and it is something that leaves a permanent mark on the soul. Weil's fullest treatment of this subject is found in an essay entitled 'The Love of God and Affliction.'[16] 'Affliction' is a translation of the French word *malheur*,[17] which implies a certain inevitability and doom, a feeling of being damned. It is like living with a death sentence. This concept became increasingly central for Weil after her 1934 experience working in the factories. She wanted to understand what the workers underwent so that she could help them discover a positive meaning in their situation. This experience, however, taught her things she did not anticipate. As a worker herself, she was subjected to the constant pressure to produce and keep up with the machines, the mindlessness of piecework, long hours, physical exhaustion, and the constant harassment of the bosses. It was a process that degraded and humiliated her. She wasted away in body and soul. This process of humiliation is what Weil named affliction. Its cause is the application of force on one against one's consent to the point where one loses all sense of dignity.

Even though human beings are fragile, vulnerable creatures, they continually seek ways to convince themselves that they matter in the world, and they expect people and events in their lives to consider their limits and needs. The experience of affliction destroys such expectations violently. While affliction includes physical suffering, it is not equated with it. One may suffer physical pain and, yet, maintain one's dignity or retain one's illusions. But everyone has a limit beyond which they break. Affliction is a point beyond this limit and involves the total loss of dignity. It is a 'complete uprooting of life, a kind of death, made immediate by attack or immediate apprehension of physical pain.'[18] It seizes life and in extreme cases includes physical pain, distress of soul, and social humiliation all at the same time. Affliction shows us how vulnerable we are and how dependent our sense of dignity is on external circumstances. Our bodies are fragile, easily plagued, torn, or crushed. Our souls are vulnerable to depression and dependent on all kinds of psychological supports. Our personality is totally dependent on our social acceptance and consideration. All these are exposed to affliction, and our dignity is easily destroyed if circumstances shift against us.

Weil admitted she knew this truth intuitively, but the experience of working in the factories revealed to her how little she was prepared for the crushing and humiliating effects of force. She felt the total loss of her dignity. She compared herself to a slave who, according to an ancient saying, loses half her soul the day she becomes one. She felt herself permanently branded a slave. A slave has no freedom to consent or to refuse and, therefore, lives only a half-life. The experience of affliction was absolutely devastating for Weil, and no social or psychological theory had ever prepared her for it.

As Weil developed her understanding of affliction through her own experience and reflection, she believed it essential that it be distinguished from sin and from ordinary suffering. Affliction is the experience of the distance separating us from the absolute good, a good which is the hidden desire deep in our souls. Sin is our location of this good in our imaginary power, goodness, or dreams of freedom in which our dignity is rooted. 'Sin is not a distance, it is a turning of our eyes in the wrong direction.' Sin is not the desire for an absolute good above us, but 'the desire for self-aggrandizement.' 'Sin is nothing else but the failure to recognize human misery.'[19] For Weil, these statements all say the same thing. Our failure to recognize the human misery in which we share, is rooted in our illusory belief that we can find the absolute good in our prestige or morality, in institutions or groups with which we are associated, in our collective progress within history, or our imaginary visions of divine providence in concord with our works. In any and all of these forms of sin, we locate absolute good within the world. In so doing, we lower the absolute good to our own fallen image of it, and we refuse to recognize how all of these imagined goods are evil and vulnerable to force and affliction.

When any of our illusions are assaulted by suffering, we seek to transfer this suffering in one way or another. If we cannot strike back, we strike those closest to us, those whom we can hurt. If we are deprived of this power, we seek out pity as a way of compensating our pain. Thus, we are drawn into a vicious cycle, adding sin to our suffering, transferring the evil we have suffered, nursing our brutalized self at another's expense. If all power of illusion or transference is taken from us and our dignity is not merely bruised but destroyed, then our suffering is affliction. Affliction is nothing less than the total loss of what makes us human in the world.

It is this loss, precisely, which distinguishes affliction from ordinary suffering. To speak of suffering as ordinary is not to lessen its intensity. When Weil speaks of torture, imprisonment, destitution, or prolonged and fatal disease, as she frequently does, she clearly has in mind severe forms of suffering that are not overcome easily, if at all. Nonetheless, even in such suffering it is possible to retain one's dignity, one's feeling of innocence, the injustice being suffered, and one's faith, be it in God or in some cause. Weil distinguished affliction from martyrdom. Martyrs know why they are suffering and are driven by some faith or cause which makes them capable of enduring tremendous suffering without losing their faith or dignity. Affliction, by contrast, reaches a point beyond which our faith, our dignity, and our feeling of innocence are lost. There is no discernible purpose to sustain one through it, and God seems altogether absent. When we have completely lost all social consideration, inner confidence, or certainty of God's presence, we cannot help feeling that we are damned. Weil refers to Job as an example of this condition:

> If Job cries out that he is innocent in such despairing accents it is because he himself is unable to believe so, it is because his soul within him is on the side of his friends. He implores God himself to bear witness, because he no longer hears the testimony of his own conscience; it is no longer anything but a lifeless memory for him.[20]

Moreover,

> affliction causes God to be absent for a time, more absent than a dead man, more absent than light in the utter darkness of a cell. A kind of horror submerges the whole soul.

Once Weil was personally confronted by the crushing experience of affliction (to which all human beings were vulnerable and which nothing in human beings could overcome), she also found in the cross of Christ the purest revelation of this condition. This pure and innocent human being was subjected to the maximum measure of affliction:

'Christ ... being made a curse for us.' It was not only the body of Christ, hanging on the wood, which was accursed, it was his whole soul also. In the same way every innocent being in his affliction feels himself accursed.

This feeling of damnation in his soul arose not only from his being forsaken and condemned by the world, but also from his experience of being forsaken and condemned by God: 'My God, my God, why have you forsaken me?' (Mark 15:34). For Weil, this testimony of Christ in the depths of affliction was sufficient to show why it was divine revelation. Even though one may experience such affliction, it is very difficult, if not impossible, to understand and articulate it to oneself, let alone to others. The cross of Christ offers such an understanding and an expression of it that is pure and uncompromising. Affliction is revealed for what it is. The loss of dignity and innocence, and the absence of justice and meaning, are, at bottom, rooted in the absence of God. If the ultimate good is God there can be nothing more distant from God than one who experiences the complete absence or condemnation of God: 'Nothing can be further from God than that which has been made accursed.'[21]

It was Weil's analysis of force and affliction, and the way in which this touched Grant's own experiences and perceptions about the way things were in the modern world, that set the standard for all other voices seeking to articulate the thing as it is.

3.2.2. Jean-Paul Sartre and Existentialism: The Tragic Vision of Life

In the 1950s, Grant also discovered in existentialism a means for understanding and expressing, in the spirit of Weil, the truth about the way things were in modern society. Existentialism was also sensitive to freedom within the human spirit and how this freedom was being crushed in the modern world. It was being crushed by overt means of coercion through war, but also by more covert, subtle means. The critical relationship of individuals vis-à-vis modern technological society was being subverted through mass manipulation aimed at adjusting individuals to society's structures and necessities. Existentialism not only gave voice to this loss of human freedom, but also to the tragedy of such loss. Those who had the courage to live honestly in modern mass technological society also had to live in anguish and despair, in the full consciousness of the meaninglessness of the human condition within it.[22]

The best representative of existentialism during this period in Grant's thought, without a doubt, was Jean-Paul Sartre. Sartre held this place of eminence, not because he was the greatest of existentialist thinkers (Heidegger was greater), but because he was the most eloquent and because he lived his philosophy to its very depths.[23] Modern thought, suggests Grant, is a mixture of scientific concepts and the remnants of older traditions of philosophy and Christian theology. This mixture is confused in the minds of most people, with the scientific aspect gaining ever more mastery. Sartre criticizes both the scientific world-view and traditional philosophical, theological language. As an existentialist, however, he addresses these themes through a focus on the problem of subjectivity. Human beings are an infinite depth and mystery to themselves. The ultimate truth about humanity is freedom. Freedom and subjectivity mean essentially the same thing: the ability to transcend ourselves in thought and practice. Like the animals, we are determined objects, but unlike and beyond them, we are free to choose how to live.

The existentialist emphasis on freedom is asserted, in part, in protest against modern technological society, which views human beings as objects to be mastered and manipulated. Such a view, combined with the modern scientific faith in evolution and progress, spells disaster for the freedom of the individual subject. Although such faith has done much to transform the external world for humanity's benefit, it has also increasingly denied human freedom and subjectivity in thought and practice. The horrors of war and suffering in twentieth-century Europe reveal the inadequacy of any optimistic faith in progress and scientific humanism.

The paradox of Sartre's thought is that even though he attempts to uphold human freedom over against the depersonalization of scientific thought, his experience of the horrors of the modern world has led him finally to view life as meaningless. It has broken him off from a Christian tradition which would uphold freedom within a higher purpose and destiny inspired by God. In fact, Sartre believes faith in God to be as destructive of human freedom as is faith in modern scientific progress. It imposes external metaphysical limitations on human freedom and responsibility. What distinguishes Sartre from other liberals, however, is that the denial of God and of ultimate purpose is cause for despair rather than rejoicing. He is not an optimist about human nature and destiny. Life is anguish and despair. It is Sartre's depth in describing the experience of anguish and despair which Grant admires. Any rational theology which does not want to call good evil and evil good, but rather name the thing as it is, must come to terms with it.

In spite of his seemingly tragic vision, however, Sartre asserts the absoluteness of human freedom. This conviction came to him during his imprisonment under the Nazis. Sartre describes their attempt to break down the prisoners physically and psychologically. The freedom to resist within himself in spite of the torture without convinced Sartre of the power of freedom. To be free under physical and mental persecution is the height for him. This also means that one is not limited by fear of punishment or hope for consolation in some system or faith which only serves to limit the height that freedom may attain. It means accepting the truth that life has no meaning outside freedom.

According to Grant, Sartre is at his best when describing the nature of evil. He understands profoundly how it penetrates far beyond the external level, to the level of the consciousness where freedom ought to reign. Indeed, Sartre asserts the radical nature of evil. It can even destroy freedom in the consciousness. His description of torture and the relationship of the tortured to the torturer, which Grant found particularly incisive, is reminiscent of Weil's descriptions of the effects of force on the souls of oppressor and oppressed. For Sartre, the loss of freedom involves the loss of human dignity. One is turned into a pathetic animal, giving up anything to live and yet having no humanity left to give up.[24] Sartre makes two important and interrelated points about evil. Like good, evil is absolute, the fruit of a free, sovereign will, and therefore one is absolutely responsible for what one does or fails to do. Second, because it is absolute, evil is irreducible and unredeemable. Their is no ultimate purpose or meaning within which it may be subsumed. There is no sovereign good or God the absence of whom constitutes evil. Evil exists independently and absolutely. The importance of these related assertions for Sartre is that it forces people to take responsibility and commit themselves to action. There is no justification for the reduction of evil to some kind of hidden good, nor is there a place for philosophical, theological contemplation which would wait upon and trust in God's redeeming purposes beyond evil.

In spite of Sartre's atheism, Grant finds in existentialism of his calibre a healthy corrective to the scientific vision of human nature, which views human beings as mere objects to be manipulated. A defence of human freedom over against such a vision is essential. Nonetheless, his assertion that human freedom survives even in the nothingness and meaninglessness of existence, Grant as a Christian cannot believe possible. The truth in Sartre is that thought must abide in the negations of what is in order to know true freedom. But the fulfilment of such knowledge cannot end there:

> It is after all, the truth of the Cross that the anguish of the soul must be made absolute before God can make it His own. It has been said of existentialism that it takes one to Golgotha to find there only two thieves dying on their crosses. Certainly I would not be content with such a vision of what happened there. Nevertheless to be at Golgotha, in despair and without vision, is better than not being there.[25]

In spite of the fact that Sartre's existentialism leaves no opening for the divine presence hidden within the negations (cross) of life, Grant found it to be a profound statement of the way things are in the world. The absence of faith in God or goodness, in the context of an expanding mass technological society which undermines the freedom of the human spirit, is not something conducive to optimistic hopes for the future of human life in the world. Rather, it is grounds for despair and anguish. Yet it is in the face of such honesty before the cross, Grant believes, that any hope for the birth of genuine faith in God and love of the world, in spite of the reality of evil and suffering, is possible. But before Grant can speak constructively about this possibility, he must attack theologies of glory which obscure the human condition in the modern context and, therefore, prevent human beings from being brought to the foot of the cross.

3.3. Western Liberalism and the Mass Society: The Theology of Glory in North America

If freedom of the spirit is the measure of the good life, and if this freedom is being undermined and crushed within human beings in the mass technological society, why is it that more human beings are not sensitive to this reality? Grant offers several reasons for this. First, Western institutions of learning, religion, and mental health have betrayed their reason for being and have conformed themselves to the necessities of the mass society. Second, liberalism in its many forms is the dominant ideology in this society, and it hinders a more honest assessment of the human condition as offered by voices such as existentialism and Weil. Freedom itself, as we have seen, has come to mean something completely different in the mass society.

3.3.1. Education, Religion, and Mental Health in the Mass Society

Very early on, Grant began to see that one of the great tragedies of modern life was the surrender of universities and churches to the necessities of the mass society. According to Grant, the *raison d'être* of universities and churches was in assuming responsibility for leading human beings into the freedom of truth through love and art, thought and prayer. Through such activity, human beings could rise above their propensity to evil. While political and economic institutions had the negative role of restraining evil and protecting the weak, schools, universities, and churches had the positive role of stimulating and inspiring the good in human souls.

But what is the modern predicament? Schools and universities have become technical colleges providing the training of specialists. And such a focus is not only encouraged by those who fund and increasingly control universities – that is, the business community – but reflects the dominant ethos of Canadian society, which places greater priority on getting a good job than on getting a good education. This is particularly true of North American society with its pioneering roots. A nation built up by pioneers naturally placed greater priority on the practical than the contemplative, and on material achievement than on profound thought about the whole. With greater material achievement, there was greater optimism about the universe and a confidence in human abilities to conquer and subdue nature. With the conquest of nature came an openness to mass industrialism, and in the light of scientific and technological advances, a belief that society as a whole could become progressively perfected. The measure of this perfection, however, has become the acquisition of comfort, wealth, and control over the human and natural environments. The purpose of education has become to provide the means to secure the ends of such acquisition and control. Through natural and social sciences, modern people are being taught the technical skills they will need to accomplish this. As opposed to the purpose of education in pre-modern society, focused as it was on developing a critical awareness of society as it is and a vision of what it ought to be, modern education is directed toward serving the necessities of mass society and helping individuals accept its assumptions and adjust to its demands whatever they are and as they are.[26]

Grant laments this trend in education, and especially as it has infiltrated into the study of philosophy. The chief schools of philosophical thought in Canada in the 1920s and 1930s were pragmatism and positivism. They taught that ideas were true insofar as they helped people manipulate the natural environment, and that all human problems could be solved by scientific techniques. Philosophy was conceived as a servant to, rather than a critic of, scientific aims. In addition, modern philosophy dreamed of freeing itself from ancient links to the dogmas of faith and, thus, supported the gradual secularization of universities founded within the Protestant tradition. But if philosophy is to be more than a purely negative discipline, claims Grant, it must have some kind of dependence on faith. Reason that is not guided by faith destroys everything and establishes nothing. Faith is an essential basis for philosophy if philosophy hopes to play more than a limited and merely critical role in society.

Such an understanding of philosophy, as can be imagined, was not very popular, and philosophers such as Fulton Anderson were very antagonistic to Grant's remarks in this regard. Basing philosophy on faith, according to Anderson, was not the means to its salvation but, rather, to its destruction. The confusion and division among theological and denominational camps could only erode the integrity and objectivity of philosophical criticism.[27]

Grant was shaken by the antagonism of Anderson's response. He had not realized how deeply scepticism and secularism had been established in Canada and how unreceptive the philosophical community would be to his thought. He realized that, henceforth, he would have to speak much more indirectly about his faith if his thought was to get a hearing. But this would not dissuade Grant from responding further to his critics. In particular, Grant wrote two articles – one on Bertrand Russell and the other on Karl Popper's critique of Plato – aimed at bringing out the essence of the scepticism and pragmatism he believed so prevalent in Canada. This time, however, he was not naïve about the cost involved in terms of the antagonism of the philosophical community.[28]

As a philosopher of science, Russell is rigorous in defining the principles by which scientific propositions are to be tested as true or false. Yet, in the realm of art or morality, he claims that philosophy has nothing to contribute. In other words, philosophy cannot teach what is right and wrong or how people ought to live. Nonetheless, Russell desires to teach people about conduct by using his authority as a philosopher. At one and the same time, he asserts a moral scepticism where reason is concerned, and a moral fervour where ethical issues are concerned. Without a rigorous philosophical reflection on moral conduct, however, he can offer no compelling reason why one 'should' act a certain way or 'ought' not to act another way. He appeals to certain virtues based on Christian charity, but cannot defend such appeals on rational grounds.

Indeed, Russell holds an instrumental view of reason whereby reason provides the means to achieve what our passions lead us to desire. Reason offers the means, passions the ends. If we desire to be rich, for instance, reason will discover the means to do this, but it cannot tell us whether such desires are right or wrong. We are left to rely on our emotions for moral direction. Reason can determine logical and empirical concepts, but it cannot formulate principles to regulate our wills. The danger here is that personal or social ethical issues are left to the arbitrary determination of power, force, or passion. Grant was sensitive to what this had led to in the twentieth century.[29]

Popper, too, offers an instrumental view of reason in the guise of a pragmatism opposed to the Western tradition of metaphysical rationalism. This tradition finds its greatest expression in Plato. He describes Plato as a 'utopian social engineer' who infers specific action after establishing general laws. These laws become chains binding human minds and preventing them from feeling free to manipulate society toward ends they deem fit. The pragmatist, by contrast, is a 'piecemeal social engineer' who tinkers with certain aspects of society without establishing general laws. The utopian model represents a totalitarian, closed society, and the piecemeal model, a democratic, open society.[30]

According to Grant, Popper has completely misunderstood Plato. Plato is concerned with politics and society only in a derivative way. For Plato, the highest end for human beings is not to be found in politics. In order to appreciate this, one has to consider the historical context within which Plato's thought was forged. The decisive event in his life was the trial and death of Socrates, and his dialogues are dominated by the memory of Socrates' bearing of affliction (in the same way Saint Paul's letters are dominated by the crucifixion and death of

Jesus). There is no greater incentive to thinking about the purpose of politics than 'the execution of a saint by the democrats.' Plato's context was the decline of religion in the name of 'science' and scepticism. With this decline also came a loss of moral and spiritual foundations for conduct. This loss led further to self-interested cynicism. Plato's early dialogues are concerned with defining concepts such as goodness, holiness, and desire. His middle dialogues seek to demonstrate that such definition requires the doctrine of ideas. The later dialogues attempt to relate this doctrine to the then current knowledge of science and theology. Plato's central concern, then, is with the operation and role of practical reason. Popper has totally missed this. Metaphysics is a necessary basis for morality if morality is to exist. Popper wants to separate metaphysics and morality. Consequently, he can only appeal, like Russell, to an irrational basis for conduct.

The basic conflict between Plato and Popper is the conflict between essentialism and nominalism. The nominalist does not believe in a metaphysical foundation for practical conduct which can be thought rationally. Without metaphysics, however, how can anyone know which action is better and which is worse? Popper's basic inconsistency is that he uses the language of morality while rejecting any rational, metaphysical groundwork for it. As a consequence, morals can only be arbitrary and irrational, based on emotions, with no strength to sustain them in the face of the growing power of mass society, scepticism, and despair.

But Popper is optimistic about human goodwill and natural intuition. He believes it is not difficult for people and rulers to know what is worth doing and to pursue it. No effort of attention is necessary. The critics of metaphysics are not bad people, yet their theories have led to the worst crimes of the twentieth century. Adjusting and manipulating people, whether forcibly in war or more indirectly in the mass technological society, is a denial of their freedom at the deepest level. The result of 'piecemeal' social engineering is the growing consciousness of anguish, despair, and meaninglessness. While existentialists have shown us how destructive this can be, superficial liberals such as Popper still hold that morality is natural and meaning is matter of fact. But in the present-day context, philosophy grounded on faith, and faith which finds its voice in philosophy, is the only hope for human freedom. Without a deep knowledge of the meaning of existence, existence can only be anguished and impotent. 'Only after finding such knowledge do men have the right to go out and, piecemeal, change the world.'[31]

Pragmatism and scepticism, rooted as they are in the instrumental view of reason in the service of the passions and detached from faith, are theologies of glory. They obscure reality by making it appear better than it is. In so doing, they trivialize evil and suffering in the world, and assert that ultimate good is within simple human reach in thought and action.

Churches within the Protestant tradition have also surrendered their foundational affirmations before the necessities of the expanding mass society. These affirmations are rooted in spiritual freedom and the worship of the infinite against all idolatry. But churches have become 'tame confederates' of the mass society. The ideal minister is seen as the active democratic organizer and positive thinker who stands for social cohesion and encourages socially acceptable activities.[32] But what can account for such a shift in focus within North American Protestant churches? Grant believes the problem lies in the alliance of Protestantism with liberalism, and he offers two historical variations to explain the process of secularization in the churches, as well as in universities, which were originally set up by the churches.

First, in the Protestant tradition the relation of philosophy to faith has always been somewhat uncertain. On the one hand, Luther and the Reformation held up the word of God as alone sufficient for salvation and became wary of rational speculation. On the other hand, the more liberal movement within Protestantism sought a closer alliance between philosophy and theology in order to provide a rational apologetic of the faith to the world. In the process, unfortunately, liberalism also encouraged certain elements which severed the dependence of philosophy on faith. Although this is not what liberal Protestantism intended, it paved the way for the secularization of the universities. Grant refers to the case of Queen's University as an example of this development. While he does not elaborate on why this happened, he seems to imply that in their quest to exercise greater influence in society, liberals sought to adapt their faith to modern scientific and technological thinking, and they were optimistic that Christian faith would retain its traditional status in society. This, of course, did not happen. In the process, universities ended up becoming destroyers of faith, rather than cultivators of a rational foundation for it. Liberal Protestant educators did not fathom that the new natural and social sciences which they welcomed with open arms would also undermine the very basis of the Protestant faith. They were open to scientific, technological expansion while failing to realize that such expansion was based on the human conquest of nature and human nature. Such expansion rejected any place for submission to God or consent to what is, without needing to change and manipulate it. Moreover, this development was linked to the democratic ideal also held sacred by liberals. This ideal encouraged the trend of education catering to the desires and passions of society rather than challenging society through its students to desire and conform to a higher good.[33]

Second, the affirmation of spiritual freedom in Protestantism was undermined by the more practical interests of freedom in liberalism. This development had already begun at the time of the Reformation. Grant's understanding of the Reformation at this point is dependent on Hegel, who saw the Reformation as the spiritual version of the Enlightenment: 'spiritual freedom in Reformed theology is seen in relation to the idea of worldly freedom in the enlightenment.'[34] Inner freedom meant that external authorities which did not support the internal consciousness of the soul before the absolute were idols which had to be destroyed. But in destroying these 'idols,' the Reformation was also responsible for destroying the moral and spiritual foundations of the medieval world-view and the Aristotelian science linking the finite to the infinite. The implications of this destruction for the future were not fathomed. Freedom as an absolute, unrestrained principle led to the modern-day hedonism that lives by the appetites and recognizes no limits to freedom. Even at this point, we can detect the beginnings of Grant's eventual rejection of Hegel. In spite of his adoption of Hegel's definition of the Reformation and the importance of freedom against oppressive and idolatrous impositions, he is too critical of human nature to be optimistic that an unfettered freedom would eventually lead to harmony with the absolute good. We will consider Grant's relationship to Hegel further below. It suffices to say at this point that the practical, world-reforming understanding of freedom is linked, in Grant's mind, to a Puritan Calvinist brand of Protestantism rather than one influenced by Luther (even though Luther's rejection of reason in its Aristotelian form encouraged the denigration of reason as a whole in Protestantism).

The biblical focus on history and the reform of society also led Calvinism into a close relation with the new sciences. This relation is based on an older relation between Protestantism and the liberal humanism of the Enlightenment. The practical interests of the liberal in reforming the world for humanity's sake and the Protestant concern for bringing about the kingdom of God in the world frequently brought them into close association. But freedom fuelled by faith and charity lost all sense of a transcendent goal and became increasingly driven by human appetite for human ends. This development was facilitated by the practical focus of Protestantism to the neglect of contemplation. Freedom to change the world still exists, in part, in the form of altruism, which is the last remnant of the Protestant vision of the divine kingdom on earth. But it also exists as a means to serving the growing self-centred hedonism so prevalent today.[35]

The erosion of the Protestant faith in the West and its separation from the modern emphasis on practical achievement has left the practical sphere without the guidance of faith. This, as Grant has asserted repeatedly, is in large part the result of the Protestant denigration of reason. A faith that could not communicate itself effectively and critically in relation to the ever new and greater achievements of practice was bound to lose its influence and significance. The split between faith and reason is seen in the modern-day universities and churches. Faith without reason remains sentimental, emotional expression and leads merely to ethical platitudes. Reason without faith leads to secularism, scepticism, and a focus on practical techniques serving selfish hedonism (the modern faith).

The result of believing that changing the world is what matters above all else is a denial that there is anything worth knowing and doing that does not lead to such change. This view of freedom is the cause of the dying away of 'personal relations, art, philosophy and prayer.'[36] Such practices have less to do with changing or manipulating the world, and more to do with contemplating it in wonder and love. But there is no need to cultivate serious thinking when it is thought optimistically that the will is naturally good. There is no need for serious art when its purpose is no longer to portray the world as it is, but rather, more sentimentally. There is no need for serious contemplation of personal relations when manipulation replaces contemplation, turning otherness into an object rather than a subject like ourselves. With the loss of genuine otherness there is a loss of the art of adoration and sexual fulfilment.

In spite of all these signs of decay, Grant claims to be unable to account fully for how the ethic of changing the world gradually lost all reference to the infinite and became worldly reformism, and how, in turn, worldly reformism is becoming ever more a democratic hedonism. Neither does he want to ignore the positive contributions of practical, technological achievement. Nevertheless, asserts Grant, one thing can be stated for certain:

> ... as the presence of the infinite fades from our minds, a society which has concentrated its energies on changing the world will more and more demand the immediate motive for so doing, and thus our society will become increasingly ruled by pleasure and force. In the next years, if we are not destroyed by war, we will watch the domination of the elite by the pleasure of personal power and the domination of the more submissive by the pursuit of those less strenuous pleasures which alleviate boredom. As thought about our proper end disappears, the busy specialists and the lazy whom they serve, will, almost without thought, pour into the vacuum the idea of pleasure, in all its manifold, fascinating and increasingly perverted forms. Beyond this chaos it is only possible to guess and to hope.[37]

Grant ends this statement with these stark words: 'How God shall reconcile the world to Himself is not a matter we can comprehend.'

Grant's affirmation of agnosticism and mystery about God's working in the world was not based on atheism or scepticism about God's intention to reconcile the world to God's self. Rather, it was a trust in and love of God in spite of the evil and suffering in the world which darken any immediate hope or possibility for salvation from the human side of reality. By obscuring this darkness in human life and history, liberalism was also hindering the possibility of a faith in God that transcended human possibilities, rooted in divine revelation and grace.

Grant's views on universities and churches in the mass society also find their parallel in his views on mental health. In one paper, he addresses the modern approach to therapy by comparing it with the ancient approach. The two most influential systems of therapy of the ancient world are (1) the Platonic progression, 'ignorance – conversion to dialectic – illumination,' and (2) the Christian progression, 'sin – repentance through grace – salvation.' The chief modern system of therapy is based on the medical model, 'neurosis – psychotherapy – normality.' All of these systems have their critical and developmental aspects:

> The philosopher must be continually aware of his ignorance if he would

persevere in the pursuit of wisdom. If the Christian is to be in true repentance before the Cross, he must face some of his past acts as sins. The patient must admit the unconscious source of some of his acts if the analysis is to be a success. On the other hand, philosophy will be frustrated by misologism if its dialectical struggles are not known as leading to the Good. The Christian's repentance will leave him a Stoic or a Pharisee if it is not seen as preparation for the divine love. The modern patient must give some meaning to the idea of normality.[38]

Although there are these strong similarities, there is one significant difference. Modern therapy has a certainty in its conception of disease, but a vagueness in its conception of health.

This problem may be seen to arise in Freud himself. On the one hand, he accepts the scientific account of knowledge as human power to change the world. On the other hand, his application of science to the mind has led to the view that human reason arises out of the 'suppression of the instinctual' in human beings. The suppression of the instinctual is the very cause of personal and social disease. Thus, the same human power that masters the natural environment is also the cause of mental disease.

Freud's ambiguous relationship to science may be further evidenced in the method by which he came to this discovery, namely, his self-analysis. While his disciples have hailed Freud's integrity as a scientist, they describe his self-analysis, through which he came to the most profound of his scientific insights, in language reminiscent of Christian witnesses describing the suffering and death of Jesus on the cross. It is difficult to defend this self-analysis as a credible scientific method of knowledge. Yet even Freud's closest followers cannot deny the profundity and depth it gave to his thought.

In later writings, Freud's therapeutic and social pessimism about the human struggle for redemption is brought out even more clearly. There is little in him of the progressive view of personal and social history popular during his time. Rather, his focus is on the necessary limits to human existence if civilization is to continue existing. The overcoming of nature by reason also means the suppression of the instincts. *Eros* – the free play of the life instinct – is suppressed, and *Thanatos* – the death instinct – is released into life and society. Consequently, health can only be a limited state which holds in check the death instinct while consenting of necessity to the suppression of the life instinct at varying levels.

While the insights and method of Freud's psychotherapy are the foundation of the psychotherapy movement in the West, in North America this movement has associated itself with the prestige and power of the medical profession and the optimism of liberal Protestantism. Therapists also adjusted themselves to the desires and interests of modern mass technological society. Reflection upon and analysis of techniques for therapy proliferated considerably, while the purpose and goal of therapy were assumed to be consistent with the goals and purposes of society as a whole. Any sense of the anguish of existence reflected in Freud was smoothed over for the sake of adjusting to things as they are.

Grant even places Carl Jung in the optimistic camp of modern therapy, even though Jung's thought and method arose out of the terrible crisis in the West during the twentieth century. This crisis manifested itself externally in the two world wars and the future potential of a nuclear holocaust. It also manifested itself internally in the sense of meaninglessness and purposelessness that Jung witnessed in so many of his patients. Moreover, unlike Freud, he appears to offer a positive place for religion in the healthy life. Yet, at bottom, Jung is an optimist about human nature and civilization. Human psychological disease arises from accidental factors. Human irreligion and confusion arise because modern rationality and technology have cut humanity off from the eternal 'archetypes,' which are linked to the very essence of human nature in harmony with the whole.[39]

Freud, by contrast, is a pessimist. Achieving whatever limited health is possible in life requires the overcoming of ambiguities and tragedies in existence that are not accidental, but of the very substance of life. Freud is closer to the biblical doctrine of the fall than are those who claim that evil is not in the will but external to it, that one can never be a slave to it, and its overcoming by human beings will lead to the good society. The conflict between Freud and others may be compared to the Protestant biblical perspective in opposition to an Aristotelian natural theology of glory, which trusts human nature's capacity for good through the will and intellect.[40]

But beyond the conflict between Freud and his optimistic disciples, there is a commonality in their faith. In the end, health is something to be achieved by human beings themselves. Jung may emphasize the capacity for ultimate fulfilment in humanity at the expense of the truth about human limits. Freud may emphasize the limited state of human fulfilment in view of the ambiguities of human life. But only Christianity believes that such ambiguities – namely, suffering and death – must be included in the movement from sickness to health, and that health in terms of ultimate fulfilment is possible for humanity only through divine grace. This is the conception of health offered by the one who said, 'Take up your cross and follow me.' Christianity believes that the human being who was most supremely free 'was sufficiently maladjusted to his community to die on a cross.'[41]

Without a doubt, according to Grant, Freud is closer to understanding and expressing things as they are. He does not share any of the liberal optimism about human possibilities for health within the expanding mass society. His North American disciples, along with Jung, however, are much more optimistic and, therefore, more representative of a theology of glory. Indeed, Freud's atheistic pessimism brings him close to an atheistic existentialism of Sartre's variety. But Freud is also a believer in modern technological science, and whatever health is possible is dependent on the aid of objective scientific methods. Moreover, freedom has more of a debased meaning in Freud than it does in Sartre. Freud shares the liberal vision of freedom as the means to get what one wants when one wants it. Freedom is crushed in the human spirit, not in terms of human dignity, humiliation, or the capacity to transcend one's social assumptions, but rather in limitations to one's material and sexual appetites – in terms of a narcissistic injury, rather than in the affliction of the soul.

3.3.2. Modern Liberalism – Hegel, Liberal Humanism, Marxism

As we have already suggested in the previous section, Grant's understanding of freedom was influenced by Hegel, who related its spiritual side in the Reformation to its political side in the Enlightenment. This primary freedom was asserted against any external limitations that imposed and inhibited its flowering in the soul. But what about the relationship of freedom to evil? In a letter to his wife, Grant claims that Hegel recognized the reality of evil in history better than any other modern, and that if a philosophy of history were possible, Hegel perceived something profound with his idea of the unfolding of freedom in the world. Yet Grant had serious doubts about Hegel. His system seemed to suggest a spirit of acceptance of necessity which included evil. This was consistent with Christianity, which recognized the importance of suffering and death in the journey of the soul toward God. But Hegel also seemed to trivialize evil by reconciling himself to evil in history too easily. This is evident in his lack of practical ethics, as opposed to his disciple Marx. It is also evident in his complete elimination of Kant's agnosticism or Plato's transcendence. He explained too much in his philosophy of history, identifying its development with the working of divine providence in the world. In so doing, he was calling good evil and evil good, trivializing the evil in history, and making God a tame confederate of his speculative adventurings. For Grant, by contrast, it should be possible to assert a transcendence that does not leave one irresponsible or a mysticism that can be combined with worldly responsibility.[42]

But there are liberal humanists who reject philosophies of history in the very name of freedom. Anything that keeps human beings from believing themselves to be absolutely free and responsible in the making of their own history must be rejected. This includes not only philosophies of history which argue for some sort of predetermined meaning imposed on history, but any metaphysics which imposes external limits to human freedom and will-power. The spirit of liberalism, for Grant, is above all

> the affirmation that 'we are our own.' To put it negatively, we are not creatures, existence is not a gift, we do not belong to some being greater than ourselves. To put it positively, we create our own meaning, we make the world for good or ill. And it is in this freedom itself, with no appeal to any higher principle, that individuals have their value. And this freedom is an ultimate beyond which we cannot go.[43]

Grant refers to empiricists such as Isaiah Berlin as the best representatives of this line of thought. Grant's criticism of this thought is, by now, evident. It fails to recognize that human freedom unfettered, human will undisciplined, and human reason unilluminated has led to the horrors of the twentieth century, which include world wars and the ethics of the mass technological society. Yet Grant also admires the deep sense of human responsibility for, and struggle against, evil that such thinking reflects, as well as the refusal to accept progressive views of history which undermine human responsibility to change the world. No theory can mitigate human responsibility or justify the passive acceptance or rationalization of evil in the world.

The best representative of a responsible liberalism which refuses to accept the evil and suffering in the world passively is Karl Marx. Marx's whole project, according to Grant, was a theodicy: 'the vindication of the divine providence in view of the existence of evil.'[44] Marx's thought begins with the reality of evil in the world. The world is not as it ought to be. Human beings are cursed by starvation, greed, and domination. Social structures are such that they prevent human fulfilment. The religious solution, he claims, is to believe that all is really well in spite of the evil everywhere. Such belief prevents human beings from facing the evils in the world for what they are and struggling to eliminate them. Religion is an opiate of the people, undermining their responsibility for changing the world. It alienates human beings from discovering their true freedom. History, according to Marx, must not become the sphere for the passive acceptance of the status quo veiled under the doctrine of divine providence, but the sphere for the rejection of God in the name of actively overcoming the evils of the world. Unlike Hegel, from whom he derives his most profound ideas, Marx limits human freedom to the domination of nature. As a consequence, he fails to recognize the need for inner freedom above all else. Marx's focus on the practical overcoming of evil in history, however, surpasses Hegel's failure to realize his philosophy in practical life.

As a modern man, Marx celebrates the accomplishments of science and technology in achieving the capacity to eliminate scarcity and overcome disease and hard labour. Yet the reality is that human oppression has intensified because the control of technological means is in the hands of the few. The task, as Marx sees it, is to remove these means from the control of the few and give them over to the control of the many. In a capitalistic society, this means taking the means of production from the control of the owners and giving them into the hands of the workers. Marx's emphasis on human responsibility (freedom) is combined with his belief in historical progress (nature). History is by nature (rather than divine providence) evolving toward a utopia in which the benefits of technology will be controlled and shared by all.

Even though Grant admires Marx's passion for social justice, he is unable to accept his doctrine of freedom. First and foremost, his conception of freedom is limited to the external, objective world, and therefore he does not recognize the need for inner freedom. He does not recognize the truth which Hegel expresses when he refers to the Reformation as the spiritual side of the Enlightenment. Revolution needs reformation. True freedom is not only transcending everything in the world that oppresses us, but everything within us that prevents us from transcending ourselves and recognizing our true purpose. Because of this failure, Marxism ends up in becoming superficial about evil. Evil is external to human beings, rooted in the objective conditions of the world. Hence, freedom is limited to changing the objective conditions of the world. This superficiality about evil has led to abuses in Marxism, be it in the lack of safeguards, practices of spiritual purification within the system, or the ruthless subordination and affliction of the individual to the interests of the state.[45]

Grant's views on liberalism are ambivalent. On the one hand, he admires its emphasis on changing the world insofar as it is a world in which evil and suffering are so prevalent. On the other hand, he is wary of its Promethean optimism about the human will, intellect, or history as a whole as the means to the overcoming of evil. Grant is forever sensitive to the depths of evil and suffering which corrupt even the human will and intellect, and hinder any ultimate resolutions of the evils of the world through human historical paths to redemption. Grant's struggle is to achieve the kind of thinking which is sufficiently sensitive to the depth of evil and suffering – not calling good evil and evil good but the thing as it is – but also open to divine grace in the desire to bring about redemption concretely in the world.

3.4. The Struggle toward a Theology of the Cross for the Mass Age: Weil versus Hegel

Grant's struggle with liberalism is rooted in his deeper struggle with biblical and Greek conceptions of freedom (as mentioned earlier). The biblical, existentialist critique of liberalism is that it is too superficial and optimistic about human freedom in the world. It fails to appreciate the inner, spiritual dimensions of freedom which are undermined by the very technological necessities that liberalism has precipitated for the sake of alleviating the external, physical evil and suffering in the world. On the other hand, the Greek understanding of freedom as obedience to the truth appreciates the order and structure of the universe and is more hesitant about changing the world, fearful of the destructive potentialities of such change. On a deeper level, however, Grant begins to perceive distinctions within biblical and Greek modes of thought. He begins to distinguish between a less reflective, reformist, optimistic, Calvinist Christianity and a more contemplative, Augustinian, Lutheran, existentialist Christianity of the cross. He also begins to recognize the difference between a more Platonic, transcendent, mystical philosophy, as opposed to a more Aristotelian, natural, speculative one. Grant's struggle along these lines is most visible when he attempts to speak positively about opening up a place for and inspiring the good in thought and practice in the mass society.

3.4.1. The Purpose of Philosophy in the Mass Society

The tension between biblical and Greek languages in Grant's thought is apparent in his attempts to define the purpose of philosophy. On the one hand, he seeks to be faithful to existential realities in the world as it is and, on the other, to the task of rational contemplation about the order of the world and its creator, without calling good evil and evil good.

In a controversial paper written in 1951, Grant makes some bold statements on the nature of philosophic study. It is 'the analysis of the traditions of our society and the judgment of those traditions against our varying intuitions of the perfection of God.'[46] Philosophy is the rational or critical form of the contemplative life. Thus, it is inseparable from faith. Philosophy, moreover, is not a discipline restricted to specialists in the university, but a reflection on the whole of life open to all and essential for people from all walks of life. As against the growing technical orientation in Canadian universities, the goal of philosophic study is to establish all enquiry and discovery within purposes dictated by the love of God. As against the growing optimism in the face of scientific and technological advances in the mass society, genuine philosophy arises out of a sense of the tragedy and uncertainty of life, and its purpose is to prevent us from becoming 'beasts.'[47]

In a speech on the purpose of philosophy, Grant points to two words: 'love' rooted in faith and 'wisdom' rooted in philosophy. The key questions are What is the purpose of existence? and How ought we to live? Those who think such questions are irrelevant for society or those who are content with an unreflective faith do not need to philosophize. Philosophy is for those who have moved beyond simple certainties, who have come face to face with the mystery of existence. This mystery arises in two ways. First, it arises in the sense of wonder about which Plato speaks. This sense is destroyed in children in our mass society, who are tamed early on to accept the assumptions and aspirations of this society as it is. The mystery also arises out of the anguish and suffering of life. It arises when one must face one's own death or that of a loved one. It arises from our disappointments, guilt, and shame, when we see ourselves as we truly are.[48]

Most will attempt to avoid an encounter with the anguish or wonder of life, either by downplaying them or resolving them in a superficial way. Philosophy, however, arises as a necessity for us when we confront the depth of life's mysteries. This task is one that each individual must do for him- or herself. As Luther said, 'a man must do his own believing as he must do his own dying.' It is also a task that each generation must do for itself. Our journey to God must be lifelong. We are no further ahead than Jesus or Socrates. The best we can do is emulate them in our own feeble way. 'We must live through the same thought, the same agony they lived through, if we are to come to the majesty of their vision.'[49]

Grant also relates the purpose of philosophy to the purpose of education as a whole. To achieve a high degree of self-consciousness in reason, will, and imagination, and to seek out freedom and wisdom in the light of God, is the purpose of education. Education, moreover, is the very purpose of human existence. Even though human beings are created in the divine image, they are also fallen and, therefore, need education to restore them toward this image again. This is a lifelong journey. Grant's model for education is Plato's allegory of the cave. Human beings are chained in a dark cave of ignorance. The purpose of life is the struggle for freedom out of the cave into 'the sunlight of knowledge which is the radiance of God.'[50] As Jesus also put it: 'The truth shall make you free.' Elsewhere, Grant describes this journey out of the cave in words which he would repeat throughout his life to define the purpose of education and life: 'out of the shadows and imaginings into truth.' For Grant, the highest knowledge is knowledge of the good or God, and we are most free when we become conscious that our destiny and fulfilment lies in obedience to God. This, of course, involves a critical function. The chains of ignorance that bind us are not easily smashed. We require rigorous self-examination and an examination of society, especially in light of the degraded purposes our passions, along with society, direct us to pursue. Rather than adjusting ourselves to society as it is, we must resist its allure and find our fulfilment in divine wisdom and charity. This also requires divine grace and illumination.

Although Grant clearly recognizes the difficulty of the journey from the cave into the sunlight, by defining the chains as ignorance does he assume that the truth revealed to the soul will lead it naturally toward the light? Not at all. The soul offers great resistance to being brought to the light. For Grant, Plato, and even Jesus as represented in the above quote, freedom is a gift of truth. Resistance to the truth, therefore, is rooted in ignorance of it or an imperfect revelation of it. Outside the grace of truth, freedom is a limited, not absolute, quality. This idea, while consistent with an Augustinian, Reformed doctrine of irresistible grace, stands in tension with the biblical view of freedom as Grant understood it in the 1950s under the influence of existentialism. According to the Augustinian view, sin and evil manifest the absence of good rather than its opposite. When we resist the truth or commit sin, we do not do so because we are free but because we are in chains. True freedom is obedience of the reason and will to the good or God. This is also the Platonic understanding of human nature and destiny, which is the basis of Augustine's teaching at this point, and it is Augustine's type of Christianity which Grant has in mind when assuming that philosophy and Christianity have a common purpose.

In the 1950s, however, Grant is not consistent in his understanding of Christianity or philosophy. We have already seen how Grant can think in terms of a more Augustinian Christianity which attempts to incorporate Platonic rationality into its biblical theology. Moreover, this type of Christianity is contrasted with a less contemplative and more activist Calvinist Christianity, or a less mystical and more rationalistic Aristotelian philosophical influence in Christianity. Elsewhere, he also makes distinctions between mystical monasticism and the political aspirations of the church in the world. This distinction further manifests itself in the separation of natural and revealed theology which leaves history as the sphere for faith and nature as the sphere for formal reason. The Reformation's rejection of medieval attempts at synthesis was in the name of freedom before God and responsibility within history. While such an assertion was essential, the consequences with regard to the denigration of reason were unfortunate. Yet Luther's rejection of Aristotelianism must not be confused with that of Calvin. Luther was more mystical and open to contemplation. This philosophical movement reached its apex in Hegel, who attempted 'to think freedom and history philosophically.'[51] In so doing, Hegel attempted to synthesize not only Western Christianity and philosophy, but also ancient and modern thought. In the process, however, the more ancient expressions of Christianity and philosophy were swallowed up by a more progressive and optimistic conception of the whole. Although Grant is attracted to Hegel's thought in the 1950s, he is never satisfied with it, and this is especially in view of his own experiences, along with his study of Weil and the existentialists. But were they able to offer a vision of light to answer their darker vision of the world?

3.4.2. Weil's Vision of the Good

Weil's importance for Grant was not only in helping him understand and articulate the darkness of the world as it is, but also a vision of the good that was consistent with his experience of faith, and in full consciousness of the evil and affliction in the world. In particular, Weil helped Grant articulate the theology of the cross in a way that brought Plato and Christ, philosophy and faith, together. Let us now consider in greater detail Weil's vision of the good/God[52] in relation to humanity and the world.

The Knowledge of God

For someone so grounded in reality, Weil had little hesitation speaking of God or her mystical experiences of God's presence. Yet such knowledge and experience could never be based on her own intellect, spirit, or will. Indeed, Weil taught that all of these aspects of human personality, rooted as they are in ourselves, are also subject to the necessity of force and affliction and, therefore, to illusion and destruction. Moreover, because such a condition is a pervasive and inescapable reality for all human beings, God can only be absent or hidden within the world.[53] If God is to be known, it is only through divine revelation. If God is to be experienced, it is only divine grace that can make one capable of receiving and experiencing such a revelation.

According to Weil, divine revelation was not limited to the sacred texts and traditions of Christianity, but was equally present in Hinduism, in the ancient mystery religions crushed by Rome, and in certain Gnostic traditions condemned by the church. At the same time, Weil rejected portions of the Bible, particularly of the Old Testament, which seemed to emphasize the exclusiveness, conquest, and interventionism of God in history, as well as the scrutability of divine providence to the human mind. Weil felt it was precisely this false image of God that influenced the Western church, with its doctrine of divine providence as conquest in history. Likewise, she rejected the church's doctrine of the Incarnation of Christ as limited to Christianity. She believed the incarnation to have been revealed in varying form and depth in other religions, and even in those who were not visibly religious at all. What made the gospel accounts of the crucifixion so unique was not their revelation of divinity but, rather, how this divinity was revealed and incarnated in one who experienced the full weight of force and affliction in the world.[54]

Weil's conception of God was influenced by her understanding of Plato's conception of the good. God is being in all its fullness and the source of all being. At the same time, however, in creating the universe God renounces being all in order to permit something other than God, to have existence. This divine self-renunciation permitted a universe to come into existence governed by a necessity other than God, and human creatures with an autonomy outside God. Accordingly, Weil's conception of divine providence is not God's intervention in the world or history, but God's self-denial or absence, allowing beings to exist outside God in an independent universe. Weil can go so far as to equate divine providence with chance in the universe.[55] This divine self-renunciation, which Weil also names love, defines the very nature of God. Love is totally contrary to force. If force is defined as that which governs the universe and imposes itself on human beings against their consent or refusal, love is a renunciation of the force or power to interfere in other life, permitting otherness to exist freely.

God's 'Secret' Presence in the World

At the same time, God, who is love, did not permit force an absolute sovereignty without manifesting an indirect, hidden, 'secret' presence in the world. While the world appears to be ruled by brutal necessity or force, there is also another side to it, another way of looking at it. The world is also beautiful. Beauty is an incarnation of divine love in the world. Weil has no hesitation equating beauty with the *Logos* incarnate in the world. Here, biblical conceptions of love and Platonic conceptions of beauty come together. Beauty is that which draws our love. It seizes our soul, even when caught in the grips of misery.[56] Beauty draws us out of ourselves and inspires us to look beyond ourselves, in love. For Weil, it is the world as a whole that can properly be called beautiful. Anything less than the world can only be considered beautiful as a reflection of the world's beauty. Weil discovers such reflections everywhere.

She finds reflections of divine love or beauty in necessity. While the world is necessity and, therefore, other than God, who is love, God has exercised an indirect, gentle 'persuasion' by which necessity submits to or 'obeys' love. Weil derives this idea from Plato's *Timaeus*. If God were completely absent from the world, it would be an unmitigated chaos. But God, through the beloved Son or *Logos*, is present in the order of the world. This order is beautiful. Its beauty is rooted in necessity's 'indifference' or 'impartiality,' as well as in its obedience to the limits marked out for it in creation.[57]

Weil explains the impartiality of necessity with an illustration of the sea. She speaks of the beauty of the waves of the sea as the force of gravity upon them creates their folds, and yet it is in these same waves that ships are tossed and people drowned.[58] To explain nature's indifference or impartiality, Weil frequently cites the gospel description of God as one who makes the sun shine and the rain fall equally on the just and on the unjust. Such impartiality on God's part, hidden in the natural forces of necessity, is not an indifference to injustice (which is how it is often experienced under force) but, rather, a love for all that is unconditional, a commitment to everyone irrespective of their virtue or vice. It requires self-renunciation to love impartially. Such love is inspired in us by the beauty of the world even when at times its movements conflict with our well-being. One must be drawn beyond one's self to experience it. Beauty is a divine snare for this drawing out of self.[59]

The idea of built-in limits in nature is also important, for each part exists in its own place permitting the coexistence of other parts. In this way, necessity is not only a brutal master, but also 'docile' and 'obedient to God' – that is, it keeps within its limits.[60] Force not only imposes itself against one's consent or refusal, but it respects no limits. Respecting limits means accepting that one is not the centre of the universe but must share one's space with other life. It involves self-renunciation. Without these limits, no one would survive, as the universe would be one mass chaos. Both self-renunciation and the respect for limits, as well as the capacity to contemplate the order of the world as beautiful, are reflections of divine love.

The idea of the limits built into necessity is also reflected in nature and society under the concept which Weil named 'equilibrium.' She derived the meaning of this concept from Anaximander and the Pythagoreans, and she explains it thus:

And like the oscillations of the waves, the whole succession of events here below, made up, as they are, of variations in balance mutually compensated – births and destructions, waxings and wanings – render one keenly alive to the invisible presence of a plexus of limits without substance and yet harder than any diamond. That is why things are beautiful in their vicissitudes although they allow one to perceive a pitiless necessity. Pitiless yes; but which is not force, which is sovereign ruler over all force. ... it is love.[61]

The limits within the natural world and within human relations in society exercise a balancing and harmonizing function in the world. Everything and everyone is subject to limits which, when transgressed, exert a counter-pressure toward equilibrium. There is a limit to growth and power as there is a limit to all life. Transgressing these limits sets a counter-movement of force toward the restoration of the natural equilibrium. These limits may be brutal and harsh for some. But they also mitigate much of the force in the world that could go on multiplying indefinitely, whether it be in the abuse of nature or of other life. The equilibrium built into necessity is an equalizing force, limiting the suffering to be experienced and the evil to be done.

Another reflection of divine love in the world is the concept of justice. In the social sphere, Weil identifies justice with equality. In a world of force, equality exists where there is an equal measure of force on both sides. If one is stronger than the other, 'that which is possible is imposed by the first and accepted by the second.'[62] This also breeds self-aggrandizement in the first and a loss of dignity in the second. On the other hand, the 'supernatural virtue of justice consists of behaving exactly as though there were equality when one is stronger in an unequal relationship.' Weil calls this supernatural because it is a reflection of divine love. It goes against nature. One must exercise profound self-renunciation not to use all the power at one's disposal.

Divine love as justice is also reflected in the love of neighbour. This love has particular concern for the weak and unfortunate neighbour, whom, according to the natural law of force, we do not even notice when passing by. The parable of the good Samaritan is particularly illuminating for Weil. The man who is wounded and afflicted by misfortune at the hands of force is inert and lifeless. He goes unnoticed, or nearly unnoticed, by those who pass him by. This is how it is with the afflicted. They are weak and are therefore rarely noticed in a world which recognizes force or power. If they are noticed, people often express revulsion or condemnation, or avoid them altogether. In other cases, they offer charity to buy off the sufferer and relieve their consciences. These responses only add to the afflicted's sense of worthlessness since affliction has robbed them of their dignity and innocence. People separate themselves from the afflicted, and this is inevitable because to confront the afflicted is not only to confront one's own fragility and mortality, it is also to accept that one is separated from the afflicted by a very thin set of circumstances that can change at any moment.[63] It is to bear the other's affliction oneself.

This genuine turn to the afflicted neighbour Weil calls 'attention.' To pay attention, whether to beauty or to affliction, is to transport oneself outside oneself to the place of the other. It is self-renouncing love. To notice the afflicted is to give them existence. Weil's experience of being treated like 'a thing' in the factories made her sensitive to how people's affirmation of their own existence is tied to this affirmation by others.[64]

It is this loving attention to the afflicted that begins to restore life in them. Weil distinguishes between charity and justice. Charity belongs to the realm of natural morality. Giving is optional and one feels the right to be pleased with oneself. Justice, however, which for both the Greeks and the gospels is equated with love, is rooted in a divine obligation to the afflicted. In the afflicted, it is reflected in the possibility of offering gratitude from the depths of one's being rather than from servile duty. This exchange of genuine compassion and gratitude allows the one to fulfil the divine law of love to the neighbour, and the other, a restoration of dignity – for to offer gratitude from within is to offer it freely and not under constraint.[65]

Finally, even in the realm of human society, Weil finds reflections of divine love. It is true that she never tires of asserting how evil society is, and calls it – borrowing imagery from Plato and the Apocalypse of Saint John – the social beast. It is also true that she includes in her condemnation of society all institutions (including the church).[66] But, at the same time, Weil speaks of *metaxu* – the Greek word for 'intermediaries.' These are relative goods in society which, albeit mixed with evil, also 'warm and nourish the soul and without which, short of sainthood, a human life is impossible.' These include family, art, culture, tradition, and country. The love of such *metaxu* can lead the soul to the love of the ultimate good, so long as they are not idolized as absolute themselves.[67]

Weil discovered the most profound revelation of divine love and beauty in the crucified Christ. Christ incarnated divine love throughout his ministry and teaching. On the cross, however, the purity of this love is especially accentuated against the reality of its opposite. Under the harshest subjection to force and the most extreme experience of affliction in which even his Father God was absent, Jesus continued to love.[68] This love is reflected, for instance, in his treatment of the thief beside him, who of all people deserved the cross but received unconditional mercy. It is reflected in his love for his enemies in the form of forgiveness. It is a love that was not destroyed or poisoned even as Christ himself was destroyed along with all the certainties and relationships that sustained him. And this is precisely what convinces Weil of the height of the cross as divine revelation. Human affliction, to which all are vulnerable, is revealed in all its horrible truth. Divine love, which is the deepest fulfilment and aspiration of the soul (albeit hidden to itself), is revealed in all its beauty. For these extremes to coexist in one human being is nothing short of a divine miracle, for there is nothing farther away from one being brutalized and humiliated than the experience of beauty. And yet hidden precisely within this distance was the truth of their redemptive link, a truth of which the crucified Christ was the mediator.

The Good 'Hidden beneath Its Opposite'

Weil perceived reality in terms of contradiction. The supreme contradiction for her was that between necessity, force, and affliction, on the one hand, and the absolute good, God, or love, on the other. Anyone who contemplates this contradiction with the clarity that Weil did is confronted by the distance between the terms. How can the love of God, which is self-renunciation, be brought together with necessity as force, which is its total opposite? Indeed, when one has seriously contemplated or experienced the effects of force in affliction, one is not able to know and experience the love of God. One is brought to the loss of all worldly supports and certainties, including one's faith. But precisely in this loss through suffering is where Weil finds the supernatural purpose of affliction. She states the following:

> A man whose family has died under torture, and is himself tortured for a long time in a concentration camp, or a 16th century Indian, a sole survivor of the total extermination of his people. Such men if they previously believed in the mercy of God would either believe it no longer, or else conceive it quite differently than before.[69]

This is as clear an example of affliction as any. If one contemplates such an experience, how can one retain one's certainties and beliefs? Nothing in this world, including our own inner confidence, can withstand such an assault on life. And yet Weil speaks of a different basis for faith after one has tasted affliction. Weil came to discover such a basis, hidden beneath the experience of affliction. Hidden precisely in this horrible, evil experience is the revelation of the deepest good for human beings. Hidden beneath the cross of affliction is the redeeming grace of divine love. But in order to perceive this revelation and grace, one must come to the end of one's faith in human thought and power. If faith and love are possible again, they can only arise through God.

Decreation

Weil explains the process by which this happens with the concept she named 'decreation.' Decreation is the form that divine redemption must take in a world of sin. Human beings have misused their autonomy. They have confused the absolute good with their own worldly aims and efforts modelled after force. God, however, has established the true purpose for human beings in the creative act: self-renouncing love. Decreation is our response to God's renunciation in creation. 'God renounces being everything. We should renounce being something. That is our only good.'[70] By using force, human beings impose themselves on creation and live under the illusion that they are at the centre. It is only affliction that reveals how false this is and how human dignity in the world is easily destroyed when the fragile thread of personal and social circumstances that hold it together is severed. Decreation is our free consent to be nothing as that which we are in reality. It is our acceptance that we are not the centre and ought not to be.

Weil develops the concept of decreation along the lines of medieval mysticism. She speaks of the annihilation of the self, the 'I,' and the total surrender of the soul to God. Such annihilation is not a destruction of the person. Weil distinguishes the two in this way: 'Decreation: to make something created pass into the uncreated. Destruction: to make something pass into nothingness. A blameworthy substitute for decreation.'[71] Elsewhere she states: '... if death is an annihilation, there are two annihilations, annihilation in nothingness and annihilation in God.'[72] The kind of 'annihilation' or suffering Weil has in mind here is what she calls 'expiatory.' It corresponds to the feeling of condemnation in the afflicted soul. One is brought face to face with the evil in oneself and the world. One is brought to the realization of one's sin and one's bondage to force. One consents to suffer evil in the same measure one reflects it. One is purified from one's illusions and idols and brought to the foot of the cross:

> God suffered in place of man – this does not mean that Christ's affliction diminished in the slightest degree the affliction of men, but that through the affliction of Christ ... the affliction of any afflicted man acquires the meaning and value of expiation, if only he desires it.[73]

This means that our suffering of the weight of our sin will not destroy us, but purify us. On the cross, Christ received the maximum measure of sin, which was not thrown back onto the world but was converted into pure suffering. Our sin is received by Christ and not thrown back to destroy us. This is divine mercy. Consequently, our suffering of our sin purifies rather than destroys us, if we are feeding on the cross. The distinction between purification and destruction, however, cannot be made easily when one is undergoing the suffering of affliction. The person, like Christ, loses all sense of purpose, faith, or hope and feels damned for eternity. If a link to God can exist at all, God alone can establish it.

Weil expresses this in Trinitarian terms, as well. God's being is the perfect unity of love, which is the Trinity. Out of this love, God renounces God's self and creates the world. At the same time, God, who is love, does not completely abandon the creation, but gives over a part of God's self to its necessities. This part is the son, who out of love renounces his divinity in the incarnation. This renunciation reaches its climax on the cross, where Christ is subjected to a maximum measure of necessity, which is affliction. The cross is the furthest distance between God and God, between God, who is absent, and a forsaken, afflicted human being. Yet the love that joins Father and Son through this distance, which is the Spirit, creates the possibility for all human beings, even the most afflicted, to participate in the divine love between God and God.[74] One participates in this love by facing the cross. The cross is the absence of God, the total vulnerability to and suffering of force and affliction, the annihilating power of God exercised to the limits permitted by love. It is both the experience of the greatest evil and the means to the deepest good. It can purify us of the evil within and prepare a place for God's spirit to enter. This is decreation.

The annihilation in God which corresponds to decreation is identified with affliction, but distinguished from it as well. Affliction is the destruction of the self from the outside, while decreation is the destruction of the self from within to which the soul freely consents by divine grace. If one is destroyed from without – that is, humiliated, degraded, and brutalized – and one is not prepared for it from within, one's soul passes into complete despair and nothingness. This happens because human dignity and faith in the world are rooted in dreams of freedom and self-aggrandizement. When such dreams are violently destroyed, so is one's whole sense of being. Those who know that they are nothing in the world and consent to this reality may be brutalized by affliction, but their sense of being is in God rather than themselves. For Weil, this mystical process of self-annihilation is also an imitation of Christ, who consented to renounce his will in complete obedience to God's will. The cross was not only a revelation of evil and affliction, but also a revelation of mystical self-renunciation imitating the divine creative act. It was not only a revelation of expiatory suffering but of redemptive suffering. Weil states further: 'Redemptive Suffering: one who through grace has destroyed the I from within and falls into affliction from outside, this is the cross in its fullness.'[75] While expiatory suffering has to do with suffering the consequences of our sin, redemptive suffering is about consenting to our nothingness and opening ourselves to God for our being. We cannot escape our affliction, nor should we. But through decreation we can endure it as a 'participation in the cross of Christ.'[76] This requires divine grace when one has lost all sense of being.

The Paradox: God's Absence–Presence

With Weil's concepts of affliction and decreation, we have already encountered her paradoxical understanding of God's presence in the world. God is absent from the world but also secretly present within it. 'The absence of God is his mode of presence corresponding to evil.' Or: 'He without God in him cannot feel God's absence.'[77] To know God's absence is to know that God is very far from a world where force governs human relationships. In such a world, God, who is self-renouncing love, can only be absent. To feel God's absence is to feel how distant this world is from God. To feel God's absence is also to feel God's condemnation of the evil in oneself. Most people must experience affliction before they become sensitive to this reality. Weil describes this feeling of absence in other terms also. She speaks, for instance, of a 'void' or 'emptiness' in the soul because nothing in the world can satisfy its desire for good when it has been marked by the reality of affliction.[78]

How must one live in this absence, void, darkness, or cross? Weil speaks of waiting 'en hypomene,'[79] waiting in patient endurance without giving in to the temptation of filling the void with illusions or false comforts, without being intoxicated by force as compensation for one's pain, renouncing it in love. This waiting in emptiness, renouncing the world of force, continuing to love despite the absence of the object of love (i.e., God); this corresponds to the decreation of the soul. Weil also identified this waiting in the darkness of affliction with faith. Faith has to do with hidden things. It is a trusting love of or desire for God against the experience of God's absence and condemnation. It is the naked hunger that remains in the soul when all else in it is destroyed. Such faith or love in the darkness was revealed most fully in the crucified Christ, who continued to love God through God's complete absence and his own annihilation. This continuing love in affliction is the love that awaits the God who is absent and refuses to settle with worldly goods or compensations.[80]

It is to such souls that wait patiently at the foot of the cross and refuse to turn away to whom God finally speaks:

> ... in affliction the soul is constrained to ... [ask] ... why? Why are things the way they are? The afflicted man naively seeks an answer, from men, from things, from God ... Why is it precisely that he should have nothing to eat, or be worn out with fatigue and brutal treatment, or be about to be executed, or be ill, or be in prison. If one explained to him the causes which have produced his present situation, and this is in any case seldom possible because of the complex interaction of circumstances, it will not seem to him to be an answer. For his question 'why?' does not mean 'By what cause?' but 'For what purpose?' ... But there is no answer because the world is necessity and not purpose ... Whenever we look for final causes in this world it refuses them. But to know that it refuses, one has to ask ... He who is capable not only of crying out but of listening will hear the answer. Silence is the answer ... He who is capable not only of listening but also of loving hears this silence as the word of God.[81]

Weil believes that this silent word of God has a point of contact in the human soul. God plants a seed of divine grace or love, secretly and silently, deep within the soul. This seed begins to grow when the soul renounces self and world, and waits upon God. Eventually God comes to the soul seeking entrance like a beggar, and upon the consent of the soul begins to fill it. The stress on divine grace is central for Weil. It contradicts the effort of the will toward the good. The will involves the assertion of oneself, which also includes the use of force and the illusions of an inflated self. Action or thought rooted in the will and not in grace only serves to bolster this false self. The realm of the will is public morality and mass society, and, for Weil, this is also the place where evil reigns most supreme and there is little room to hear the silence of God speaking in the void, seeking to enter secretly into the soul and transform it.

Those who are oriented toward the grace of God, however, know that they can do nothing toward genuine goodness, but consent to be nothing, renounce their will, embracing the cross, in order for God to fill their souls. It is only out of this decreation that self-renouncing love becomes a human possibility. Often, it takes severe affliction and a lingering for a long time in the void before God comes to the soul in silence.[82] Weil experienced her mystical possessions by Christ during severe attacks of migraines which completely paralysed her. At other times, Weil's solidarity with the afflicted, as well as her own failings, caused her so much distress that she was unable to feel the love of God.[83] Grace alone is able to give birth to love in the soul when it has been confronted by affliction.

Life under Grace

It is this divine birth of love in the soul which then makes the soul capable of turning to the world in love. For Weil, even though God may be present in the world through the beauty of nature's impartiality, a respect for limits, the natural equilibrium of forces, justice, attention, and *metaxu*, such revelation is 'secret' and hidden from the soul living under the illusions of force or the despair of affliction. The one exception is beauty itself, which can draw us out of ourselves in love. But this does not always happen consistently. It is only through decreation that the beauty of the world becomes consistently manifest to the soul. When one is reduced to nothing and then is graciously turned outside oneself toward God, then God's love fills the soul. This soul then turned toward the world is a vessel of divine love flowing into the world. The love born within the decreated soul is self-renouncing, and this is the divine image restored at the centre of the human being. It is impartial and humbly respects its limits. It is committed to justice beyond personal convenience or suffering. It treats the weak with the highest respect. It is creative in that it can restore life to souls who have lost their sense of beauty and dignity because of affliction.

This, for Weil, is also the life of faith. She states: 'Faith is the experience that the intelligence is enlightened by love.'[84] Faith is the knowledge, beyond appearances, that love is a higher and truer reality than force and affliction. As one experiences such love from God, one loves God and the world through God. Knowing is no longer trying to understand in order to manipulate, but humbly standing under and allowing the truth and beauty of otherness to be revealed to one's intelligence.

Weil also speaks of the life of faith and love rooted in decreation as obedience. Obedience is a very central idea for Weil. It has to do with complete consent to God's will which is love, even through affliction. It is the consent to be nothing in order for God to be everything. Such consent in obedience to God is the basis of true freedom. Freedom is not about choices one can make. One is either obedient to God or obedient to the forces of necessity which govern the world. To consent to divine obedience is not a matter of human choices but, rather, of that mysterious grace by which the soul is opened to the truth of its condition and its need for God to whom it consents, even through affliction.[85]

Living with Force

How is one who desires to be obedient to God and has consented to decreation to live in the world of force? Here, Weil appeals to the concept of equilibrium. In *The Iliad*, she speaks of an equilibrium in nature by which the powerful, who inevitably exceed the limits of their strength under the intoxication of force, eventually fall. Elsewhere, however, she questions how often the powerful receive justice through a natural equilibrium, and the great suffering that follows the rise and fall of those in power. Such suffering falls disproportionately on the powerless. Consequently, she suggests a more intentional involvement in the social order in order to create an equilibrium in which 'injustices punish each other through a perpetual oscillation.'[86] Without a social order based on limit and law, people would be subject to the unlimited force of the powerful and the lawless whim of the tyrant. Promoting social equilibrium also implies finding out which way society is unbalanced and then doing what one can to add weight on the lighter side.

This is how Weil defined the purpose of her own activism. But does adding weight not involve the exercise of force? Yes it does. Weil suggests, however, that although the weight may consist of evil, in handling it with the right intentions, perhaps, we do not become defiled. But she also admits that a moderate use of force by which one is not intoxicated 'would demand a more than human virtue, one no less rare than a constant dignity in weakness.'[87] This brings us back, once again, to the need for divine grace and decreation.

3.4.3. Grant's Earliest Encounters with Weil and the Insights Arising Therefrom

It would take a lifetime for Grant to absorb all that Weil taught. But even in the 1950s, her thought dominates his thinking, and especially as he attempts to speak about the good/God in relation to the individual and society in positive terms and in a way faithful to the requirements of a theology of the cross. Many of Weil's ideas are already anticipated in Grant's thinking after the war and during his studies: ideas about the world of human relations as governed by force; how such force is visible not only in war but in mass, technological civilization; the limits of human beings changing the world for good; the crushing effects of force on the soul; the reality of affliction; faith as a divine possibility beyond human possibilities; God as not intervening in human history but hidden, absent, or 'waiting'; the concept of natural justice or 'equilibrium'; the distance of the world from God; the purity of divine love revealed on the cross; and the centrality of revelation and grace for receiving intimations of divine love, as well as opening one to the beauty of the world.

In the 1950s, however, Grant's thought was engaged by his reading of Weil in a direct manner. He admired deeply her profundity and intelligence as a thinker. But even more so he admired her 'sanctity.' She thought and lived her faith at the highest level. This faith was one that included the anguish, horror, and affliction of the world. Her account of evil and suffering was as profound as that of Sartre and, indeed, superior to him, because she believed nothing whatsoever in the human will, intellect, or spirit was invulnerable to destruction if affliction was severe enough. This included freedom. Even though Sartre, too, believed that human freedom could be destroyed, he also believed it to be the irreducible core of human life and the source of human salvation, however limited this could ever be. For Weil, by contrast, the irreducible core of human life was not human at all, since anything human was destructible. Rather, it was the presence of the divine in the human soul (or the 'divine image' in Christian terms) through which God moved through the soul and drew it upwards. Only such divine initiative and movement could overcome the destructive effects of affliction, for it incorporated affliction in the soul's journey to the good/God. As a Platonist, she believed in the ultimate desire of the soul for the good/God and that evil was the absence, not the opposite, of good. God was sovereign in the universe and divine providence pervaded every movement of life, even as evil under harsh necessity and chance reigned supreme. The contradiction between necessity and the good was an anguish in Weil's soul. Nevertheless, she refused to reduce either side of it in order to achieve synthesis or reconciliation. There was an absolute, uncompromising integrity in her honest assessment of the irreducible depths of evil and affliction, as well as her faith in, love of, and obedience to God through it all.

Weil, nonetheless, also frustrated Grant. In notes he wrote to himself while reading the *Notebook,* he is suspicious of her language of love of and consent to necessity as somehow reducing evil and suffering to divine providence, and collapsing the distance between necessity and the good. At the same time, in these and other notes, he admires her understanding of evil and suffering and how these are also related to modern industrial, technological society.[88] In an essay written in the early 1960s, he speaks of her call to give oneself away, which is also the essence of Christian charity. But he questions how much this is possible for tortured, alienated, or neurotic souls who do not have a developed self to give away. Weil had a strong self. Had she fully fathomed the difficulty and injustice of demanding this of those who were not so fully developed? Should they not be helped and encouraged to gain their selves before they would be called to give their selves away? In spite of these comments, Grant was quite hesitant in making any criticism of Weil. It was presumptuous of someone like him, who was not a 'saint,' to judge someone who was. Moreover, because Weil linked her thought to her life, it was difficult to make final judgments on her ideas. One had to wait upon them until further illumination and insight was granted.[89]

In several sermons given in the early 1960s, and in one in particular, the positive influence of Weil on Grant along the emphases of a theology of the cross is clearly evident. Humanism, which is the modern

faith in either liberal, existentialist, or Marxist forms, believes that
when faced with suffering human beings must make a world in which
it does not exist. Christianity, however, sees things differently. 'In some
strange way suffering must be consented to; it is part of the divine purpose.'[90] This does not mean consenting to something one can change
that needs to be changed. Rather, it is consent to what cannot be
changed in the present or the past. But how difficult it is to consent to
that and to love God in and through that. Obviously, for most of us, it
is too difficult. But we can contemplate its beauty.

We see this consent in places of affliction all over the world, where
nothing seems able to break through the cycle of evil and despair. It is
broken only when one person consents to bear the evil upon her- or
himself. Such consent is innocent and pure. We see the abyss of such
consent in the writings of Homer and Dostoevsky. But the supreme act
of perfect consent is that of Christ at Gethsemane:

> Here the absolutely pure – the absolutely just – the absolutely innocent,
> consents to bear, to accept the full weight of the evil of his day, the full
> weight of the evil of the Roman Empire, [of the] ecclesiastics of his own
> race. And think what it cost him: His sweat was, as it were, great drops of
> blood falling down to the ground.

This act was nothing less than the act of God's own self, 'for only God
can consent to be nothing.' In the garden of Gethsemane there is a consent within God, between father and son, a consent which is love. It is
this act of consent at the heart of the gospel on which we must fix our
attention.[91]

Grant also speaks of the act of loving consent or 'acceptance' in an
earlier unpublished work. 'The traditional idea of God,' he states,

> demands from man the spirit of acceptance. To believe in God is to affirm
> that all events fall within an ultimate purpose so that the believer, to be
> consistent, must strive to accept all the events of the world in joy.[92]

This is the ideal of Christian faith, however difficult it is to achieve.
Even theologians who assert the illusory, evil character of the world
are not asserting an ultimate pessimism about it, because they also see
this reality as a passage necessary for human redemption. Here,
clearly, Grant has in mind theologians of the cross, of whom Weil is
one. Because of the biblical roots of Western theology, moreover, the

spirit of acceptance must include the affirmation of the created world and all life within it as ultimately good. Even when the depth of evil in the world has pushed theology to assert an extreme transcendence of God, as, for instance, in the doctrine of the *Deus absconditus* in Protestantism, life in the world, which includes its evils, must be accepted in joy. With the assertion of divine transcendence also comes the assertion of mystery. Without such assertions, theology either trivializes evil or makes God a 'tame confederate' of some human intellectual or practical adventurings:

> Religious joy had to be either an imminent realization which complacently disregarded evil (often by calling it good) or else a joy which held, in some mysterious sense, that the ground of its possibility was beyond the world. Because of the cross the Christian religion, if it were to be true to itself, could never hesitate but choose the latter. But transcendence and mystery implied the ultimate reliance of the believer on faith which was beyond any intellectual foundation.[93]

These themes are taken up in Grant's personal life, as well. In a letter to his mother, he refers to a painful incident which involved his uncle, Vincent Massey. When Massey had come to visit Halifax, he failed to call the Grants and invite them to any of the public functions in which he was engaged. This hurt them deeply. Grant tells his mother that on one level, this hurt has to do with the vanity and pride of wanting to be in the company of important people. But on a deeper level, he knows that life is a continual process of 'remaking oneself,' and this is part of the 'wonderful mystery' of divine providence through which disappointments teach one what is worth trust and what is vanity and pride. Indeed, it is only the love of God that matters, and no earthly love can compare with its infinite depths. For one who has faith, whatever one learns and experiences in the journey of life can only lead to this truth. Hurt is tragic for those who experience it without knowing this truth. For those who believe, however, it reveals one's limitations and failings, and reminds one 'of one's complete dependence upon things that are not worthy of being depended on.'[94] It is spiritual humbling and purification before God.

Weil was able to help Grant base philosophy on a theology of the cross. We see the beginnings of this process already in the 1950s. We see it also in Grant's attempts to think of faith and philosophy as one. In a poem entitled 'Good Friday,' faith and philosophy are joined in the cross. This poem asserts the centrality of the cross. It is in the crucifixion, not the resurrection, that human redemption is accomplished. Imagery from nature is linked to the imagery of Plato's allegory of the cave, pointing to Christ on the cross as the vision of the sunlight, which is final illumination. The meaning of the cross is love in the form of forgiveness, which reveals 'God's Will most fully done,' transcending any freedom of choice on our part. Christ on the cross reveals 'the backside of God,' God's hidden face.[95]

In lecture notes written in the late 1950s, Grant makes even more explicit the connections among a theology of the cross, Weil's thought, and Plato. The crucifixion is the revelation of the infinite distance between the necessary and the good. This distance is also revealed in the 'Just Man' of Plato's *Republic*, who, in the name of supernatural justice, suffers the loss of all prestige, rights, and dignity according to the categories of worldly justice. The Just Man reveals that true justice is not of this world and is not recognized in this world in any apparent or visible form. Thus, it is transcendent, supernatural (or hidden), and must be revealed in order to be known to the human mind or awakened in the human soul. Moreover, the Just Man reveals that true justice necessarily suffers in the world. The Just Man, for Grant as for Weil, is an image of the crucified Christ. His suffering is absolute, for he is perfect innocence and pure justice in a world of profound corruption and injustice. He suffers the absolute distance between the necessary and the good – 'My God, my God ...'[96]

Yet the suffering of the Just Man is also 'redemptive' (Weil) or 'persuasive' (Plato). In order to understand this, Grant suggests, we must 'assume that suffering, struggle, and even dereliction are seen as part of the life of the Godhead.' It is only in this way that the redemptive work of God in Christ can be perceived and appropriated. To explain this further, Grant refers to the two 'theories' or ways of interpreting the crucifixion. First, he refers to the 'ethical theory of redemption,' which interprets Christ as the supreme example of the Just Man. On the cross, he suffers the loss of all prestige, comfort, and consolation, even from God. He consents to deny himself and give up his very life in the name of divine justice or love. This consent is no simple matter. Grant refers to Jesus' great inner struggle at Gethsemane. Moreover, the suffering he endures is so absolute that any inner certainty, purpose, or sense of God's presence becomes absent. This example of self-denial or 'decreation' is the central path of redemption for all who would consent to the rule of divine justice in their lives. It may be the human path to redemption, but it is not one humanly possible. One cannot simply choose the cross. Yet hidden in the cross is also the divine power of love, which manifests itself through Christ. Grant associates this divine love with the 'sacramental theory of redemption,' which is rooted in the mystery of the incarnation. God consents to become absolute necessity, or matter, crucified in the world. God consents to this because God is love. By becoming part of necessity, God becomes one with us and joined to us, in order to raise us up to the divine life. This life is the divine love, which is the one thing present in Christ when all else is stripped away. It is the source of our life when we consent to our own decreation through which all that is corrupt and ugly in us is stripped away. We can consent to decreation, but only God can grant us life through it.[97]

Finally, however, Grant finds both theories of redemption inadequate. The ethical theory can easily turn the cross into a kind of martyrdom, while the sacramental theory can obscure the human struggle and doubt involved in the cross. Both of them fail to maintain adequately the absolute distance between the necessary and the good, which is, finally, a mystery. We must strive to maintain both the importance of struggling against the evil in the world as well as consenting to the suffering of evil through which the mystery of the good may be revealed to us. In making this latter statement, however, Grant asserts that we must never confuse evil with good, trivialize it, or assume that good will arise automatically out of necessity. Rather, the distance between the necessary and the good must be maintained in order to account for reality as it truly is. He then quotes Luther's Heidelberg theses, which, he suggests, describe this in the best possible way. The theologian of glory obscures the distance between the necessary and the good and, in the process, trivializes the evil and suffering in the world. The theologian of the cross speaks about reality as it truly is. The distance between the necessary and the good can, therefore, only be bridged from the side of God. The mystery and the truth of this redemptive link is revealed in the cross and in the decreated soul.[98]

Grant, along with his wife Sheila, also wrote on Dostoevsky. Their presentation of his thought is within the larger framework of Weil's thought, which, far from being a weakness, brings out the depth of Dostoevsky's vision. Like Sartre, Dostoevsky affirms the absoluteness of freedom and the absoluteness of evil. Human freedom is an essential prerequisite for a meaningful and fulfilled existence, yet, on its own, it either is crushed or goes wild in self-assertion and self-worship, leading finally to destruction. Only the grace of God can save human beings from being destroyed or destroying themselves and others in their freedom. This is in contrast to modern views of freedom, which have either minimized the need for redemption – as in the case of liberalism – or minimized the truth of human freedom – as in the case of social science, evolutionary theory, and behaviourism. Dostoevsky denies that human beings are naturally good (as optimistic liberalism would have us believe), or that they can be made good through manipulation as objects (as other sciences would have us believe). Indeed, without a recognition of the human need for God, freedom which is not crushed easily turns into nihilism.

According to the Grants, Dostoevsky's greatest contribution is his understanding of faith and doubt. As a man broken and afflicted, he portrays the great struggle of the soul to reconcile necessity and the good. The good is revealed most fully in Jesus Christ. In spite of the profound doubts etched in his soul because of the suffering and evil he experienced within and around himself, Dostoevsky held an unwavering love and adoration of Christ. His doubts are compared to those of Weil, who speaks of the difficulty of loving God through and beyond the misery of others. He, like Weil, is granted faith and believes in an ultimate unity beyond the distance between necessity and the good, even though he cannot think it. The inability to think it is a source of great agony for him, an agony that is revealed most fully in the crucified Christ. Christ is subjected completely to force, crushed and swallowed up by it. And yet his response to his torturers is infinite compassion and forgiveness. 'Here is the infinite weakness in which the second Person of the Trinity crosses the void of separation.'[99]

3.4.4. Loving the World Concretely

From his earliest years, Grant was concerned about the practical implications of thought and how practice was a test of the validity of thought. Thinkers were ultimately praised or criticized according to the concrete implications of their ideas. The weakness of Oman's theology of the cross, for instance, was evident in his practical prescriptions, which reflected a modern liberal theology of glory. From the 1950s onward, it was Weil who would serve as Grant's guide on practice in the world. Grant made frequent reference to Weil as an authority in this regard:

Love is only love in so far as it has passed through the flesh by means of actions, movements, attitudes which correspond to it. If this has not happened, it is not love, but a phantasy of the imagination by which we coddle ourselves. As far as love is concerned, and particularly love of justice, 'matter is our infallible judge.'[100]

We see Weil's influence in Grant's practical prescriptions for building community within the mass society. Is it possible to build true community (a collection of persons before God) within this society or will we end up with nothing but a 'slave' community? The one force, argues Grant, that can build a community and hold it together is love. Love binds people together and allows their spirit to thrive, while a slave society must be held together by 'naked force.' Against the idea of the 'survival of the fittest,' the Bible teaches that all things, from the stars to human beings and communities, are held together by love. To deny this is to deny faith in God. Because such faith is so difficult, religion has been rejected as an illusion. Others believe that the spirit of love will work itself out automatically in human society. Grant is not so optimistic. Even though his vision of humanity is darker than that put forth by modern psychologists, progressive educators, democrats, politicians, universities, and churches, he believes that love is the greatest, yet rarest, quality in humanity, achieved by the very few. True love springs from faith in God, and truly good works from the spirit of such faith. The difficulty of true faith and love is why Christianity holds divine grace as the only authentic source of genuine human community. But does this imply that we turn our back to the reality of modern mass technological society and its institutions? Not at all. The great task ahead, however, is not further expansion and quantitative progress but, rather, the attempt to bring a greater quality and beauty of existence into the technological world.[101]

Another problem area that needs to be addressed concretely within the mass society is capitalism. Although Grant has great sympathy for the socialist critique of capitalism, he challenges contemporary socialists to deepen this critique. Too many criticize capitalism within the progressive doctrine of history and the celebration of scientific, technological developments as the solution to the problems of modern existence. Grant challenges socialists to develop a deeper understanding of the ideal good out of which standards of social order and justice can be established, standards which are not so easily undermined in the name of profit, progress, or self-interest. In this regard, Grant argues for a deeper basis for the doctrine of equality so precious to socialist theory. Equality implies that all human beings are persons with an equal right to consent to or refuse whatever is imposed on them. Yet it is also true that there is a natural inequality of talents among human beings. Many capitalists would like to accept this as the natural order of things in the form of 'the survival of the fittest.' They argue that the failure to recognize and respond to differing talents reduces society to a dead level without the possibility of true excellence. As a Platonist and conservative, Grant recognizes the truth of a hierarchy of talents. But he also believes that any recognition of inequality must be subsumed within a greater recognition of equality.[102]

The basis of the doctrine of equality in the West is the biblical, Puritan understanding of all people as made equally in the divine image. Indeed, asserts Grant, without a recognition of this equality, hierarchical arrangements in society become too entrenched and oppressive. The effect of prolonged relationships of inferiority and subordination can have devastating consequences on people's spirits. Such arrangements must always be seen within a larger purpose of bringing people toward greater inward freedom and self-realization. This would involve greater participation of people in the decisions, goals, and directions society will take. Even though technological society has brought us greater opportunities for education and inner cultivation, its capitalist ethic stands in the way of such opportunities. Human sin continues to be a constant, however much its forms may vary historically. The only way to counteract it and bring human destiny to its fulfilment in the technological society is by an 'ethic of community which understands the dignity of every person and is determined on ways of fulfilling that dignity in our new conditions.'[103]

3.4.5. The Growing Influence of Weil and the Allure of Hegel

In spite of the growing influence of Weil on Grant's thought, Hegel would continue to be influential in the 1950s. Although Weil was beginning to help Grant in bringing together philosophy and Christianity in a way that perceived the connection between a Platonic, mystical philosophy and an Augustinian, Lutheran, existentialist theology, Hegel's particular understanding of the Reformation and the Enlightenment would continue to inform Grant's thinking. The biblical conception of freedom was related to modern liberal Enlightenment thinking without distinguishing, consistently and finally, the more contemplative, Lutheran reading of the Bible from the less reflective, Calvinist one. Moreover, Hegel tempted Grant to seek for a higher unity or 'synthesis' of the truths of biblical (modern) and Greek (ancient) conceptions in the very data of human history being unfolded in the mass technological society.

We have already seen this problem as the search for a unity in 'Two Theological Languages.' It is also articulated in other ways elsewhere. Grant refers, for instance, to the 'paradox of democratic education.' He explains this paradox thus: 'On the one hand there is much in democracy to which we must give loyalty; on the other hand, isn't there something in democracy which we must fear as the enemy of true education?'[104] To question democracy may be unpopular, yet we must never give absolute allegiance to anything as relative as the ordering of society. The loyalty we owe to democracy has to do with its doctrine of social equality, which has its roots in Christianity. People may not all be equal in talents, and this needs to be stressed against naïve liberal democrats, who speak so ecstatically about equality. But above the inequality of talents lies an essential equality of personhood. Such an equality is rooted in the Christian mystery of every human being as equally the object of divine love. Not only is divine love a possibility in the life of any person, but even rulers and leaders of the highest education are not free from corruption and sin. Democracy is both a check on those who rule, and the opportunity for all persons to be educated and involved in social life.

Yet democracy also undermines true education. In Plato's *Republic*, democratic society is viewed so negatively because the rule of the masses also means the rule of the lowest common denominator of the appetites. Reason, which may be inspired by love but not equally open to all in talent and ability, is dethroned from its rightful place of leadership. The present transformation of schools and universities into technical colleges aimed at serving the degraded ends dictated by society is the result of democracy. Today these institutions are places where youth are taught 'to adjust themselves to the common denominator of achievement.'[105]

Grant admits that it is difficult to reconcile the contradiction between loyalty to democracy and the recognition of its destructive tendency on education. But this is no excuse for seeking to escape this tension by pretending it does not exist. Rather, one is called to live within it. Grant also admits that when one faces this contradiction, one is tempted to despair. Yet if one has faith in God, despair is not the answer, nor is escape from one's responsibility in the world. Instead, the Christian believes that the resolution of history is not, finally, in his or her hands, and is content to trust God through the uncertainties and mysteries of life.

The paradox between Christianity and philosophy in relation to education is also articulated in another way by Grant. In this case, it has to do with the expanding economy in North America. Grant sums it up in this way:

> On the one hand, an expanding economy has given us a society in which more people than ever have the chance for education. On the other hand, in building that economy we have created a world in which the idea of real education is darkened in the human soul as perhaps it has not been since the end of the Roman Empire.[106]

The expanding economy has led to the prosperity of more people than ever before, and certainly to greater financial comfort and stability. This also means that people have more leisure time than ever before. With leisure time comes increasing opportunities for education. Yet while these practical developments conducive for education are taking place, the very conceptual foundations by which leisure has been achieved are destructive of the purpose of true education. It is the instrumental, technical view of reason which has found in science and technology the means to achieve what degraded desire has dictated. Prosperity and success, which lead to leisure, have become the goal of education rather than the means to opportunities for deeper education. But leisure without any greater purpose can only bring meaningless or perverted forms of pleasure-seeking. Social science tries to help by providing techniques for adjusting the masses to modern society. This has also provided these disciplines with their *raison d'être* in modern society.

In spite of these developments, Grant can also express some optimism. The new reality of greater leisure for a greater number, combined with the dissatisfaction of many youth with scientific humanism in their quest for meaning, offers a golden opportunity for education. The newer existentialist humanism, which is attractive to many youth, may still deny the existence of God, but such denial is anguished and there is greater insight into the destructive and meaningless drive of modern scientific, technological civilization. In such a climate, at least, people are ready to pay attention to thought rooted in a faith that is willing to face the darkness of reality.[107]

The paradox between biblical and Greek, modern and ancient, thought, the search for a higher unity, the hope in the younger generation within the mass society, and the growing influence of Weil, all find their way into Grant's major writing of the 1950s, *Philosophy in the Mass Age*. In the preface, he states what is now commonplace for him: the need of philosophy for faith if it is to be a moral philosophy addressing moral questions in life and society. In the first chapter, Grant asserts that moral philosophy is concerned with principles 'by which we should direct our lives.'[108] At the same time, it must formulate these principles within a particular historical context in order to be meaningful and relevant. In the modern world, this context is the mass society. The mass society has been realized most fully in that of North America, which is the only society without a history before 'the age of progress' and, hence, the society in which the values and principles of this age are incarnated most fully. The mass society is one of 'mass production and its techniques, of standardized consumption and standardized education, of wholesale entertainment and almost wholesale medicine.' It is the new and all-encompassing environment that influences every facet of our lives.

Two characteristics distinguish the mass society from others that have existed in the past. First, it is scientific, which means that human domination over nature is the framework for knowledge and its application. The practical benefits of science have also made possible the satisfaction of more basic human needs with less work than ever before in history. But second, the mass society is characterized by an unprecedented domination of some human beings over others. This takes place through mass institutions and structures and, above all, corporations, through which certain ends are imposed on all people. The paradox is that this domination is becoming so complete that no one, including the elites, are free from its grip. It is a liberal illusion to think that one is simply free in any situation to choose for or against the forces of society which shape our lives. Neither is it easy to change the direction society is moving. The way, however, is not to be found in a defeated pessimism. Inner freedom only comes with serious thought about what is and what ought to be. Serious thought arises when an old system of meaning has come to an end and the need for a new one is recognized. The old Protestantism, with its simple faith in the Bible as its source of meaning, held the minds of people in small pioneering communities. This is no longer the case in the mass society. It is necessary to incorporate the truth of that faith with serious thought about modern society as it is. In a context 'when meaning has become obscure' or 'when God seems absent' there is a need for profound theology and philosophy to establish principles based on new meaning rooted in an old faith.

The problem, according to Grant, is the alienation of individuals who are free beings. Inner freedom is compromised by mass means that seek to adjust individuals to the goals and aspirations of society as it is. Art is used no longer as a critique of culture but as a means of glorifying society as it is. To assist in this adjustment, reason has been deprived of its real function (thinking the truth of inner freedom) and turned into an instrument for the service of the degraded goals dictated by society. The irony is that the instrumental view of reason, which is the basis of scientific successes in the domination of human beings over nature, is also the cause of the domination of some human beings over others. Nonetheless, even though human freedom is being crushed under the pressure to conform within the mass society, this society has been instrumental in eliminating scarcity, disease, and back-breaking labour as never before in history. Grant's hope is that as these external benefits to humanity are further realized, human energy will be liberated in leisure to pursue the true life of reason as more than mere domination over nature. This is particularly pressing for the young people of modern North American society who know themselves as free, standing over against a society which has bound them in an impersonal grip. In their search for greater freedom, they will not easily be bound by the dictates of the mass society. Rather, they will be driven increasingly to philosophy and theology for meaning and purpose.[109]

In the second chapter, Grant compares the consciousness underlying modern society with that of ancient society. His purpose in so doing is to bring out the assumptions and beliefs of modern society more clearly. With the help of Mircea Eliade, Grant defines the ancient consciousness as a vision of 'the temporal as the mere image of the eternal.' According to this vision, human fulfilment was not to be found in the making of history but, rather, in living out divinely established patterns or 'archetypes.' In imitation of these archetypes, human beings would achieve meaning and redemption. Moreover, justice and law were rooted in the divine rather than in the human. Any existing human laws ought to be 'mirrors' of eternal law. This conception found its fruition in the doctrine of natural law, which was the foundation for all law in the West. The ancient consciousness was most beautifully expressed in Plato, who saw time as the moving image of an unmoving eternity, and the passing events of time as having meaning in the unchanging reality of God. The movement of life in death and death in life was a movement out of the shadows and imaginings into the sunlight of truth.[110]

The difference between ancient and modern consciousness is brought out most clearly in comparing their respective views on history and freedom. The ancients believed the human will would find fulfilment in obedience to reason, and freedom in obedience to the good. Consequently, history was of little significance except as a moving image of an unmoving eternity. The moderns, however, saw history as a series of unique and irreversible events of supreme consequence. Human freedom was freedom to shape history according to the human will and toward the goal determined by human beings. Humanity, not God, was the maker of history. Because historical events were significant and human beings were responsible for shaping them, belief in the progress of history also arose. Because North Americans have no history before the age of progress, this faith in human historical progress has become an unquestioned good. While, for most people, lingering influences from the past still exist in conjunction with the modern faith, as any such influences continue to disappear, Grant questions whether there will be any limits to, or goals in, the making of history other than the making of history as an end in itself. This unfettered history-making orientation combined with technological advances raise fearful prospects for the future welfare of life on the planet. Grant is not suggesting that we should turn back the clock. Modern achievements in technology and democracy have eliminated the curses of scarcity, disease, and hard labour under oppressive social structures. Yet the vast dangers implicit in modern developments can no longer be ignored.

The particular strength of the ancient consciousness is brought out most profoundly, for Grant, in the doctrine of natural law. He explains this doctrine in the following way:

> There is an order in the universe which human reason can discover and according to which the human will must act so that it can attune itself to the universal harmony. Human beings in choosing their purposes must recognize that if their purposes are to be right, they must be those which are proper to the place mankind holds within the framework of universal law. We do not make this law, but are made to live within it.[111]

The implications of this doctrine are twofold. First, any law which is based on the divine law of justice is not relative, subject to one's whim, but absolute and eternal. Moral conduct is not a matter of convenience, but an attempt to live out eternal law in one's own life. The force of this assertion can be gauged in the conception of human rights. If laws are held to be relative and a matter of convenience, what prevents anyone from degrading and abusing another? But if law is absolute and eternal, no reason can justify its disobedience, and no end can justify its setting aside. A second implication is that reason, which is the means of deriving natural law, can lead us to know what is right. Through reason one can derive moral principles of practice. This view stands in sharp contrast to the modern view of reason, which sees it merely as an instrument.

The key question that arises for Grant with the doctrine of natural law is the following:

> ... are we truly and finally responsible for shaping what happens in the world, or do we live in an order for which we are not ultimately responsible, so that the purpose of our lives is to discover and serve that order?[112]

For natural law theory, human beings are not finally responsible for what happens in the world, and they choose to conform to or disobey an order they did not make. In this line of thinking, freedom is much more limited a characteristic of human nature. We lose our freedom when we disobey the universal order, and we gain our freedom in obeying it.

In the next few chapters, Grant focuses his discussion on the modern consciousness. He begins by considering the modern conception of history as progress. In contrast to a view of humanity in subordination to divine law and as part of a natural order, the modern consciousness is one which views human beings as makers of history and asserts human freedom without external limits. The chief source of this view, Grant claims, is Christianity.[113] With its biblical doctrine of human responsibility and divine intervention in history, it paved the way for the destruction of the ancient view of reality and the coming to be of the modern, now secular, view. Grant traces this view through the Bible and through the Western church. Theologians like Saint Augustine tried to synthesize the biblical, Hebraic view with the philosophy of Plato. The doctrine of the Trinity 'incorporates into the timeless God of the Greeks, the God of project and of suffering; that is, the God of love.'[114] In spite of his ultimate failure, Augustine set the pattern for medieval civilization, which continued this attempt at synthesis.

What is important to see is how the idea of progress has its origins in the biblical, Christian view of history as the sphere for divine providence and human responsibility. Human responsibility is rooted in the idea of freedom. As freedom in the name of inner spiritual honesty before God in the Reformation gave way to freedom from all external impositions, including the belief in God, divine providence was increasingly conceived as human progress in history. The idea of God was seen as a limit to human freedom, and any belief in God was attacked in the name of a pessimism which was unable to reconcile the evil of the world with a divine purpose. Rather than leading to a sad humanism, as it did in ancient Greece, such a belief was displaced by an optimistic humanism which believed in the progressive elimination of evil from the world through human activity. Human freedom combined with science and technology would be the means. Thus, beginning in the eighteenth century, the doctrine of providence is replaced by the doctrine of progress, and any pessimism about the evils of the world is replaced by an optimistic faith in human freedom in and responsibility for building the divine kingdom on earth. Any doctrine or belief that placed limits on human freedom or questioned historical progress was rejected outright.

Grant then goes on to describe the thought of Karl Marx as the best representative of this shift between ancient and modern views. Earlier we discussed the reasons Grant admired Marx's analysis of society as it is, as well as his passion to change it for the sake of alleviating the evil and affliction in modern capitalistic society. Nonetheless, Marx's superficial view about evil as external to the human soul made his thought superficial about evil and about the basic human need for the realization of inner freedom of the spirit.

In North American society, in contrast, there is still a recognition of the truth of inner freedom, however much this is being challenged and denied within the new conditions of the mass society. Yet, in saying this, Grant also recognizes that the idea of progress in history and the human making of it is the true God that is worshipped in our society. The real question, therefore, is whether,

the progressive spirit is going to hold within itself any conception of spiritual law and freedom; or whether our history-making spirit will degenerate into a rudderless desire for domination on the part of our elites, and aimless pleasure seeking among the masses. Can the achievements of the age of progress be placed at the service of a human freedom which finds itself completed and not denied by a spiritual order?[115]

The rest of the book is devoted to this critical question. The difficulty of this question is evident when we consider the truths of natural law and the history-making spirit side by side. The truth of natural law is that we live in an order we did not make and our purpose is to obey that order and measure all our actions according to it. The truth of the history-making spirit is that we are 'free to build a society which eliminates all the evils in the world.' Both are true, yet contradictory, and neither can stand on its own. The idea of a divine order has often contributed to the complacent acceptance of evil and hardship, and a failure to struggle to eliminate these in the world. The truth of the history-making spirit is a rebellion against this complacency. Nevertheless, the modern history-making spirit has been responsible for the worst crimes of the twentieth century. The question to be put to this spirit is whether there is any limit to human freedom in manipulating and controlling the world. 'Is there anything that we should never under any circumstances do to another human being?' This question is especially critical when one considers the vast powers to manipulate the natural and human environment which are made available through scientific knowledge and technological invention. The idea of limit is the idea of God. God is the limit to our right to change the world. God represents the standard of value, justice, and law, a standard that we cannot manipulate but to which we must submit in order to be spiritually whole. The alternative is aimless nihilism or pleasure-seeking.

Grant sees these dangers particularly in modern North American morality. The roots of these dangers are found, as has been said earlier, in Puritan Calvinism. Unlike Lutheranism, which was more mystical, Calvinism was driven to the practical as a means to receiving assurance of salvation from a God whose will was hidden and inscrutable. Unlike Roman Catholicism, which believed in seeing God's footprints in the world and in the human formulation of natural law, Calvinists saw in practical action the source of their freedom and the fulfilment of God's will and providence. The strength of Calvinist Puritanism was its emphasis on egalitarianism originating in the doctrine of the priesthood of all believers. Its weakness was its singular focus on the Bible to the neglect of serious philosophical thought. The focus on equality and on the practical over contemplative studies is clearly evident in North American society today. What is particularly critical, historically speaking, is how the practical spirit, which encouraged changing the world in conformity to God's will, became freedom to change the world in conformity to the human will. Without serious thought, Puritanism could not anticipate and engage these gradual changes rooted in the sinful nature of humanity. Divine providence became historical progress, practical achievement for the glory of God became practical achievement for personal success and wealth, and hope in the progress of providence in the world became a shallow liberal optimism in the human establishment of a paradise on earth.[116]

Grant questions this Protestant-turned-modern spirit of freedom to make the world. Any philosophy which is unable to declare that some actions are categorically wrong is, in his mind, iniquitous. It cannot address evil with the depth it requires. It cannot address the degradation and affliction to which souls are consigned through force, nor the manipulation of the world according to the purposes of the powerful. Hence, it is a philosophy of glory, trivializing evil and making good a tame confederate of human thought and activity. There is no transcendent standard of judgment and justice the free obedience to which leads to ultimate fulfilment. The question is, can such free inner obedience to the good be consistent with the free changing of the world, involving as it does the use of manipulation and force on the human and natural environment?[117]

There are two contradictory realities this question must engage. On the one hand, there is the North American history-making spirit which manifests a complete lack of any transcendent purpose other than the making of history for its own sake. On the other hand, there are Jesus' words to Peter, 'When thou wast young, thou girdedst thyself, and walkedst whither thou wouldest; but then thou shalt be old and another will gird thee, and carry thee whither thou wouldest not.' By 'another' Jesus meant not only the evil Roman authorities but, ultimately, God hidden beneath them. Limit here is revealed in all its ambiguity. The consent to go where one does not want to go is consistent with a theology of the cross, which consents to obey God even through the evils of life. This also implies an acceptance of one's impotence to change the world through one's will, and the joy of obeying God through a dying to life. This, of course, is no easy feat. Grant refers to the difficult statement of Weil about loving God not only through one's own miseries, but through the miseries and sufferings of others, sufferings which one cannot alleviate, redeem, or atone for. To love God through these is, depending on one's level of purity, expiatory or redemptive suffering. Such redemption or 'reconciliation' beyond the distance between the necessary and good is no human possibility but a divine one alone.

For those who are not so reconciled (and Grant thinks particularly of Sartre), despair about the world must not lead to a defeated pessimism but an active rage for changing the world. In modern liberalism of the optimistic North American variety, however, we have seen where such change, unrestrained by faith in and obedience to God, is leading. But can such faith and obedience be freely consented to from within? Can such consent be viewed as the goal and fulfilment of human freedom? Or are any limits to human freedom to be seen simply as external hindrances to human fulfilment in history? On a deeper level, is nature simply there to be manipulated or to be recognized in its authentic otherness? Will we find our fulfilment in changing the external world or being changed within to see the world as God's world? Grant has no immediate answers. He does hope, nevertheless, that 'a morality which does not scorn joy and relates it to suffering may perhaps arise.'[118]

In *Philosophy in the Mass Age*, Grant has related many themes he has discussed elsewhere. His formulation of key questions confronting the modern world, however, is clearer here than anywhere else. Grant has great respect for the modern spirit in spite of his criticisms. Modernity has brought us unparalleled goods in terms of the elimination of the curses of scarcity, disease, back-breaking labour, and oppressive rule for the masses. Yet the bulk of his work is a criticism of modernity, and this is for contextual reasons. The modern spirit is becoming ever more sovereign. This also means that many essential truths about the nature and destiny of human beings in the world are being lost, while new curses of unprecedented depth are emerging. The conflict between the ancient and the modern, for Grant, is centred in the conflict between a transcendent order, justice, and law that are the measure and limit of human freedom, and a human freedom to change the world without any limits.

The idea of limit, as Joan O'Donovan has pointed out, has a twofold meaning in Grant. On the one hand, it is an unconditional limit whose measure we do not determine, but rather, which determines and measures us and all that we do. On the other hand, limit is a binding necessity which 'carries evil within itself' and 'is the very negation of freedom and power.'[119] The one meaning understands limit as consistent with the good, the other as consistent with necessity or affliction. The parallels between Grant and Weil at this point are unmistakable. What Grant fails to resolve, however, is not only the relationship between the two, but how each understanding of limit is related to the modern spirit. He begins, for instance, to distinguish between a liberalism which still retains a belief in a limit to human freedom – that is, practical freedom to make the world must serve the needs of human emancipation from the traditional curses that humiliate and enslave human beings – and a newer historicism without any limit and, hence, without direction or purpose in its pursuit of freedom. He also begins to distinguish between a liberalism that seeks to serve its idea of the good by eliminating the evils of necessity, and an understanding of the cross which sees in the limits of necessity (evil) a hidden divine means to a human humbling which is a basis to true inner freedom.

Yet Grant continues to fail in distinguishing clearly between, on the one hand, an Aristotelian, rationalistic, Calvinistic form of Christianity and a modern optimistic liberalism, both of which trivialize evil and make the good a human intellectual or practical possibility; and, on the other hand, a more Platonic, mystical, Augustinian, Lutheran form of Christianity and a more passionate, anguished modern liberalism which recognizes the full depths of evil and the absence or distance of God. Existentialism experiences the death of God in the soul without any rebirth of faith to sustain human freedom. Later, Grant will accuse existentialism of asserting a 'heroic humanism' with its emphasis on human freedom standing alone against the principalities and powers. For others, however, beyond the death of God in the anguish and affliction of their soul, faith in God is experienced as a divine gift. Moreover, the life of faith becomes one of struggling to change what can be changed and consenting to love God through what cannot be changed, trusting through grace in the mysterious, unfathomable truth that 'all things work together for good for those who love God.' Grant will continue to struggle with and clarify these contradictions and issues in the years ahead.

One final word needs to be said about Hegel. In later work, Grant makes much of his Hegelianism in the 1950s, and particularly in *Philosophy in the Mass Age*.[120] And there is, no doubt, an implicit attempt at setting up a Hegelian synthesis. Ancient traditions of philosophy and theology (the Greeks) discovered the truth about inner freedom. Yet these traditions were also complacent about the evils of history. Modern (biblical) thought criticized this complacency and, through science and technology, struggled to eliminate the traditional curses of scarcity, disease, and back-breaking labour. In the process, however, contemplation itself was lost and, consequently, the truth of inner (biblical) freedom. But the next stage of history is a new and greater synthesis. External leisure and comfort combined with a renewed search for meaning will lead to a flowering of freedom for a greater number than ever before in history. Grant saw the future with youth who knew their external freedom and were hungry to find it internally. This would lead them inevitably to the study of theology and philosophy. If this is altogether where Grant was headed, it would have been Hegelianism and a theology of glory, attempting to fathom the mysteries of divine providence, or how God was going to reconcile the world to God's self. Yet Grant also expressed deep scepticism about this happening. If he reflected a Hegelianism, it was a 'reluctant' one.[121] A central characteristic of the modern world was that even though it had brought greater leisure for a greater number, it had also undermined the basis and eliminated the need for contemplation. It had become the new faith supplanting any faith before the age of progress. Even at this point, it was more Weil and a theology of the cross than Hegel and a theology of glory that informed Grant's vision of the truth about necessity, the good, and the mysterious, hidden link between them.

Chapter Four

Intimations of Deprivation

In the 1960s, Grant's thought undergoes a profound deepening. This deepening has to do with a broader, and what for him is a clearer, understanding of the nature of modern technological society (the thing itself), as well as the nature of the liberal thinking which gave it birth and continues to sustain it (a theology of glory). We shall argue that this deepening moves Grant further toward a theology of the cross and helps him clarify some of the confusion encountered in his earlier thought. This deepening and the clarification it brought to Grant's thought is related to practical events and experiences as much as to theoretical influences. In 1960 Grant accepted a job offer at the newly established York University in Toronto. This would bring him close to his mother, who was now elderly, and to the centre of modern technological civilization in Canada. Both the impact of his coming to Toronto and his inability to accept the terms of the job at York, leading to his immediate resignation, had a profound impact on him. Also profound was his growing 'lament' for the gradual loss of a distinctive Canadian identity before the 'universalizing' and 'homogenizing' forces spearheaded by the United States. This loss was crystallized for Grant in the fall of Prime Minister John Diefenbaker as well as by the death of his mother. Finally, the Vietnam war was the cloud hanging over Grant's thought in the late 1960s. It unmasked the true nature and destiny of modern technological civilization and the liberalism which served as its theoretical grounding.

Along with these practical events and experiences, Grant came upon the thought of several figures whose writing would have a tremendous influence on him. Jacques Ellul, the sociologist, would help Grant understand the thing itself (the technological society) in a way he had not done previously. Leo Strauss, the political philosopher, would help Grant connect biblical and Greek thought, and to distinguish both from modern liberal and historicist thought in a new way. In so doing, Grant would also reject Hegel's thought completely. Finally, Philip Sherrard, a scholar of Eastern Christianity, would help Grant understand the Western tradition as a unity, and to distinguish it from a more 'Eastern' tradition of Christianity and philosophy. In this regard, Sherrard would prepare the ground for Grant's deeper appreciation of Weil's critique of Western civilization, with its brand of Christianity and philosophy.

4.1. A Deepening of Perspective

Grant explains the deepening that took place in his thought in the 1960s in a preface he wrote for a new edition of *Philosophy in the Mass Age*, published in 1966.[1] He begins by stating: 'This book was written seven years ago and since that time I have changed my mind about certain questions in moral philosophy.' The change in Grant's mind is centred in a deeper understanding of the nature of modern technological society. Quoting Ellul's definition of technology, Grant asserts that the modern pursuit of technology is not just an option that society can utilize for good or evil ends, as liberal doctrine suggests. Rather, it is an all-embracing fate, and more, it is a religion. It is that which North American society trusts to solve all of its problems and realize all of its dreams. It is the dominant 'faith' and 'morality.' As is already evident in earlier work, Grant held religion to be much more than a voluntary choice of the will. One did not simply choose the sacred but was grasped and fashioned by it. 'Choosing' technology also meant being shaped and driven by it and toward it in all aspects of existence, from one's thoughts to one's activities, from the private to the public realms, out of one's fears and toward one's hopes. Thus, to choose technology was to be transformed in oneself, transform society as a whole, and, in the process, eschew other choices in terms of faith and morality. Indeed, claims Grant, the pursuit of technological advance defines modern society's standards of excellence in a way that denies all other standards. So pervasive and deep is this faith that one is hard pressed to find any remnants of an alternative faith (i.e., pre-modern) anywhere in society.

Grant's more particular criticism of his book is that when he wrote it his mind was divided between ancient and modern religious and philosophical traditions in the West. As much as he criticized the modern progressive dogma rooted in technology, he was still held too deeply by it to stand apart from it. He admits that it was difficult to free himself given the fact that he was raised within mainstream North America and could not conceive of giving up the modern faith without giving up his very identity. He began to see the evils of technological society but was also bewitched by its benefits. Thus, he believed that what was lost with the coming to be of modern technological society would be regained on a higher level with the 'progressive incarnation of reason' in North America. Society would take up once again 'all that was good in the antique world and yet keep the benefits of technology.'

This line of thinking was connected to Hegel, whom Grant held to be the greatest of philosophers. This was because Hegel seemed to synthesize ancient and modern traditions so completely. This synthesis hinged on Hegel's understanding of the Western doctrine of providence, which, Grant confesses, Hegel perhaps understood better than anyone else. Grant had begun to question this understanding in the 1950s, and his espousal of Hegel's synthesis had been ambivalent. Nonetheless, he had been unable to conceive fully of an alternative way of thinking about Christianity, philosophy, and the modern world, in spite of the growing influence of Weil on his thought. In the 1960s, however, Grant questions Hegel to the point of rejecting completely his synthesis of ancient and modern ways of thinking and believing. This rejection is the result of Grant's deepening understanding of ancient thought, particularly as associated with Plato. While in *Philosophy in the Mass Age*, Grant had placed Plato in the Western tradition and, hence, within Hegel's synthesis, he now sees Plato outside that tradition and superior to Hegel. Plato's understanding of what constitutes human excellence and its realization in the world stands in contrast to that of Hegel, and it cannot be synthesized with the modern vision inspired by liberalism and realized through technology.

Grant concludes the preface by declaring his debt to two contemporary thinkers who have helped him see things more clearly. In helping him better understand the nature of modern technological society, he is indebted to Jacques Ellul. In helping him understand the conceptual foundations of modernity and their profound opposition to ancient thought, he is indebted to the writings of Leo Strauss. Let us consider, in greater detail, the thought of these men and how they influenced Grant's thought.

4.2. The Darkness of the Technological Society: Its Nature and Essence

4.2.1. *Jacques Ellul: The Technological Society 'As It Is'*

Ellul's influence on Grant is based primarily on one book, *The Techno-logical Society.* This book helped Grant 'see things as they are'[2] in a way that he had not done previously. Ellul states his aim in the book to be a sociological description of the nature of technological society. Such a description is critical, given the unique relationship between technol-ogy and society in the modern world. Whereas in pre-modern society technology was simply a secondary means to human ends, today it is an all-embracing reality that transforms all things into means for its own exclusive ends. Because of the uniqueness of technology in the modern world, Ellul gives it a special name: technique. He defines technique as 'the totality of methods rationally arrived at and having absolute efficiency (for a given stage of development) in every field of human activity.'[3] This definition points to the fact that all aspects of thought and activity in society are subsumed within technological necessity.

Ellul rejects the liberal idea that human freedom is an 'immutable fact graven in nature and on the heart of man.' Human beings have always been determined by various necessities, and freedom to tran-scend such necessities has always come with great struggle. What is different in the modern world is the nature of necessity. While in the past it was natural necessity that enslaved human beings, today it is technological necessity. And because the nature of necessity today is so different, it is useless to mine the wisdom of the past for a solution to the problem of freedom today. If there is any solution, it is not in getting rid of necessity, which is not possible in any case, but in tran-scending it. Such transcendence can only arise with awareness of the workings of necessity. In the modern world, technique is the all-embracing necessity. Moreover, 'the artificial necessity of technique is not less harsh and implacable for being much less obviously menacing than natural necessity.'[4] What Ellul desires to do in the book, therefore, is to arouse awareness by articulating the thing as it is.

In language reminiscent of Weil's account of force, Ellul goes on to describe in detail how technique transforms everything it touches into a machine, including human beings. All of society, nature, and human existence must adapt to technological efficiency and expansion. Every limitation or problem that arises is met with ever new and increased technique. Rapid technologization began with the advent of modern science and spread with the standardization and rationalization of economic and administrative structures. Today it has become an autonomous, unquestioned end that brings every other end into question and, eventually, into oblivion. All cultures and traditions are progressively being swept aside before technological culture. It is becoming increasingly universal and homogenizes all ways of thinking and living. Those institutions it has not created, it forces to adapt to its standards and goals. This includes schools, universities, and churches. It forces human beings to adapt to its artificial structure, and for this function of adaptation modern social science has discovered its place. Through psychology, propaganda, and education, human beings are manipulated into accepting unnatural concrete, mass environments and becoming the servants of technological efficiency. While the promise of comfort and wealth was the initial enticement into technological expansion, it has now become an end in itself independent of such basic human desires.

But how, asks Ellul, can we account for the emergence of technique in so forceful a way in the West? Ellul confesses that this is a difficult question. Plato and the Greeks treated science devoted to technical application with contempt. Technical research was unworthy of intellectual effort, and the goal of science was not application but contemplation. An obsession with harmony and order led the Greeks to value the virtues of moderation and restraint, fearing the force inherent in technical application. Christianity, too, cannot be held responsible for the technological revolution in the West, in spite of what many have argued. Medieval Europe, which was saturated by Christianity, was a-capitalist and a-technical. Moreover, Christianity always held a clear distinction between the city of God and the city of the world, maintaining a moral distance between the divine and the human. Yet technique explodes in the eighteenth century, and Ellul does not know why. Nor does he suggest that the history of ideas can help in this regard. Philosophical ideas are not important in shaping history or society and only influence the minority elite. More important are social circumstances and necessities. Ellul points to the bourgeois class, who saw in technical expansion the means to greater comfort and, drawn by self-interest, led the masses into it. This led further to the development of a common will to exploit the possibilities of technique and a common agreement on the excellence of this goal.[5]

For Grant, Ellul is at his best in his description of the nature of technological society. Ellul helped Grant to see that he could not simply accept the benefits of technology and reject the evils. It was all or nothing. Accepting the increased comfort and leisure also meant accepting the destruction of nature and all traditions and cultures before and outside technological progress. Nor was technology something morally neutral that individuals or society could use for good or ill, opt for or reject at will. It was an all-embracing fate for everyone, beginning with North Americans and progressively spreading throughout the world. Where Grant finds Ellul wanting is in his failure to take philosophical thought seriously and, as a result, his inability to perceive the inherent connection between biblical, Calvinist Christianity and the progress of scientific, technological expansion. This is because Ellul is himself a Calvinist Christian who 'scorns' serious thought and holds an instrumental view of reason.[6] Grant had already written about the connection between modern technological society and biblical, Calvinist Christianity in the 1950s. What is new in the 1960s is how he connects the emphasis on freedom and will (theology of glory) in biblical, Calvinist Christianity with Western Christianity as a whole, and through Western Christianity, all of Western civilization. This accounts for its dynamic, activist, mastering, conquering mentality and its emphasis on the shaping of history in a way that makes it unique among civilizations. We shall consider this further below.

4.2.2. Leo Strauss: The Irreconcilability of Ancient and Modern Visions of Society

Grant concludes his preface to *Philosophy in the Mass Age* by stating what a great blessing it was for him to have come across the thought of Leo Strauss, and he cites two books in particular: *What Is Political Philosophy?* and *Thoughts on Machiavelli*. Whereas Ellul's strength was in describing the nature of modern technological society with such clarity, Strauss's gift was in understanding and articulating how profoundly modern thought stood in contradiction to ancient thought.

What Is Political Philosophy is a collection of essays and also the title of the first essay in the book. Philosophy, according to Strauss, is the quest for wisdom or for knowledge of the 'whole.' Knowledge of the whole includes knowledge of all reality – God, world, humanity. It is not a possession of such knowledge but a quest. The philosopher is one 'who knows that he knows nothing' (Socrates). Political philosophy, however, is distinguished from political theology. The former is rooted in knowledge based on the unassisted reason, whereas the latter is based on divine revelation. Strauss is implying that the philosophical quest is one that may respect divine revelation but is also independent of it. Even further, he argues that reason can proceed quite a distance toward a knowledge of the whole, including metaphysical knowledge. This belief stands in sharp contrast to the assumptions of modern thought, following a Kantian framework, which limit the capacity of reason to the discovery of empirically verifiable, factual knowledge. This does not include the knowledge of values (metaphysics). In fact, the natural evolution of modern thought has led from a basic Kantian agnosticism toward metaphysical knowledge and values, to a complete devaluation of them.[7]

This is reflected in modern social science with its fact-value distinction. Accordingly, any legitimate knowledge about reality must be based on scientific, empirically verifiable criteria in order to be considered factual and credible. To this social science aspires. Moral judgments are not thus verifiable and, therefore, stand outside the purview of true knowledge. The genuine quest for knowledge, according to modern thought, is for morally neutral, 'value-free' knowledge. Yet, argues Strauss, there can never be a quest for knowledge that is value-free. If values are not gained through rigorous thought on the whole, then they are hidden uncritically and arbitrarily within the rubric of factual knowledge. Indeed, without serious thought and discourse on values, society is in danger of simply conforming to what is, as it is.

The dangers of such conformity are severe for the political regime and its citizens. According to classical political philosophy, the best regime humanly possible depends on chance. Human beings are enslaved in so many ways that it is almost a miracle when a human being, let alone a society, achieves the highest virtue. Moreover, being a good citizen is necessarily in tension with being a good human being. If being a good citizen means being patriotic and loyal, and if the regime is not in complete accord with the good, then love of the good, which characterizes a good human being, comes into conflict with love of one's own, which characterizes the patriot. Love of the good, then, must transcend love of one's own. In order for this to be possible, however, there must be some content to the good which transcends society as it is. It is for this reason that classical thinkers rejected democracy as the ideal political order. For them, the goal of human and social life was not freedom but virtue. Freedom as a goal is ambiguous for it can be a freedom for good or evil. The rule of the many who are patriotic in a state that commits crimes against humanity is evil and must not be loved. Virtue emerges through education, which is the formation of character through habituation, and this requires leisure on the part of children and parents. But leisure requires material means which are not available for the many. Consequently, democracy can only be the rule of the uneducated – those who have not been formed in the virtues oriented to the good. Moreover, because classical thinkers knew that only the few could be educated properly, they believed that the popularization of technology and the arts – giving powerful tools into uneducated hands – would not lead to good, but to tyranny and dehumanization.[8]

Modern political philosophy was a conscious rejection of classical political philosophy in fundamental ways. Beginning with Machiavelli and continuing in Hobbes and Locke, it lowered the standards of the best regime in order to make its attainment more realizable. In order to do this, it had to reject the view that human nature was properly directed toward the good, and begin on the basis that human beings are selfish and driven by the desire for self-preservation. Thus, in order to organize a successful regime, human beings had to be manipulated through fear of death or lust for glory. It would require that charity be replaced by calculation or utilitarianism, and contemplation with manipulation or mastery. Strauss calls this development the 'narrowing of the horizon.'[9]

But Strauss also refers to a second wave in modern political philosophy beyond Machiavelli, Hobbes, and Locke. The origins of this wave he associates with Rousseau, and its fulfilment in Hegel and Kant. For Rousseau, human beings are innately good, and all they need for direction toward the virtuous life is supplied by the human conscience. Thus, the free democratic rule of all, based as it is on self-preservation, will lead to the care of all out of mutual need. Freedom inevitably leads to virtue, and the freedom of each individual leads to the good of all. Society as a whole is now the standard by which the good is measured. There is no value or good that transcends society or the way things are. With Hegel, there is the introduction of the historical progression of freedom culminating in the universal and homogenous state in which everyone is equal. This is seen as a possibility because everyone is measured by the lowest common denominator – one's need for recognition. It is also based on the optimistic premise that human nature tends toward the good of itself, and compassion is common to humanity (Rousseau). Thus, values can take care of themselves while scientific knowledge will bring about whatever changes are needed to make human beings as free externally as they are so directed internally.[10]

While the first wave of modern political philosophers – Machiavelli, Hobbes, Locke – were much less optimistic about human nature, they too measured society and the individual by the lower standard of self-preservation common to all human beings. Morality was based on the needs of society, rather than on the order of the good toward which the human soul was directed. For classical thinkers, the highest virtue was the life of contemplation rather than action. Their focus was on peace over war, leisure over business, and thinking over doing or making. They consented to the fact that the best regime depends on chance, whereas the moderns sought to conquer chance through the power to mould nature and humanity. The first wave of modern development sought to conquer necessity. The second wave sought to conquer human nature. It had to break the hold of older conceptions of human nature and destiny which saw virtue, not freedom, as the right order of the soul. It had to break the conservatism of classical influences which distrusted political, social, and technological change, with a liberalism which worshipped change and welcomed technical expansion. It had to destroy the idea that human limits built into the nature of things, along with the cataclysms of nature, were to be accepted as part of the larger order within which humanity was set. It had to replace this idea by one that viewed humanity as subduing nature, human and non-human, in order to shape it toward human interests. According to Strauss, it is not that classical thinkers were passive or indifferent to the brutality of nature. Rather, they feared that human mastery and control of nature through technical invention could lead to greater evil and destruction than a consent to the rule of nature.[11]

While many of Strauss's ideas appear throughout Grant's work beginning in the 1960s, Grant wrote one major essay in which the extent of Strauss's influence, as well as its limitations, are clearly evident. This essay centres on a controversy between Strauss and the renowned Hegelian philosopher Alexander Kojeve. This controversy, according to Grant, is the most important controversy in contemporary political philosophy, and the key question it raises is 'whether the universal and homogenous state is the best social order.'[12]

Strauss admits that modern-day tyranny is of a form different from that of ancient tyranny. There has been great progress in the conquest of nature through modern science, along with the popularization and diffusion of philosophical and scientific knowledge. Yet, argues Strauss, classical political philosophy can understand the nature of tyranny – ancient or modern – in a way that modern science and philosophy cannot. The ancients knew of the possibilities of the conquest of nature and the popularization of scientific knowledge, but rejected them. Moreover, their assumption, as well as that of Strauss, is that tyranny is a form of government common to all ages and, thus, identifiable by clear characteristics. The form that modern tyranny takes is the universal and homogenous state, and it is toward this state that modern philosophy and science are directed.

Kojeve agrees with Strauss about the goal of modern political philosophy and science. But he disagrees with him fundamentally that the universal and homogenous state will be a tyranny. Rather, the establishment of such a state is the best possible social order, and he is optimistic that humanity is advancing progressively to its establishment. According to Kojeve, it is Hegel who has proven this in the most comprehensive way, and he has provided a comprehensive analysis of history as it moves toward the establishment of such a state. Although Christianity is also part of this history, the final stage achieved in the modern world involves a necessary rejection of faith in God in order that humanity obtain absolute freedom to be. According to Kojeve, the final stage of historical progress has been achieved in our time, for the philosophical idea of the universal and homogenous state based on freedom and equality has also become a political goal. Even though Grant, like Strauss, questions whether this is finally true, or whether the content of this goal is actually emptying 'into little more than the pursuit of technical expansion,' he also believes there is a need to think the truth or falsity of this modern liberal ideal.

The distinctions between the visions of the ancients and moderns are clear to both Strauss and Kojeve. Is being eternally identical with itself and independent of historical change, or is being created through historical becoming, leading to completion in the totality of historical epochs? Both of them realize that any eternal, unchanging order to which human beings must submit is a limit on freedom to change the world. The question is whether such change can lead to a greater good or whether it will lead to greater evil. Hegel, argues Kojeve, realized most fully that human freedom to make the world necessitated a rejection of theism. The realization of the universal and homogenous state would be the end of philosophy, for the goal of wisdom will have been attained. Strauss, in contrast, argues that human beings are unable to build an ideal social order and that the universal and homogenous state is not the ideal order but the worst form of tyranny, destructive of human excellence.

The difference between them lies essentially in their differing conceptions of human excellence and fulfilment. For Kojeve and Hegel, human fulfilment is rooted in human recognition, dignity, and equality. The universal recognition of all must be the measure of the greatest excellence. In order for this to be achieved, however, there is need for revolutionary struggle. For Strauss, this bloody historical struggle is precisely what dehumanizes humanity and destroys dignity. It is in thinking rather than in recognition that human fulfilment and excellence are to be gained. Because the attainment of wisdom is possible only for a few, however, universal human fulfilment is not possible, and the only way of making it possible is by lowering the standards of excellence to the common denominator of human nature and society as they are – that is, the need for recognition, self-preservation, and freedom from transcendent norms. But this also means that any ideal standard above the actual which can judge the actual must disappear. If such a 'lowering of the horizons' is to be the basis of the universal and homogenous state, any independent, critical thinking has to be stifled and all differences, distinctions, and natural inequalities must be denied. In the process, however, the possibility for genuine human excellence will also have been obliterated.

Throughout his presentation of the controversy, it is clear that Grant sides with Strauss. In the last part of the essay, however, he puts some critical questions to Strauss which reveal the limitations of Strauss's influence. First, he addresses Strauss's claim that classical political philosophy considered the possibility of science issuing in the conquest of nature as unnatural and destructive of humanity. We encounter this idea also in Ellul. But Grant asks whether (1) this is true of classical thinkers, and (2) if so, were they right? We have already encountered how Strauss spoke of classical thinkers as conservatives who distrusted change and believed the purpose of science to be the contemplation and admiration of natural necessity rather than the conquest of it. Moreover, classical thinkers taught a consent to natural limits on human existence and that such consent was more beneficial than the desire to overcome them. Yet Grant also points to the Marxist criticism which suggests that classical thinkers belonged to the privileged class of aristocrats and, consequently, were more comfortable keeping things the way they were than changing society for the greater freedom and fulfilment of all. In line with this perspective, Kojeve believes that unlimited technological progress is not worth pursuing for its own sake, but for the sake of human freedom from heavy labour and disease. Even though Grant agrees with Strauss that modern progressive society is increasingly committed to unlimited progress for its own sake rather than for universal liberation, he still questions whether Strauss has sufficiently considered the justice of the liberal ideal. To say no to change, one must also contemplate a world of hunger, disease, and poverty, and the 'poor, the diseased, the hungry and the tired can hardly be expected to contemplate any such limitation with the equanimity of the philosopher.'[13] Although Strauss is aware of this fact, Grant wonders how integrally the virtue of charity is related to the virtue of contemplation in his thought. Is charity more primary than thought for Strauss, as it is for biblical religion?

This questioning leads to Grant's second concern about Strauss's thought: the relation between biblical religion and classical philosophy. This, of course, had been a central concern in Grant's thought since his thesis on Oman. Where Strauss helped him was in understanding how both biblical religion and classical philosophy made strict demands with respect to self-restraint and, therefore, were both incompatible with modern philosophy, which viewed humanity as lacking an awareness of sacred restraints and driven by nothing but the desire for self-preservation, recognition, and freedom of the passions. This, according to both, was also a lowering of the horizons of the good. But what remained to be answered in Grant's mind was the relation between the Bible and philosophy, as well as the Bible and technology. Was Christianity a worldly, historically focused religion, or an otherworldly, transcendent one? Were these two views completely contradictory? Finally, did revelation have authority over philosophy, or were philosophy and contemplation independent of it?[14]

While Grant criticized Ellul for not taking philosophy seriously enough, he also came to criticize Strauss for not taking revelation seriously enough. The relationship between faith and philosophy, reason and revelation, was something that concerned Grant in a central way from early on in his thought. Revelation meant the primacy of charity and how this was incarnated in the world through Christ, revealed most fully on the cross. Thought that did not serve the more primary standard of charity was as suspect in Grant's thinking as was Christian theology that did not take the discipline of philosophy, as perfected by classical thinkers, seriously. It is not only Ellul, but Strauss also, who has failed to see the inherent connection between modern philosophical, political, scientific developments and biblical (Western) Christianity. The revolutionary call for democratic equality or for conquering nature to bring about human freedom from hunger, disease, and overwork, was inspired by the virtue of charity taught in the biblical tradition. This was inherited and secularized by thinkers such as Rousseau and Hegel in Europe, and brought over in a simpler, more practical form to North America by Calvinist Puritans. Even though this development has led to the terrible state of modern technological society, as is shown by both Ellul and Strauss, Grant's commitment to Christianity causes him to have a sympathy for the ideal envisioned by modern liberals like Kojeve that Ellul and Strauss do not share.

Strauss helped Grant to think more consistently about how the revolutionary call to freedom from ancient necessities left human beings without any standard above them that limited and restrained their free pursuits for good or evil. Both biblical and Greek thought knew well that human freedom unrestrained by a transcendent faith and morality was bound to be destructive. Any doctrine of freedom that was not rooted in a self-denying obedience to the good was bound to lead to evil. It was this lack of critical thought, combined with a biblical hope cut off from the biblical experience of repentance before the cross, that led to an uncritical and triumphant espousal of modern science in the West. Although Grant had begun to think this way in the 1950s, he had also been influenced by the Hegelian doctrine of providence as secularized in the liberal doctrine of progress, which saw in history the unfolding of the reconciliation and synthesis of the truth according to modern and ancient visions. There was hope that the benefits of the modern world could be maintained and combined with a new focus on critical thought and restraint on human mastery. Strauss helped him to see how classical thinkers did not hold any doctrine of historical progress or providence understood in this way. Their thinking about the whole was irreconcilable with the thinking of the Western tradition. Necessity was further from the good than Grant had perceived. The challenge for Grant in the 1960s was to think Christianity, with its central teaching about the primacy of charity, outside the Western doctrine of providence. In this regard, it was not Strauss, but Sherrard and Weil, who would help him (as we shall see further below).

Indeed, Grant came to see that Strauss was more an Aristotelian than a Platonist. Plato held the good to be beyond being, whereas Aristotle saw the good within human intellectual and moral capacities. The idea of the good beyond being made it possible for Plato to be brought together with the biblical understanding of revelation as the divine source of truth, coming to human beings beyond their intellectual and moral resources. For Aristotle and Strauss, however, reason as discerned by the human intellect is sufficient for all knowledge of truth about the whole.[15] Thus, while modern liberalism (ending up as it did in atheism and secularism) was a theology of glory worshipping the liberated human passions, was this not also the case for the Aristotelian tradition, leading as it did to an atheism and immanentism worshipping the human intellect as divine? The question to Plato, however, whose thought was more open to the mystical and transcendent, was whether he also held to the primacy of charity for thought? Here again, Weil would lead the way for Grant.

4.2.3. Philip Sherrard: The Corruption within Western Civilization As a Whole

The questions that remained unresolved in Grant's mind from his study of Ellul and Strauss found considerable resolution in his study of Sherrard. Here Grant discovered the connections between Greek (Aristotelian) philosophy, biblical (Western) Christianity, and the modern technological society, in a way he had not done previously. Sherrard's influence on Grant was centred primarily on one book, *The Greek East and the Latin West*. In the book, Sherrard attempts to address the reasons for the East-West split in Christendom. He suggests that this split went far deeper than simply political considerations. It represented a split between world-views.[16]

Sherrard begins to trace the reasons for this split in the differing philosophies of Plato and Aristotle. He argues that the Roman, Aristotelian appropriation of Platonic thought also constituted an 'exteriorization' and rationalization of his thought. Plato's thought was dualistic, but not absolutely so. Form and matter were opposites, yet both had their origin in a supreme reality. Moreover, Plato's 'ideas' or forms were not simply transcendent and ideal in relation to the multiplicity of sensible objects which they determined, but also immanent or present within them. Creatures were linked to the divine source of their creation through their intelligible nature, which participated in the transcendent ideas.

The exteriorization of this thought took place when Aristotle rejected the objective reality of these creative ideas. The opposition of form and matter was now absolute, with no transcendent reality embracing both. This had severe anthropological implications. For Plato, the highest purpose of human beings was their contemplation of and participation in the transcendent realities through a process of spiritual dying and rebirth. Such contemplative participation presupposed the existence of a supernatural order and a recognition of some faculty in human beings through which this participation took place. This faculty was not associated with the mind or reason, but with something higher which needed to be awakened through intuition and illumination. Aristotle, however, rejected the existence of anything transcending the human mind. In so doing, he located the highest faculty in human beings to be the mind and the highest purpose for human beings to be reasoning. This also led to a shift in the method of reasoning after truth, from an inductive, intuitive approach to a deductive, analytical one. Finally, it led to the limitation of any concept of transcendence to the human mind and to the dualistic opposition between mind and matter with no greater ground of unity linking them. Sherrard associates this Aristotelian way of thinking with the early Roman emphasis on the subjugation of nature and the organization and ordering of society to serve human purposes.[17]

Sherrard then traces these differing views on, and approaches to, reality through the early Christian church. The earlier influences were the Platonic ones, which moved Christianity into a contemplative, mystical, and more inductive spirituality. But with the advent of Constantine and the crowning of Christianity as the official religion of the empire, there was pressure to exteriorize the faith. Suddenly, the church was obligated to pronounce itself on all issues related to society and to shape society in a Christian way. This went hand in hand with the expansion of the empire, requiring greater order over a growing territory. The Platonic form of Christianity was not well suited to such 'secular' responsibilities. The focus now had to shift toward the shaping of history and society, and in biblical terms it meant the more external, concrete conception of the Mosaic law rather than the more internal, metaphysical interpretation of this law revealed in Christ. Matter separated from its divine origin was now seen as evil and, thus, to be subjugated. Moreover, the human mind was now the ground of transcendence and, therefore, responsible for subjugating nature and shaping society to the order of its own reasoning.

Sherrard then goes on to relate these two different ways of thinking to the doctrine of God. The Greek East, influenced as it was by a Platonic philosophy, asserted the transcendence of God in a way that the Latin West did not. God's essence, which transcended every human thought and conception, was finally unknowable. Only God's being as revealed in the three persons of the Trinity was comprehensible to human understanding. The assertion of unknowability protected the transcendence of the divine beyond human conceptions of the divine. At the same time, however, God was immanent in all that was, as the ground of being. Human beings could be opened to such knowledge by means of their intuition and, through a process of deification – a dying and rising with Christ – could be raised to a greater likeness to the divine image. But in order to protect both the immanence and the transcendence of God, which was, finally, a paradox, Eastern theologians asserted the distinction between the essence (unknowability) and the being (Trinity, immanence) of God. All three persons of the Trinity had a common essence in the Godhead, but they were revealed to the human mind as distinct persons. The essence of God was related to all that is, but not open for human beings to understand. There was a mystery that transcended the revelation of God in Christ, although not contradicting or diminishing this revelation in any way. Far from being ground for human speculation outside revelation, this meant that human thought about God was restricted to that which was revealed, as well as open to the intuition of manifestations of God in the world transcending human speculation.

Theologians of the Latin West, however, simplified and, as a result, undermined the paradox of the transcendence and immanence of God. They rejected the distinction between God's essence and being, and simply asserted God's being. This also meant that even though they still spoke the language of God's unknowability there was no longer any substance to this understanding. The move to insert the *Filioque* clause into the creed – namely, that the Spirit proceeds from the Father *and the Son* – was a further attempt to circumscribe the mystery in and transcendence of God. This doctrinal development, combined with an Aristotelian rejection of the transcendence of ideas and the deification of human reason, led to a tradition of speculative rationality opposed to the Eastern tradition of mystical contemplation. It also led to the natural theology (medieval theology of glory) of the West as opposed to the negative theological tradition which was stronger in the East and in theologians who were more dependent on Plato than Aristotle. Sherrard then relates these differing philosophical, theological perspectives to the church's understanding of its place in the world. He sees, for instance, a connection between the Western church's doctrine of God and its increasing preoccupation with worldly power and conquest. He sees it also in the advent of modern science and technology, along with an emphasis on the human reason and will in the shaping of history and the world.[18]

The influence of Sherrard's ideas on Grant's thought are only too obvious. The distinction between a Platonic approach to philosophy and an Aristotelian one, as well as the connection between an Aristotelian philosophy and Western history and thought as a whole, are also evident in Grant. What was new for Grant was how these conflicts manifested themselves at the very beginning of the formation of Christian doctrine and extended themselves thereafter. Sherrard, however, was not a theologian of the cross, emphasizing the resurrection of Christ and the human soul more than the crucifixion, and offering no place in his discussion for the suffering of God and its relation to the human condition in the world. Yet his arguments for the Eastern Platonic understanding of God's transcendence and unknowability are consistent with the idea of God's absence in the world or hiddenness in the cross beyond all natural human understanding. For a theology of the cross, however, the hidden God is also the God revealed in Christ, and particularly in Christ crucified. This revelation was perceived with a faculty beyond the human intellect – the soul's openness to God in faith. In Luther and Weil, the mystery of God's transcendence beyond human understanding is also related to God's immanence or hidden presence in all that is.

4.3. The Theology of the Technological Society: The Consequences of Liberalism in Education, Religion, and Politics

With a deepened clarity about the way things are and how they came to be in the modern Western world, the bulk of Grant's writing in the 1960s is an attempt to name liberalism for what it is (i.e., a theology of glory), and to show how its practical fruit in the technological society is all too consistent with its theoretical foundations. Again, by naming things as they are, including the theology of glory, which both obscures the darkness of this reality and ultimately feeds it, Grant's hope is to inspire a humbled openness to a reality and truth transcending the darkness of the world as it is.

This task, however, is complicated for Grant by several factors. On the one hand, he desires to attack the modern liberal vision, which is an outgrowth of a Western Christianity scorning classical philosophy and embracing modern science and technology uncritically. On the other hand, he is confronted by the way in which the process of secularization is cutting itself off even from its liberal roots, roots which at least provided a minimal rudder guided by the Christian virtue of charity. During the first half of the 1960s, Grant appeals to churches, educators, and social workers who are animated by a liberal vision, in the hope that they will awaken to see the process of secularization for what it is – a rejection of any values whatsoever as restraints on freedom. His hope is that they will seek to fortify their social, practical vision inspired by charity with a critical vision in thought inspired by classical philosophy. In the later 1960s, however, Grant sees that this hope is not possible or realistic, that he has been too naïve, too blinded by his hope of success, and too much in denial about the extent of secularization and technologization in modern society. Technique was expanding its grip at an accelerated pace, outside and beyond any values or restraints. The challenge for him was to face the truth of the darkness of modern technological society in thought, and not despair. Here again, he would come to Simone Weil for inspiration. These developments in Grant's thought are highlighted in his reflection on education, religion, and politics within the technological society.

4.3.1. Education and Religion

Resignation from York University and Arrival in Toronto

The reasons for Grant's move to Toronto have already been mentioned (p. 121). Accepting a position at the newly formed York University would bring him closer to his mother, as well as to the centre of technological society as it was unfolding in Canada. Yet he was not prepared for the overwhelming impact that coming to Toronto would have on him. Despite his intense awareness of technological expansion, he was still surprised at how accelerated a pace Toronto had undergone expansion. Things began to fall apart, however, even before Grant arrived in Toronto. His intention in coming to York University was to create a philosophy department as an alternative to the modern, secular department at the University of Toronto. What he had not understood was that there was an arrangement between the two universities whereby York would be an affiliate of Toronto for five years. This meant that York's department of philosophy was under the control of the philosophy department at the University of Toronto, which was headed by Fulton Anderson. Needless to say, such an arrangement was far from comfortable.

In his letter of resignation, Grant explains in some detail his difficulty with this arrangement. Accepting the job would force him to teach philosophy according to the modern, secular approach represented by Anderson and others. This approach presumes modern analytical (English-speaking) philosophy to be superior to that of the Continent or that of the ancient world. Moreover, Christian faith is considered as mere superstition and, hence, completely irrelevant if not detrimental to philosophy.[19] We have already encountered Grant's reaction and response to such an approach.

Grant may have retained his integrity in resigning over his Christian faith and philosophical perspective, but he was out of a job with a family to feed. He proceeded to look for other work and received some interesting offers, including one from the Institute for Philosophical Research in San Francisco. With the understanding that he could work out of Toronto, he accepted the job and moved his family. Upon completing some of the work, however, he concluded that the orientation of the institute was 'Aristotelian' – lacking an appreciation of the transcendent, mystical side of Christianity, and driven by worldly ambition.[20] But Grant did eventually find a job he could live with. In 1961 he was offered the chairmanship of the newly formed department of religion at McMaster University in Hamilton. Here, unlike the arrangement at York, he was given the freedom to teach religion and philosophy as he believed they should be taught – in close relationship and interdependence. In a letter to a friend, he explains the importance of this:

I have had too long at Dalhousie been careful to draw the line between philosophy and Christianity – and I want now to be able to speak directly. It has not been philosophy but Xian doctrine that has got me through the necessities of life – and I think there is a crying need for young people to know what Xian doctrine is.[21]

Grant approach to the teaching of religion and philosophy is reflected in a series of interviews he did for a local paper at the time. He makes reference to the many profound questions young people are asking today – How should one live? What is the meaning and purpose of life? Perhaps people from a previous generation who are still held by a tradition may find such questioning hard to understand. But modern technological society is progressively destroying any remnants of such traditions, necessitating a new quest for meaning by the young. Nor are the old answers sufficient. These questions must be re-engaged in an existential, open way. Some questions may be answered easily through factual information about religious traditions. But other questions point to mysteries that must be contemplated. The big question of all time, for instance, is what is the meaning of evil and suffering if one is open to faith in God? It takes a whole lifetime to begin to understand such a question with greater depth and wisdom. Yet there is great merit in such questioning and contemplation. It teaches the young a broader perspective on life and helps them make wiser decisions in practical life.[22]

In a paper also written at this time, Grant focuses on the requirements for the 'academic study of religion in Canada.' He distinguishes the study of religion from that of theology. Biblical religion 'has centred round the assertion that a unique revelation of deity has been given to man and that this revelation concerns what is most important for man to know: the purpose, in obedience to which he can alone fully realize himself.'[23] Theology, on the other hand, is 'concerned with the attempt to think systematically about that revelation and its relation to all else.' But universities in the modern world are organized so far outside these assumptions, that ecclesiastical bodies must now move outside the university and set up their own theological colleges to fulfil the needs of theological study. Yet can universities offer a complete education without the study of religion, which is coeval with humanity? Nor does Grant find the modern secular approach to the study of religion adequate. This approach interprets the great religious figures and traditions through modern sociology and psychology. In the process 'there is the tendency to reduce these figures to tame confederates of transitory hypotheses.'[24] What is needed, then, is a study that takes the truth of a given religious tradition seriously, and teachers who are not only scholars but practitioners in a given tradition. A real education must consist of a dialogue of mutual respect and learning among people who consider the truth of religion, their own and that of another, with ultimate and absolute seriousness. In a society that worships 'positivist technocracy' as its religion and morality, and according to which the purposes of our society are fashioned, it is essential that there be a means of study through which one can be genuinely opened to the truth of alternative, older traditions.

The Religion of Progress and Education

Grant's emphasis on the needs of education in a modern secular technological context is taken up in several papers in the 1960s. In an early
paper entitled 'Religion and the State,' he addresses the debate over
the teaching of religion in the public schools of Ontario. Grant's intent
is to critique both liberal and conservative positions on the issue. Liberals argue that religion should be removed from the schools in order
to protect religious pluralism or a broader pluralism of opinion. But
what liberals fail to question altogether is the reigning religion of our
society: the religion of 'democracy,' or of 'progress, mastery and
power.' The inculcation of this religion is prevalent in public schools
and in society as a whole. Believers of this religion, 'assuming their
religion to be self-evidently true to all men of good will ..., are forceful
in advocating that it should be the public religion. They work for the
coming of the universal and homogenous state with enthusiasm; they
await its coming with expectation.'[25] Conservatives are not as eager
about the loss of traditional religion and the expanding religion of
technological progress. Nonetheless, they fail to realize how advanced
this religion is within society. They assume that Canadian society is
still essentially Christian and, therefore, Christianity should be given a
central place in the school curriculum. But Grant wonders how serious
modern-day conservatives are about Christian instruction in the
school. Do they want such instruction in order to serve a social function in civilizing the masses? And if so, how can such instruction be the
genuine article? Those in the church who do take their Christianity
seriously should awaken and realize what is happening in modern
society.

   In a book review written during the same period, Grant speaks of
the author as an 'educated American liberal' who believes that the
modern democratic state is the greatest human political achievement
in history. Grant sympathizes with his liberalism because the author
speaks of moral virtue, justice, right and wrong. Moreover, he has reverence for the older moral traditions of the Bible, the Greeks, and the
Chinese, and does not assume that these have been superseded by the
wisdom of modernity. Yet the author fails to relate his concept of
democracy to the 'religion' of scientific mastery and progress which is
the reigning morality within modern society. Moreover, he fails to give
adequate reasons why justice that transcends the subjective values of
the individual should be maintained and on what basis. Indeed, argues

Grant, without a strong tradition of faith, virtue cannot be maintained. This is not being taught in the schools and universities of the modern era.[26]

In a paper he wrote later in the 1960s, Grant develops some of these themes in greater depth. How does the religion of progress and technology affect the university curriculum in modern society? Basing his argument on Ellul's definition of technology, he states:

> The dynamism of technology has gradually become the dominant purpose in Western civilization because the most influential men in that civilization have believed for the last centuries that the mastery of chance was the chief means of improving the race ... one finds agreement between the corporation executive and union member, farmer and suburbanite, cautious and radical politician, university administrator and civil servant, in that they all subscribe to society's faith in mastery.[27]

Grant questions whether mastery in terms of technological progress is still justified by being linked with the improvement of the race, or whether it has become an autonomous quest outside any purpose other than expansion for its own sake. Indeed, argues Grant, in the face of this century's imperial wars, a growing space program, a superficial fun culture, and art whose purpose is nothing more than titillating, cajoling, and shocking people into fitting into a world where the question of meaning is irrelevant, he, following Strauss and Ellul, sees the latter to be the case.

Yet the more particular issue Grant seeks to address is the liberal faith behind technological progress to which society still pays lip service and which is the theoretical framework behind the university curriculum. This liberal faith is centred on freedom as being the most essential human characteristic and the shaping of the world as the most important human activity. The university finds its purpose in producing personnel for the service of this faith. In a technological society, this means the development of scientific mastery over human and non-human nature. The role of science is important here. With pressure from the public and private corporate elite, science motivated by wonder has given way to science motivated by power (domination, control, and manipulation).

The social sciences, on their part, have found their purpose in providing a theological rational for such motivation with the fact-value distinction. Following the lead of Strauss, Grant proceeds to criticize this distinction. The belief that facts alone constitute objective knowledge while values are human creations, is in contradiction with the pre-modern belief that values are derived from knowledge of the whole. This contradiction reveals how the fact-value distinction is a modern religion. It stands against the perspective of the more ancient religious faiths. The Greeks believed that the good could be discovered only through openness to the whole, in the sense of contemplating and waiting upon the most important questions. Biblical religion believed contemplation to be fulfilled in the service of making revelation intelligible.

Grant then puts several key questions to modern technological liberalism. Is it possible to gain any knowledge other than that derived from quantitative and experimental methods? If not, can these methods provide answers to the question of human purpose and what are better and worse purposes? Finally, does liberalism with its fact-value distinction not end up asserting that purpose is merely 'what we will in power from the midst of chaos'?[28] If this is so, does it not, on the one hand, cut itself off from pre-modern faiths which did believe in ultimate purposes above that of human invention, and, on the other hand, lead to historicism and the eclipse of all values from the public realm other than technological progress as an end in itself? According to Grant, 'our present forms of existence have sapped the ability to think about standards of excellence and yet at the same time have imposed on us a standard in terms of which the good is monolithically asserted.'[29] By serving this 'monolithically asserted' good, the university curriculum ensures that the universities will cultivate no serious criticism of themselves or society as they are and as they have been shaped. The confusion as to the end result of liberalism arises from the fact that in its early stages liberalism was influenced by the Christian virtue of charity in its striving for equality in the public realm, and freedom from poverty, disease, and overwork in the private. Yet the form of Christianity that dominated was one that gave up contemplation because it believed it to be an obstacle to the purposes of charity. Unfortunately, this led to the opposite effect of leaving liberalism vulnerable to the basest of human passions, which have been progressively unleashed via mastery through science and technology. A universe without God as ruler in the human heart and intelligence becomes a universe where humanity becomes God. The liberal illusion was that the human God would be a kinder and gentler one than the traditional God of Western Christianity. But rather than rethink the true nature of God on the basis of the revelation of the cross, liberals have rejected the Christian God altogether for one of their own making. They have carried over merely an emasculated love, which is incapable of withstanding the true evil in the universe, rooted in the human soul.

But where is it, then, that those who experience the barrenness of modern technological society and its liberal faith will go to find transcendent ground for human excellence and fulfilment? Modern technological liberalism has progressively killed even those mediators such as art, community, common sense, and reverence that help humans bridge the separation between the world and the eternal in modern society. If there is any hope, Grant suggests, it will not be through 'those who think of it [human excellence] as sustained simply in the human will, but only by those who have glimpsed that it is sustained by all that is.' This will require an intense openness to the whole in the midst of the present barrenness. For most, this openness may arise only with much suffering, for, as Grant states, 'Who is to recount how and when and where private anguish and public catastrophe may lead men to renew their vision of excellence?'[30]

The End of Western Christianity

In the later 1960s, any residual optimism Grant held in the possibility of reform or change in the directions of technological society was purged from his thought. In earlier work, he had believed in the possibility, however faint, that the churches along with concerned social workers and teachers could be mobilized to restrain and redirect technological progress according to a vision 'conservatively appropriated' from the 'wonderful truths from our origins in Athens and Jerusalem.' Grant attributes this blindness, not merely to intellectual limitations, but to personal vice. More specifically,

> if one is raised in the North American dream one so wants one's society and its institutions to have potentialities for nobility. For example, I hoped for years that our ecclesiastical organizations (being the guardians of the beauty of the gospel) might continue to be able to permeate this society with something nobler than the barrenness of technical dynamism. I hoped for this when every piece of evidence before me was saying that it was not true. I could not face the fact that we were living at the end of Western Christianity. I could not believe that the only interpretation of

Christianity that technological liberalism would allow to survive publicly would be that part of it ... that played the role of flatterer to modernity. Beyond such foolish hope lay the vice of ambition. One wants one's thoughts to be influential. Thinking in any era requires courage to sustain it. But courage always tends to fall over into ambition and as such corrupts the very thinking that courage must sustain. To want one's thoughts about the practical to be influential can lead to this corrupting ambition.[31]

Grant's struggle to be open to the whole or to God had to include a confrontation with those personal vices which served to distort the truth about the way things were.

But what did Grant mean about the 'end of Western Christianity' and his earlier illusions about the church? In 'Religion and the State,' Grant appeals to churches to awaken and see the secularization that is taking place around them. Grant's assumption (although ambivalent) is that somehow the churches may be free enough from the technological society in their worship and thought to respond to such a call and stand as prophetic witnesses against it. In another paper also written in the early 1960s, Grant urges those in the helping professions – clergy, teachers, social workers – to set aside any prestige they hope to gain in modern society, in order to see how the dominant faith in technique is co-opting all other purposes and priorities in society. At this point in history, they are confronted by two options. The first is to keep the present system running as well as possible. This means patching up wounds that are sustained in this tough society and keeping the system from being too harsh. The motivation for such work two generations ago was inspired by biblical religion, and one generation ago by liberalism. But the second option, asserts Grant, is 'not simply in patching up the wounds but in trying to incarnate meaning into the structures of the automated age.' To do this will require a higher degree of sophistication on the part of these workers than that provided by a naïve and optimistic liberalism, and a greater readiness to assume the weight of the present suffering in society, a readiness to enter the 'pitface,' for 'it is only in the pitface that the coal of meaning can be dug.'[32]

What Grant came to see as wrong in his hopes was not the nobility of attempts to enter the suffering and affliction of the world, but, rather, to assume that the churches and social workers were sufficiently capable of disentangling themselves from the North American dream to engage its evils in a self-denying way, open to the whole of reality, their 'fallenness' included. Grant's thought about the end of Western Christianity coincides with his growing disillusionment with the church, particularly his own Protestant confession. In one book review, he accuses a Roman Catholic theologian of joining Protestants in maintaining 'a profound optimism about the modern experiment of universal technological civilization.' Moreover, 'this optimism expresses itself in a theology which affirms that history is the unfolding of the divinely ordained process of man's salvation and that the world-wide civilization of technology and freedom is a step forward in that plan.'[33] This affirmation is deeply rooted in Protestant theology and particularly in that found on the North American continent, with its roots in a Calvinist reading of the Bible and a modern existentialist and empirical approach to philosophy. Grant is thinking here of the emphasis on human freedom and will. This tradition is opposed to Greek philosophy and earlier theology influenced by it, which limited the place of human freedom and will by an openness to the divine working, and which did not map divine providence in the world but affirmed an agnosticism and mystery surrounding God's purposes. This further implies a limitation on human freedom outside obedience to the good and human thought outside divine revelation and illumination. Grant associates this kind of faith and thought with a more Platonic tradition within Christianity, and whereas he had associated it earlier with Augustine and the mystical tradition in the West (including Lutheranism), he now sees the Platonic 'eastern' tradition standing outside the Western tradition altogether. Here he is influenced by Sherrard, as we have seen, and Weil, as we shall see further below. Grant ends by stating that the Western approach has led Protestantism into being co-opted by the religion of progress, thereby becoming nothing more than a 'flatterer' of the present age.[34]

The reference to modern Protestantism as a flatterer of the age is a common theme in Grant.[35] It is also the focus of an extended commentary on a book by the renowned liberal theologian Harvey Cox. Cox represents North American liberal Protestantism in his attempt to synthesize biblical faith with modern technological society. According to Grant, however, Cox's attempt only serves to give up the very essence of the gospel. Grant agrees with Cox on one fundamental aspect of Christian faith – that love is the supreme virtue. 'To love is to pay attention to other people and this means to communicate with them.'[36] This also means communicating with people in the context of the modern technological society. But the desire to understand this society and

communicate effectively with people in it can easily turn into an acceptance of it. This is a temptation for many church people who feel the
church today must be modernized in order to relate to the mass technological society. The grave danger in this endeavour is that of losing
any standards that transcend this society and can judge it. Some want
to eliminate judgment altogether from Christianity. But does love
really mean the elimination of transcendent standards of judgment?
Must communication in the world mean an acceptance of it as it is?

Cox's book proposes a marriage between Christianity and the 'secular city.' Through marriage, it is believed, 'Christianity will be able to
impregnate modernity with the spirit of Christ.' But in this union 'who
is going to seduce whom?' Cox associates the modern world with the
rise of secularization. This involves the building of urban civilization
and the collapse of traditional religion. Cox argues that we must welcome the process of secularization as good, for secularization brings
freedom with it. Human beings are no longer slaves to an old metaphysical, religious order which imposed restraints on human freedom.
The emphasis on human freedom to shape the world by reform,
human creativity, and activism finds its roots in the Bible and should,
therefore, be accepted joyfully. But in order to see things in this way,
argues Grant, Cox must see only the bad side of traditional religion
and the good side of modern secularism. The ferocious wars of this
century, the imperial aggressiveness of America, and the political
orders of Nazism and Communism, can only be insane ideologies
unrelated to the essence of the secular city. But is not the power of
Nazism and Communism related to the Western collapse of traditional
religion, which Cox celebrates? Is not the growing imperial aggression
of the United States (i.e., in Vietnam), or more covert corporate colo-
nialism, also related to this collapse?

The basic questions that Grant puts to Cox and to modern liberal
Protestantism are the following:

> Are our technological societies really producing free men or are the
> masses given over to passive pleasure-seeking and the elite to a more and
> more ruthless pursuit of prestige and power? Are the multiversities of our
> society producing wise or even educated people, or are they turning out
> units who keep the technological system going? It is the claim of the liber-
> als that the secular city will be a pluralist society; that is, a society where
> men will be free to pursue divergent aims in tolerance of each other. But
> is this happening? Isn't the greatest of secular cities (the United States)

turning into a monolithic tyranny in which the dominant aim in life is sophisticated vulgarity?[37]

Cox has simply smoothed over these questions. But the criticism of Cox must go deeper. It must engage his whole account of Western history. It is true that the process of secularization can be linked to biblical religion, and the age of progress to Western Christianity. But can this secularized Christianity be identified with the religion of the gospels? What Cox has not understood is that the origins of modern liberalism are not only rooted in biblical religion, but in a basic revolt against biblical religion. Founders of modern thought and society such as Machiavelli, Hobbes, and Rousseau sought to establish a ground for human beings and society in which the idea of supernatural purpose was completely discarded. Cox seems totally ignorant about this side of liberalism.

Grant concludes by addressing two areas in which the irreconcilability of liberalism and genuine Christianity is clearly evident. First, biblical Christianity, particularly in the Gospels, makes high demands on self-restraint for the individual. Self-restraint is not applied merely to sexual matters but to the desire for prestige, wealth, and power. Self-restraint is not simply a repression of the emotions and desires, but their fulfilment in obedience to Christ. This stands in sharp contrast to the liberal emphasis on the liberation of the passions and a deprecation of the language of restraint as simply a remnant of an old oppressive religious system. Cox smooths over these differences with much talk of love. But the issue is not simply whether one should be in favour of love. Rather, it is about how loving is to be achieved. Liberalism believes that with the liberation of the passions people will the better love each other. Christianity believes that loving is much more difficult, and that a lack of restraint is detrimental for the common good. This, of course, has nothing to do with a freedom from the restraints that technology imposes on us all. Christianity is surely sympathetic to such a revolt. Yet unlimited freedom is not the answer.

Second, Christianity and liberalism have different understandings of the word 'freedom.' For the Gospels, true freedom is the ability of individuals to give themselves to God. For liberalism, it is the ability of individuals to make themselves and the world as they want them to be. For Christianity, God is the measure by which human beings are to be measured and defined. For liberalism, human beings are their own measure. For Christianity, absolute freedom is atheism. For liberalism,

it is the essence of humanity. There is a great gulf between the two
ways of thinking. The question, then, is how are we to live in the modern world and communicate the gospel without giving it up? Certainly
it is not with the spirit of flattery or the denial of the gospel. Rather,
'the answer will come out of much contemplation and anguish.'[38]
Cox's gospel is nothing but a theology of glory.

In the 1960s, Grant is concerned once again with maintaining the necessary interdependence of faith and philosophy, revelation and reason.
Where he has developed clarity is in his delineation of what constitutes
a genuine Christianity and a genuine philosophy. Grant makes his
choice for what he now calls a more Eastern Christianity as opposed to
a Western one, and a more Platonic philosophy as opposed to an Aristotelian one. He still retains a high regard for Aristotle, yet he also sus-
pects him of moving along the path of a theology of glory, obscuring
the great distance between the necessary and the good, a distance that
cannot be bridged by the human intellect or will, but by God alone.
This is what Western philosophy and Christianity have tried to do.
Grant further perceives this Western tradition to have sown the seeds
of modern technological society and its liberal religion. The whole
movement of freedom from and a rejection of transcendent standards
above the human intellect or will, is simply a continuation of the theology of glory tradition. Idolizing freedom, history, or progress, and
identifying these with the working of divine providence, is as much a
deification of human activity and thought as was the medieval natural
theology that Luther opposed. Grant's contention with Western Christianity is that it has bought into the modern dream too deeply to be
able to stand apart from it and judge it. It has obscured the distance
between the necessary and the good, the world and God, a distance
that can only be bridged from the side of God. Its emphasis has been
on a possessiveness of, rather than an openness toward, the truth, on
the human will rather than on divine grace, on the human intellect
rather than on revelation, and on freedom rather than on charity.

The liberal Protestant celebration of modern technological society
also trivializes evil. It trivializes the deep suffering, anguish, and
meaninglessness that are so prevalent within technological society.
Even though Grant came to see that it is not simply by further action
that human beings will address these crises successfully, he stressed
the need for entering the suffering of our times through contemplation,
attention, and solidarity. It is only out of such 'passive' activity that one

could be open to the whole, to God's hidden presence and redemptive working in life. Does this activity lack sufficient hope or remain too pessimistic? Grant increasingly came to see his task as honest reflection on the way things are. But more than that, the idea of openness to the whole, to the truth hidden or absent in the modern world, is one of patient trust and hope in a God whose working and purpose transcend our understanding and comprehension.

We must, nonetheless, also question Grant's account of modern Protestantism. The limitations of this account were already noted in his thesis on Oman and in 'Two Theological Languages.' While it may be true that modern Protestantism has been suspicious of Greek thought and has sought to distinguish biblical religion from it, there have also been more mediating theologians such as Paul Tillich who have incorporated a deep appreciation of the Platonic tradition in their thought. Moreover, the whole neo-orthodox movement was based on a profound criticism of modern liberalism in philosophy, theology, and society. Indeed, Grant's criticism of theologians such as Cox is not unlike that of followers of Niebuhr, Barth, Bonhoeffer, or Tillich. Finally, the whole issue of communicating effectively in the modern world, but in a way that retains the essence of the gospel, was very much the focus in the methodological debate in Protestantism between Kerygmatic and Apologetic approaches.[39] Grant's struggle to communicate the gospel in its purity, in language that modern people can understand – that is, contextually – is very much a struggle to incorporate the best of both approaches. Grant was much more of a Protestant theologian of the cross than he realized.

4.3.2. Politics

Lament for a Nation

Without a doubt, *Lament for a Nation* has been Grant's most widely read book, but also the one that has generated the greatest controversy. As in much of his other work, Grant offers a fundamental critique of modern technological society from the perspective of his philosophical, theological orientation. Unlike other work we have considered in this chapter, however, he offers this critique through a biting commentary on the history and politics of Canada. Perhaps the controversy was generated because he combined his commentary on specific political events with universal philosophical and theological themes in a way that gave these events a highly concrete significance. He was able to relate these events to the larger movement of history toward the universal and homogenous state, and revealed in practical terms how this would be a tyranny.

Grant admitted later that what motivated him to write the book was anger more than anything else. Such anger was in response to several factors surrounding the pressure, primarily from the United States, but also from the Canadian public, to test nuclear warheads on Canadian soil.[40] While the Conservative government had seemed to be prepared to acquire nuclear weapons in 1959, its views had changed by 1961.[41] The government saw its international role increasingly as that of broker for nuclear disarmament. Acquiring these weapons would damage its international credibility to lead in this initiative. Nonetheless, the pressure from the United States, the Canadian public, and big business was so arrayed against this change in policy that the opposition parties, with the implicit support of the majority of Conservative politicians themselves, combined to defeat the government and force a general election in 1963. For Grant, this defeat symbolized nothing less than 'the defeat of Canadian nationalism.' The form this nationalism took was the resistance of Prime Minister John Diefenbaker and his minister of international affairs to bowing to American pressure. Grant had been committed to pacifism and internationalism from early on in his life. This was related to his Christianity as well as his belief, inherited from his progenitors, that only internationalism could be a counterbalancing force to the growing power of the United States and the escalating tensions in East-West relations.

It was also during this time that Grant's mother died. For him, her passing symbolized the passing of the national dream of his progenitors: that of building in the northern half of the continent, along with the French, 'a more ordered and stable society than the liberal experiment in the United States.'[42] Grant's lament is associated with the fall of Diefenbaker because 'his inability to govern is linked with the inability of the country to be sovereign.' Although the book ended up being more an indictment of Diefenbaker than praise, Grant saw in him 'the apotheosis of straight loyalty.'[43] This loyalty was to Canada, to the belief that the continued existence of Canada as a sovereign state was consistent with the good transcending the political order. In searching for a publisher, Grant explains that the book is 'a closely written book and full of passion and regret about Canada. It starts with a lot of factual material about Canadian history, but ends with a logic, which is deeper, about the age of progress.'[44] The book begins from the particulars of the Canadian political situation and gradually builds to more universal themes of philosophical and theological reflection. Let us consider its argument more closely.

The situation that animated Grant's anger was the attack of the Canadian establishment – business, intellectual, church, and media – on Diefenbaker. The purpose of his 'meditation' is to consider why this has happened. But why use the concept of 'lament' for such a meditation? Grant explains it thus: 'To lament is to cry out at the death or at the dying of something loved. This lament mourns the end of Canada as a sovereign state.' The idea of a lament stands in contrast to popular expectations in an age of progress that things are always improving. But a lament is not 'an indulgence in despair or cynicism.' Rather, it expresses both 'pain and regret,' but also an appreciation or 'celebration of a passed good.' Grant puts it another way:

> One cannot argue the meaninglessness of the world from the facts of evil, because what can evil deprive us of, if we had not some prior knowledge of good? The situation of absolute despair does not allow a man to write … When a man truly despairs, he does not write; he commits suicide. At the other extreme, there are the saints who know that the destruction of good serves the supernatural end; therefore they cannot lament. Those who write laments may have heard the proposition of the saints, but they do not know that they are true. A lament arises from a condition that is common to the majority of men, for we are situated between despair and absolute certainty.[45]

The idea of a hidden or absent good that allows us to mourn its deprivation in a world of evil, as well as the idea of the faith of the 'saint' who trusts that God's purposes are realized even through the tragedies and evils within the world, clearly reveal the influence of Weil on Grant at this point. Grant has reverence for such faith and considers it the ultimate standard of moral excellence. Yet he also recognizes his distance from this standard, and thus his lament.

Grant's purpose in the book is to describe the particular evil in the history and politics of Canada along with the good that is being lost. This good is the existence of Canada as a sovereign nation. The evil is how this sovereignty has been progressively eroded. Diefenbaker's role in all this has been to represent the minority resistance to this loss. Grant acknowledges that Diefenbaker has done a poor job in working consistently for this resistance. But he is also disgusted at the establishment's readiness to give up Canadian sovereignty altogether. Canada's disappearance may be inevitable, a matter of necessity or fate, given the larger modern movement toward the universal and homogenous state. But Grant laments its loss as the loss of something precious, that 'tenuous hope that was the principle of my ancestors.'[46]

The battle over Canadian sovereignty was very much centred on Canada's relations with the United States. While the Liberals saw the threat to Canadian sovereignty coming from the traditional connection of Canada with Great Britain, the Conservatives saw the continuing British connection as a counter-force against the growing influence of the United States on Canada. This influence was expanding via the growth of corporate capitalism throughout the continent. It was in the interests of the ruling classes, who ran the private and public corporations in Canada, to welcome this expansion. Expansion meant wealth, and the ruling classes were more committed to wealth than to a sovereign nation. In order to receive American capital, Canada had to be transformed into a 'branch-plant economy'· of the United States. The Liberals welcomed this movement. For them, expansion of the economy in any way was good for everyone. They could not see all that would have to be given up with this expansion. The strength of Diefenbaker's defeat of the Liberals in 1959 reflected his support by all those excluded from the expanding economy of corporate capitalism. Diefenbaker's stand against pressure to acquire nuclear weapons in 1963 and the antagonism toward him from the Canadian ruling classes, the United States, and the military revealed two things. It revealed Diefenbaker's commitment to Canadian sovereignty, as well as how economic dependence on the United States would also imply subservience in all facets of public life, including national values.

Diefenbaker's failures are related to his inability to define consistently what Canada should be and, therefore, what it was that made it distinct and worth saving. Grant then goes on to catalogue a number of decisions Diefenbaker made that undermined Canadian sovereignty. These failures notwithstanding, Diefenbaker's stand against pressure to acquire nuclear weapons reveals in principle the nationalism he held. He did not think it right that Canada's defence policy should be determined in Washington. Diefenbaker's minister of international affairs, Howard Green, was even more eloquent a spokesman for what was at stake. Canada's best military role within the international community was as an influence toward disarmament. The acquisition of these weapons would diminish that role considerably. Moreover, he referred to the growing power and aggressiveness of the United States in the world, and how such power could tempt them to be 'bullies' in relation to smaller nations. His vision for Canada was influenced by a gentler tradition of international morality. All this, however, had little support in Canada. Diefenbaker and Green assumed that an appeal to Canadian nationalism, Canada's unique role in the world, and its counterbalancing presence to the growing power of the United States would find ready acceptance in Canada. They failed to realize that the Canadian ruling class was no longer nationalist and found any remaining ties with Britain a burden.

The Canadian ruling class and the Liberals, however, did not see themselves as anti-nationalist. Indeed, they believed that they were the better defenders of Canadian nationalism. Liberals were committed to the corporate rule of Canada, with government simply playing a supervisory role. Moreover, they made greater advances vis-à-vis Quebec, with their readiness to do away with any hated British symbols left in Canada. Both they and the French failed to realize that the real enemy to nationalism was not Britain but the United States. Liberals accepted the necessity of American rule. Canada had to do its part in the defence of the West, with the United States as leader. If this also meant Canada had to become a branch-plant of the United States, so be it. But the consequence of having a branch-plant economy is the development of a branch-plant culture, and, eventually, any distinctive national identity or sovereignty is bound to disappear. The liberal idea that individuals, or society as a whole, are free to choose how deeply it is desirable to buy into this development is an illusion. The whole idea of democracy is brought into irrelevance in the modern world. Capitalism is the great 'solvent' of all traditions in the modern era. Everything is relativized before the ideal of profit-making, and this includes all traditions of virtue such as love of country. But liberalism is the perfect ideology for capitalism. It destroys any apprehensions that would restrain expansion.

The broader question, however, is whether anything could have been done to save Canada after 1960. The larger aspirations of the age of progress have made the existence of an independent Canada meaningless. It is toward greater universalism and homogeneity that the modern world is moving. The liberal hope is that universalism will eliminate the curse of war among nations, and homogeneity will eliminate class conflict. But Grant questions whether this is, indeed, where the world is heading, and whether all that will be lost has been fully contemplated. The tools for this universalization and homogenization are the sciences, which issue in the mastery of human and non-human nature. But is such mastery not control, be it of mind, society, or heredity? And if so, is this good? Moreover, the continued existence of local cultures will be a thing of the past. Is this good? Yet this is not how moderns think of what is happening. They accept that fact that the larger movement of history is toward greater universalization and homogenization, that Canada is located next to the most modern of societies, and that nothing essential distinguishes us from the United States and, hence, nothing essential is to be lost. Canadians, as much as anybody, 'oblate themselves' to the 'American way of life,' which is the 'reigning Western goddess.'[47] But the founding of Canada was based on the determination of both French and English not to be swallowed up by the great republic to the south. Both peoples held some common ground in their emphasis on social order, law, and public virtue. Both believed that the state should be given greater powers in the promotion of the common good and that there should be more restraint on individual freedom than was recognized in the American constitution.

Why, then, have these traditions failed? Grant offers historical and political reasons why both British and French traditions in Canada were undermined by the larger liberal movement toward the universal and homogenous state. Moreover, to those who do not celebrate the liberal vision, liberals argue that we should at the very least accept historical necessity. They are prepared to lead us so that we can do this with as little pain as possible, for 'fate leads the willing and drives the unwilling.'

Grant concludes by offering some larger philosophical, theological analysis. The view that Canada's disappearance serves the larger good is consistent with the philosophical view, common in the age of progress, that identifies necessity and goodness. The movement of history is upward. This view, as Grant has repeatedly stated, is rooted in a Western reading of the Bible and secularized in the modern period in Hegel's identification of divine providence with world history. Grant questions this view:

Is it possible to look at history and deny that within its dimensions force is the supreme ruler? To take a progressive view of providence is to come close to worshipping force. Does this not make us cavalier about evil? The screams of the tortured child can be justified by the achievements of history. How pleasant for the achievers, but how meaningless for the child.[48]

Grant then goes on:

> As a believer, I must reject these Western interpretations of providence. Belief is blasphemy if it rests on any easy identification of necessity and good. It is plain that there must be other interpretations of the doctrine ... It must be possible within the doctrine of providence to distinguish between the necessity of certain happenings and their goodness. A discussion of the goodness of Canada's disappearance must therefore be separated from a discussion of its necessity.[49]

If consumption is everything, nationalism is irrelevant. But the disappearance of Canada is about the disappearance of important principles. While earlier liberalism was more virtuous, being the voice of freedom in an oppressive context, today it is the voice of oppression and the legitimater of a universalization that may become even more horrific in violence and tyranny. It is essential that those who criticize our progressive technological society take into account the basic improvements of life that it has made possible. But we must also face the new problems it has brought:

> ... increasing outbreaks of impersonal ferocity, the banality of existence in technological societies, the pursuit of expansion as an end in itself. Will it be good for men to control their genes? The possibility of nuclear destruction and mass starvation may be more terrible than that of man tampering with the roots of his humanity. Interference with human nature seems to the moderns the hope of a higher species in the ascent of life; to others it may seem that man in his pride could corrupt his very being. The powers of manipulation now available may portend the most complete tyranny imaginable.[50]

At least the ancients understood human nature sufficiently well to foresee the possibility of such tyranny. The moderns are completely blinded in their pride and lust for freedom.

Grant's lament is based not on philosophy, however, but on tradition. His lament is over the passing of a particular tradition and way of life. He does not know whether this loss serves the greater good. Yet to lament is not to fall into self-pity, but to have courage and, beyond courage, faith. And this 'ancient' faith trusts that any and all change in the world, be it toward the good or toward evil, takes place within a larger 'eternal' order whose goodness, justice, and love are not corrupted or destroyed.

Lament clearly reveals the influence of Grant's progenitors on his political thought. While he rejected their naïve optimism about the progress of history, he imbibed very deeply their nationalist vision and their definition of what Canada ought to be.[51] Some critics accused Grant of indulging in a nostalgic longing for his Loyalist past, which is romanticized, offering an interpretation of the founding Canadian vision more mythical than real, and seeking to escape the realities of the present. They contend that the idea that technological determinism transcends any institutional control (an idea adopted from Ellul) is wrong. Technology is controlled by political power, and political power can be swayed in different directions. The determinist view leads Grant into a complete pessimism and, ultimately, a defeatism.[52] The charge of pessimism is levelled against Grant from many quarters. A. Kroker finds the roots of this pessimism in Grant's 'religious temperament,' which 'leaves no room for emancipatory politics' or any 'celebration of human creativity in the face of dismal odds.'[53] G. Horowitz accuses Grant of lacking faith and hope altogether. His determinism is overpowering and his pessimism uncompromising. This is because he 'identifies the inevitability of technological progress with the inevitable failure of any attempt to control and use it for human purposes.' [54] G. Horowitz and M. Hurtig, as socialists, and W.L. Morton, as a conservative,[55] are unable to accept Grant's pessimism about the possibility of genuine politics in the modern progressive era, or that Canadian nationalism is, indeed, defeated.

The irony is that *Lament* had the opposite effect to what many critics feared. It inspired a renewed nationalism among many of the young.[56] Moreover, an honest description of the way things are, did not mean that Grant did not also promote participation in politics. As he stated at the beginning of *Lament*, a lament is not an indulgence in cynicism or despair. If one cannot bring about the best result in society, one must work to prevent or slow down the worst from happening.

But more essentially, Grant accuses his critics of having grasped the practical part of the book while missing completely the more important philosophical, theological affirmations. Others have read it as a call to nationalism when it was speaking about the end of Canadian nationalism. This is because their hopes are limited to the finite realm, and they cannot entertain the thought that the larger continental forces may be leading to an unprecedented tyranny.[57] In the preface to an edition of *Lament* published in 1970, Grant addresses his critics more formally. The charge of pessimism does not engage the fundamental issue: whether hope must be offered at the expense of truth; or, whether things are to be presented as they are. Grant has obviously chosen the latter option. Yet is this pessimism? No, argues Grant, for,

> it would be the height of pessimism to believe that our society could go on in its present directions without bringing down upon itself catastrophes. To believe the foregoing would be pessimism, for it would imply that the nature of things does not bring forth human excellence.[58]

Clearly, Grant felt that the deeper philosophical, theological affirmations in *Lament* were more fundamental than his political, historical commentary. The fate of Canada was simply a particular case of the global trend in the progressive movement of history toward the universal and homogeneous state. He tried to show how this would be a great loss for Canadians and, ultimately, for the world. When every culture and tradition that has developed over centuries becomes swallowed up in a universal technological culture which reduces everything to self-centred consumerism, pleasure-seeking, and mastery without limits, true excellence in humanity is lost, and tyranny in manipulation and control is imposed on human beings on an unprecedented scale. Moreover, with the erosion of any transcendent order restraining and guiding an expanding human freedom, the burden of meaning and purpose is borne by the individual soul. Existentialists may be atheist, but at least they realize the weight of such a responsibility.

But Grant also argues that beyond tradition stands philosophy. The philosophical affirmation for Grant is the ancient one which distinguishes between the necessity of certain happenings and their goodness. Indeed, in contemplating the loss of Canada with its traditions, necessity is very far from the good. For those who affirm the philosophy of modern liberalism, necessity and the good are closely identified because the loss of Canadian sovereignty serves the larger progress of history toward universal freedom and equality. For Grant, this is blasphemy and idolatry. It is identifying the good/God with something human and, beyond that, with something that will lead to great suffering and inhumanity. To worship necessity, as Weil taught him, is to come close to worshipping force, and this also leads to a cavalier attitude toward the evil and suffering in the world, which are its fruit. For many who could understand Grant's logic, such a state of affairs would be cause for despair, and hence the charge of pessimism. But they were only able to see hope or redemption on the horizontal plane of history.

For Grant, however, genuine philosophy is undergirded by faith. Faith is the mean between absolute certainty and despair. Faith is not despair, for it is a trust against the darkness. It 'asserts that changes in the world, even if they be recognized more as a loss than a gain, take place within an eternal order that is not affected by their taking place.'[59] Faith is also not absolute certainty. It has glimpsed the truth of the eternal order of divine perfection, the good which is love and the hidden presence in all of reality. But it has glimpsed this love from afar, crucified on a cross. It knows this love by experiencing its absence. Through his faith, Grant was able to discern that the loss of Canada would be a loss of good. The inhumanity, suffering, and corruption of the soul that would also come, would reveal how absent, hidden, or crucified divine love was in the world. Grant knew about and revered the experience of 'saints' like Weil or Luther, who, in spite of their many doubts, could consent to love God through all that happened in the world and, as a result, affirm all that is as good and beneficial with absolute certainty. But Grant was too attached to the particularities of his life to come even close to doing this. Faith is, finally, to endure such suffering without escaping into the illusion that necessity is good, while remaining open to God, even a God absent or crucified. Weil and Luther were much further ahead on this path than Grant. But he recognized their path to be the right one, and their standard of excellence to be his own measure.

Finally, as we have already noted earlier, Grant's understanding of the doctrine of providence undergoes a fundamental change in the 1960s. Providence is no longer identified with progressive history. This Western interpretation is replaced with a more 'Eastern' one which identifies providence with the soul's union with God through all the vicissitudes of life in the world. Salvation is no longer tied to history or to a redemption of society on this side of history. Obedience to and fulfilment in the love of God, as well as a commitment to the world in the name of that love, is not linked to any optimistic outcome or results.

This is also consistent with the truth revealed by the one who affirmed God's love even on the cross.

The Vietnam Era

The Vietnam War was the significant political event that affected Grant's thought in the latter half of the 1960s. The nature and motivations of American involvement in this war revealed to Grant the brutal possibilities of the modern technological society and the end result of liberal ideology. It revealed to him just how distant necessity was from the good. In one article, Grant compares American action in Vietnam with what was being done to Jews in Auschwitz. Moreover, by supporting the United States, Canada is directly implicated. But most either justify what is being done or simply treat it as an aberration in an otherwise sound political order. They fail to see the inherent connection between modern liberal ideology and what is happening in Vietnam. When freedom is combined with power and mastery made possible through technology, human nature easily becomes corrupted and destructive in a way blind even to itself. But our modern North American society is unable to judge itself fundamentally. Its intellectual roots are a shallow liberalism legitimated by a morally shallow Protestantism. It promotes pluralism in words but subsumes all traditions and cultures loosely planted on the continent into a great stream whose defining element is 'affluence through technology.' The worship of such affluence and the freedom it promises, however, leads to great evil; not the evil, perhaps, of an Auschwitz, but a 'bland, impersonal wiping out' of a people who cannot otherwise be brought under submission to the American way of life. Grant explains this philosophically with the Platonic, Augustinian doctrine of evil as the absence of good. This absence is evident when 'your moral roots lead you to exalt affluent technology as the highest end' and as a consequence to 'a use of power, when deemed necessary to comfortable self-preservation, which perpetuates evil from its very banality.'[60]

In his struggle to uncover the evil hidden beneath the banality of what was happening in Vietnam, Grant was encouraged by the reaction of students. Great opposition to American policy in Vietnam developed on university campuses in the United States and elsewhere. This opposition broadened into an attack on Western capitalism and imperialism, and students mobilized themselves for protest. Leading the attack were radicals who called themselves the 'New Left' to distinguish themselves from older Marxists and Social Democrats. Many of them had already encountered Grant through their reading of *Lament for a Nation*. But it was his political, social criticism and nationalism they admired, not his philosophical, theological affirmations. With Vietnam and the broader issues surrounding it, Grant shared common ground with the New Left and agreed to support their protest any way he could. But it also became clear that there were some fundamental differences between them.

First, the students wanted to extend their protests to acts of civil disobedience. As a conservative, Grant could not countenance this. Civil disobedience was a last resort to be used only when the government was directly responsible for evil.[61] Second, what was the purpose of protest? Grant addressed this question in a short article. Protest, he states, is an extreme act for an extreme situation. The Americans are willing to engage in a genocidal war in order to bring the Vietnamese into submission. Canadians are implicated in this war, although indirectly (they have not sent in troops) because of whatever nationalism they still retain. Nonetheless, their support of the United States undermines their international credibility as peacemakers. Thus, opposition to the war is a matter of self-interest as well as conscience. But can protest accomplish anything given the escalating intensity of the war? Yes, affirms Grant. In every situation, it matters ultimately what one does. Without protest, things would be worse. Canada would be more involved in the war. Protest puts pressure to stop or limit what is being done in Vietnam. It also voices the truth in a society where truth and lies are no longer distinguished. We must always be concerned to stop terrible suffering in any way possible. We must also be concerned for society and for individual souls being destroyed by lies and perversion.[62] The students and New Left could agree with all this. But they also hoped for much more. They believed policy in Vietnam, as well as the broader currents of imperialism and capitalism, could be changed by protest. Grant, as can be expected from one who was influenced by Ellul, Strauss, and Weil, was more realistic about these necessities.

Grant addressed this and related issues in a speech he gave at a student teach-in and later published as an article. He begins by stating his political stance and the nature of the North American context. He is a Canadian nationalist and conservative who lives next to an empire controlled by huge public and private corporations whose bureaucracy increasingly spreads its control over much of the world and beyond it (i.e., space exploration). The nineteenth-century idea of democracy, by which a citizen participates in public decision-making through political parties and the vote, is fast becoming meaningless. Such citizenship is incompatible with a growing technological empire. Grant then goes on to offer his critique. He agrees with the New Left's account of the inhumanity of North American institutions. But when they speak of overcoming these conditions through protest, Grant thinks 'they are indulging in dreams and dangerous dreams.'[63] For centuries the chief pursuit of the West has been, first, the conquest of nature and, more recently, the conquest of human nature. The motive of such a pursuit was freedom. Under freedom we have built massive institutions, which may have helped free us from nature but have also enslaved us in fundamental ways. Why should anyone believe that through some 'dialectical process of history' there will arise out of technological society a 'free and human society' ? Where is the evidence in our democracy, our universities, or the autonomy of the space program? Even dissent is built into the system.

Grant, however, is not advocating 'inaction or cynicism.' Neither does he deny the 'nobility of protest' or that justice and injustice, good and evil, must be distinguished openly. 'To live with courage in the world is always better than retreat or disillusion.' But he is arguing against 'the politics based on easy hopes about the future of the human situation,' and the idea that the technological structure in North America can be radically changed. Hope in the future is the 'chief opiate' of the modern world because it teaches people to dream rather than come to terms with reality. The danger of such dreaming is that it can lead to serious disappointment, which in turn can lead to despair or bitterness. 'Moral fervour is too precious a commodity not to be put in the service of reality.'

Effective protest today, then, must be combined with deep and careful thought. True freedom that will keep us human and effective is to know the truth about the way things are without illusion or false hopes. Freedom is not achieved by mastery of human and non-human nature, nor is it simply a political slogan. Rather, it is the quest for knowledge of reality, the whole of it. What we have to do, then, is to learn what it means to be a citizen in the technological society. We must learn how its structures operate in their potential to liberate us from natural necessity, but also how they bind and dehumanize us. We need to contemplate where in this vast system there are spaces for human excellence and community to exist, how we can bring pressure most effectively on the North American empire to use moderation and restraint in its dealings with the rest of the world, and how to maintain as much of our national identity as is possible.[64]

In an article on President L.B. Johnson's 'vision' of the 'Great Society,' Grant develops further what it would mean to be a citizen in the midst of a technological empire. The vision is of the prosperous coexistence of free and equal human beings. The principles for this being carried out are, first, the sciences issuing in the mastery of human and non-human nature; and, second, the application of these sciences within a state corporate capitalist structure.[65] North America is certainly the society that has furthest applied these principles. But what are the results thus far? Grant gives a list of facts that reveal the dehumanization being lived out by many, and this does not even include what is being done by the 'Great Society' around the world (namely, in Vietnam).

But supporters of the Great Society point to all its benefits and achievements. Any poor results or limitations can be overcome with time and with more advanced technological application. Moreover, once the threat of communist tyranny has been overcome, it will be possible for the whole world to enjoy the benefits of the Great Society. This, however, does not bring us to question the basic principle of the Great Society: that mastery of human and non-human nature through scientific application will create a society of free and equal human beings. This principle is the religion of our society, that which people trust to save them. But will it save or destroy them?

In order to answer this question, Grant offers his own understanding of the human condition and the purpose of human existence. We live in a world where we are victims of forces beyond us. These forces (chance) limit the possibility of our participation in excellence. Human excellence can only be understood in relation to the purposes of human existence: 'to live together well in communities and to think.' Human excellence consists in the virtues necessary for the achievement of these purposes. Modern science, in the name of charity, turned from contemplation to mastery in order to overcome chance and make the good life possible for all. Yet through this mastery, we have created a monolithic structure which is more tyrannous, and a greater barrier to human participation in excellence, than any previous. It denies the possibility of serious thought outside the technical or the maintenance of a genuine community of free persons. As the structure grows, it needs to control and manage people more completely.

How, then, is one to live meaningfully in such a society? Grant stresses the need to maintain one's active commitment to the world. There are many wounds to be bound up in the world. It is an illusion to believe that through some form of mysticism or LSD one can arrive at ultimate joy and bypass one's immediate responsibilities and relationships in the world. The virtue that is most necessary for such an active commitment is openness. Openness is the opposite of control or mastery:

> Mastery tries to shape the objects and people around us into a form which suits us. Openness tries to know what things are in themselves, not to impose our categories upon them. Openness acts on the assumption that other things and people have their own goodness in themselves; control believes that the world is essentially neutral stuff which can be made good by human effort.[66]

The virtue of openness is exceedingly difficult to realize in our era. It requires the discipline of confronting one's 'closedness, aggressions and neuroses, be they moral, intellectual or sexual,' in an age obsessed with control.

In another essay, Grant struggles with these themes as a Canadian. The fate of Canadian existence is to be bound up in the interplay of various world empires. The language of 'fate,' which Grant borrows from Weil, stands in contrast to the language of freedom, for it implies that 'human beings come into a world they did not choose and live their lives in a universe they did not make.'[67] To speak in this way is not to be pessimistic, for Grant also affirms that the world and 'nature' are good. Implicit in these twin affirmations of fate and the goodness of all that is, is a theology of the cross which is open to the transcendent good (divine love) even in the face of the afflictions and evils of the world as it is. But this is also to speak in the language of faith and philosophy. As a Canadian and a conservative, Grant sees the particular fate of Canada being bound up with the American empire at a time when that empire uses brutal means to expand itself (i.e., in Vietnam). What is the moral predicament of Canadians caught in this bind? On the one hand, they are not so completely destitute of ancient traditions to realize the evil that is being perpetrated in the name of liberal democracy. On the other hand, they have been caught up in the North American dream and, therefore, feel no choice but to support the United States. They have entrusted their soul to faith in progress through technology as the means to their meaning and purpose in life.

Where did such a faith originate? Grant offers some historical connections which we have already encountered in his thought. What saddens him most deeply, however, is 'the disappearance of indigenous
traditions, including my own.' Although no tradition can incarnate the
universal good adequately, one can only access the universal good
through some particular tradition or 'roots' which serve as an image or
gateway. Here again, we detect the influence of Weil's understanding
of the importance of human roots and *metaxu*. But tradition, for Grant,
has to do with his conservatism, which is a practical stance. Philosophy
transcends practice. Did this imply that at the higher level of philosophy (or faith?) one could live in the void or absence of concrete good in
the world? Whatever the case may have been, Grant states the bald fact
that the modern faith in the universal and homogenous state as the fulfilment of human excellence leads inevitably to the undermining of all
particular traditions in the world.

This Western 'imperialism,' which began several centuries ago,
reached its apex in the war of 1914. There, Canada's fate and the violence of that fate were clearly manifested. The war killed many of the
best Canadians and left the survivors 'cynical and tired.' They abandoned public life, retreating into the private world of money-making.
The war also forced French Canadians to participate against their will.
This created deep scars within Canada. The war also brought Great
Britain closer to the United States and, therefore, closer to dependence
on it. All these factors contributed to the progressive supremacy of the
American empire in the West. This supremacy exists not only in economic terms, but in ideological terms also. It is the supremacy of the
progressive spirit, a faith in technology, scientific mastery, and imperialism as the means to fulfilment and purpose. Finally, such supremacy
unchecked becomes violent in imposing itself, and traditional liberal
doctrine, which identified technological expansion with the progressive evolution of the species, could not anticipate this outcome.[68]

The moral dilemma for Canadians, who are bound to this Western
fate, is one between love of their own and love of the good. As was
stated earlier, love of one's own, be it a person, tradition, or nation, is a
means to love of the good. But the two loves must be separated; otherwise, love of one's own can become absolute and, therefore, idolatrous.
What happens if love of one's own and love of the good come into conflict? This happened to many Germans, for instance, during the Second
World War. It is also happening increasingly to Canadians in the face of
Vietnam and Canadian support for it. Although here Grant has bor-

rowed the language of Weil and Strauss, he has applied it to his own particular situation as a Canadian who sees clearly how the nation he loves has been caught up in the North American, and increasingly global, dream. This also means that he has to account for the Vietnams which manifest the violent dealings of the empire with those who resist being caught up in the dream. For most, however, there is no conflict. They can easily separate what is happening in Vietnam and what their aspirations are as North Americans. Others acknowledge Canada's implication in Vietnam, but also rejoice that there is freedom for criticism. Grant does not see this position as much better. Dissent, too, is factored into the system as a means of releasing the tension, but it does not lead to a serious alternative.

For a minority, however, the conflict is so serious that they can no longer love their own, and, indeed, it almost ceases to be their own. There is no greater alienation than to be separated from one's own, while feeling disgust because one is still a part of it. Nor is there much hope for radically changing the directions in which modern society is going. With the student protests, Grant felt some hope that if enough people realized what was happening, there could be a serious challenge to technological expansion.[69] In this essay, however, Grant emphasizes the Weilian view that the move for radical change or revolution only hardens the directions in which society is already going. To question the ruling religion of progress in scientific mastery is 'to invite an alienation far greater than the simply political.' This does not mean that one must not do whatever one can to preserve whatever sovereignty still exists in Canada. Yet it must also be admitted that 'what is worth doing in the midst of this barren twilight is the incredibly difficult question.'[70]

In his writing on Vietnam, Grant has become more concrete about the violent and destructive nature of progressive technological society and the moral foundations out of which he condemns it. Freedom for conquest, mastery, control, and manipulation, which modern science initially applied to nature as a means of freeing human beings from the basic oppressions of life, has expanded through technology to the mastery and control of human beings, cultures, traditions, and nations. Any resistance to this movement is met with ruthless force. Moreover, because of the level of the expansion or universalization of technique, North Americans can abstract themselves from the evil their society is responsible for perpetrating – namely, conformity to the North Ameri-

can way of life through violence and force. This abstraction or 'banality' permits a much more subtle and, therefore, wider application of
mastery in the world. Against this universal tendency, spearheaded by
the American empire, stands the conservative who believes in order
and restraint. Order and restraint are related to the virtue of charity,
which, negatively, involves self-denial and self-emptying, and positively, openness to the other as she or he is rather than as one wants the
other to be. Contemplation is related to charity in terms of this openness to the other. Contemplation stands over against mastery, and
seeks to understand in order to admire and wonder rather than to
control.

Grant was also confronted by the student protesters, whose natural
openness to the good revealed to them the evils of Vietnam and how it
was linked to broader elements of Western imperialism. Yet these
students were still caught within Western assumptions when they
expected their protests to lead to radical change in the structure of society. Grant shared their outrage, but he also challenged them to separate
the justice of their revolt from the expectation of a positive outcome. In
order to do this, however, the students were in need of something that
they did not share with Grant, that is, a deeper philosophical perspective undergirded by faith. This perspective was based on a person's
ultimate allegiance and orientation toward the good/God, independent of where history would lead. It was also based on the philosophical, theological affirmation that the realm of necessity is contrary to the
realm of the good and the only bridge from one to the other was from
God's side. This bridge, as Grant learned from Weil and Luther, was
the cross. This meant that being open to the evils and sufferings within
the world – that of one's own and of others – was a means to spiritual
purification, a purification that was purer the deeper one confronted
the evil and suffering for what it was. It also meant that the struggle for
justice would lead inevitably to suffering in a world whose structures
radically contradicted it.

The further problem of attaching protest to outcome was that the
students were also operating within the grid of mastery and force.
Grant knew from Weil, as well as from his own war experiences, how
the victims of force could become just as brutal as their oppressors if
and when given power. This is also why on a deeper level Grant
opposed civil disobedience. Restraint and order rooted in charity and
openness, even toward one's enemies, was the only means of keeping
oneself pure and unstained from the world. But Grant did not believe

in cynicism or inaction. The practical aspect of charity was the struggle to maintain whatever independence Canada still held and to attempt to influence society toward whatever measure of restraint and order was possible in its dealings with people. Such activity before God and in obedience to the good was not only 'delay tactics,' but also a means to further purification and maturity as a Christian. It was also very much part of Grant's Protestant heritage inherited from his progenitors.

4.4. Charity and Contemplation Inspired by the Cross

4.4.1. The Eastern Tradition of Christianity

While Grant used Sherrard's terminology with regard to Eastern Christianity, it was Weil more then anyone else who gave it content. Weil was able to relate the Platonic Christianity that Sherrard wrote about with a theology of the cross. In 1963 Grant wrote an essay on Weil with the purpose of introducing her thought and writings. Weil's obedient attention to God led her into the sharing of the afflictions of the modern world, and these afflictions in turn made her that much more acutely aware of its evils. Moreover, adds Grant, 'the afflictions of modern civilization taught her to question the philosophic principles on which modern civilization is based, and so enabled her to read and participate directly in what the Greeks and Hindus have said about alternative principles ...'[71] Grant has in mind her mystical experiences and spiritual insight. This is also related to her Platonism. Weil appropriates and interprets Plato with such purity because she stands so outside modern assumptions in her thought. Her Platonism also places her within the 'extreme wing of Greek Christianity.' This type of Christianity is at the opposite end of the Western type (Catholic or Protestant) or one of its 'secular offshoots' (Marxism or Liberalism). Moreover, it transcends institutional forms. It is a Christianity closest to Buddhism or Hinduism and farthest from the Christianity prevalent in North America. Weil's adoption of Greek Christianity is related to her experience of affliction in the Western world – its wars, factories, and ideologies.

   In substance this means two things. First, faith in God is a matter of knowing and not of willing. It is a matter of attention and open receptivity in thought before the truth, rather than an act of human will or choice. One cannot simply choose to have faith. Such faith is an illusion and a human construct. The afflictions of the world taught Weil that only the certainty of divine grace and a knowledge based on divine revelation could suffice. Second, she rejects the language of individual personality. She speaks of a dying to self and an openness to the whole or God. It is out of this openness to God and all that is, that one can then be filled by divine love and be opened to all that is as good – the particular being of another, or one's particular relationships, roots, and traditions in the world.

The influence of the Eastern tradition of Christianity is also evident in an unpublished fragment in which Grant attempts to define the essence of authentic religion. Western religion, and particularly its shallower North American Calvinist version, is focused on controlling and changing the world rather than contemplating it in open wonder and love. This is also related to whether God is perceived as the transcendent ground of all that is – distant from our reason and will, yet imminent in all things to the eyes of open faith – or whether God is a construct based on human reason whose working in the world (providence) is discernible to human thought and reducible to human freedom and action. The genuine religious experience consists in being enraptured by the other so that we do not want them to be other than they are – be it a human being or a landscape. It is to love the goodness of the other. This stands against the idea of loving the other only insofar as we want to change them according to our image, failing to see the goodness in who they are. At a deeper level, religion is the experience that the whole is good even when it includes evil and suffering. The beauty and excellence in Jesus Christ is in how he accepts his 'appalling fate' as good – that is, as the good in an otherwise evil set of events. Obviously this requires change, but not external change in order to suit our passions. We need, rather, to admit change within ourselves in order to see otherness and all that is as good.

Grant's more particular concern is to enquire as to what type of action is legitimate for a genuine religious orientation? He makes a distinction between action that is used to help others be what they are by nature, and action that is used to change people to what one wants them to be. It is a very different kind of action, for instance, to do whatever one can to provide for a child because one loves that child for what he or she is, than to help others (e.g., as in the case of the Americans with the Vietnamese) because we want them to be whatever we want them to be. But one is also left with the question of theodicy. How is authentic religion possible in the face of the evil and suffering which surround us in the world? Can we affirm all that is as good and want it to be as it is when this includes Vietnam? Being open to the whole also means being open to evil, which may lead one to say that the whole is not good. The true religious act, however, is the experience of otherness as good. And this requires knowledge of something further: that otherness may cease to be altogether. 'Tragedy haunts us at any moment.'[72]

In an interview, Grant offers some deeper insights. According to biblical tradition (that reading of it consistent with Eastern Christianity), the human journey to happiness in the world must incorporate the experience of suffering. This is not to say that 'suffering is good in itself' or that 'suffering is necessary to good.' Yet the complete overcoming of chance and limit in the world leaves it 'a banal place full of bored and tired people.'[73] It is absolutely essential to overcome suffering wherever it is possible to do so. Yet the ancients also acknowledged that human excellence and nobility arise with moderation or restraint in the passions and courage in the face of limitations. What restraints of the passions are finally liberating? At what point is the acceptance of limit a necessity for building character and reverence?[74]

Grant also addresses these issues in a letter in which he attempts to explain the distinction between necessity and the good. The strength of such a distinction – be it in Plato or Kant – is that 'it squarely faces the problem of suffering and does not swallow it up in any easy explanation.'[75] To exist is to suffer, and 'in human terms it is to learn that we cannot have what we want.' The primary thing the philosopher must try to understand, then, is 'what is the purpose (if any) in the fact that our immediate desires are broken and trampled on from the earliest age.' According to the Christian tradition, it is through a consent to this brokenness, a self-denial, that redemption is achieved. This is also to 'bring suffering into the Godhead,' which is the strength of Christianity and the reason it is considered a 'religion of slaves' (Weil). This is something that liberal Protestantism does not understand. Christianity shares the truth of the negation of desire with all the great religions.

In terms of philosophy, Grant suggests that Plato seems to understand human suffering in a way that Aristotle does not. Plato's assertion of the transcendence of the good, which comes to us from beyond our comprehension or possibilities and demands the death of our worldly desires, is also consistent with a greater agnosticism in the face of the evils of the world. The statement at the beginning of the *Republic* about the sufferings of the just man, Grant has taken to be 'a straight affirmation of the transcendence of the good.' But Strauss, who is more of an Aristotelian, denies that in this passage suffering and absolute justice go together, for this is also to deny that absolute justice is possible in the world as it is. Grant's reading of Plato, however, is that suffering, which is a consequence of evil, also manifests how distant necessity is from the good – so distant that the good is totally outside it. Yet, at the same time, it must be asserted that Plato does not suggest an absolute dualism, for both necessity and the good have their origin in the transcendent good. Here below they appear as separate and so they must. This is why Plato, like Kant, claims to be an agnostic – the philosopher is one who knows that he knows not. To see both the separation and common origin of necessity and the good is the strength of Christianity and the mystic saints who come to a vision of the beauty and goodness of the world only after submitting to its afflictions and loving others who are so afflicted.

For his part, Grant claims to be unable to know these truths from experience, as do the saints. His perspective is drawn from the experience of practical life in the world, which must maintain a distinction between the order of necessity and the order of the good. The affirmation of this distinction is essential in order that the purpose of the whole is not circumscribed to the reasoning of the human mind. This, in any case, would only be possible for those who live in abstraction from the depth of evil in the world, which veils any such purpose.[76]

4.4.2. Intimations of Deprival

These deeper religious themes are incorporated with the other themes of Grant's thought in two important essays he wrote at the end of the 1960s: 'In Defence of North America' and 'A Platitude.' Grant begins with several familiar statements. Western technological achievement has shaped a unique civilization in the history of the human race. North America is the most advanced form of this type of civilization. Technological civilization is not simply external to us but moulds us in all that we are, from our practical activities to our thoughts, dreams, and imaginings. The pursuit of technology has become the dominant purpose of our existence; it is our religion. It has brought us unprecedented wealth and comfort, as well as the power to impose its purposes on other peoples and cultures.

Grant then goes on to analyse in greater detail how North America is European by birth, and yet significantly other. The primals of European civilization were contemplation founded on Plato and Aristotle, and charity based on Christianity. In North America, the primal is founded on the encounter of a particular form of Christianity – English-speaking Calvinism – with an 'alien yet conquerable land.' While much has been written about the relation of Calvinism, Puritanism, and capitalism, less is known about the deeper connections between Protestant theology and the new sciences. Negatively, this connection is related to the rejection, by both Protestant theology and modern science, of medieval science rooted in Aristotelian teleology. According to science, this tradition prevented human beings from observing the world as it is. According to Protestant theology, it led to a natural theology outside a fundamental reliance on revelation. It did this because 'it encouraged men to avoid the surd mystery of evil by claiming that final purpose could be argued from the world. Such mitigation led men away from the only true illumination of that mystery, the crucifixion apprehended in faith as a divine humiliation.'[77] In a footnote, Grant adds: 'Luther laid down the whole of this with brilliant directness at the very beginning of the Reformation in some theses of 1518.' He then quotes theses 19–21 of the Heidelberg disputation.

Beyond this negative rejection, there are also positive elements that brought them together. We have already encountered Grant's perspectives on how Calvinism was open to empiricism and utilitarianism, and why it was so amenable to the modern scientific, technical spirit. Grant also offers a quote by Ernst Troeltsch to support his view. But Troeltsch was writing in 1914. Since then, modern catastrophes combined with secularization have made the religious feeling and ethical discipline of Calvinism very tenuous. Once the will becomes severed from obedience to God, it becomes the servant of the human passions. When any faith in God and obedience to God's loving will (the source of restraint and discipline in thought and action) are lost, human faith serves the freedom of the passions. This, according to Grant, is what has happened in North America. Nonetheless, Grant respects the practical focus and discipline reflected in the North American primal. This focus was necessary in order to conquer a tough, harsh land. Mastery and the conquest of nature was a matter of survival for the early pioneers. But when the pioneering context, combined with a Calvinist faith and ethos, is no longer present, we are left with large cities, where consumption competes with abject poverty; the emancipation of greed, which feeds on the resources of the whole world through imperialism; a middle-class majority cushioned from these brutalities, who believe they live in a pluralistic society but really live in a monolithic structure which defines what is worth thinking and doing; reason narrowly defined as technical, while openness and awe, questioning and listening, have been reduced to the drive toward technical expansion as an end in itself; and slogans of progress which can no longer lift the young above boredom and meaninglessness, if not despair.

In spite of all these realities, it is amazing how mastery of human and non-human nature is still the governing faith and source of hope in North American society. It is still believed that what is being done today is a continuation of the basic drive of early science, motivated by Protestant Christianity, to free human beings from the natural necessities of hunger, disease, and overwork. There is a basic failure to see how dependent we are on technology, to the point where we impose it on the rest of the world, and seek solutions to whatever problems we face with further technological expansion and sophistication. We see many of the major catastrophes and problems of technological society as 'difficulties of detail' which further technology will solve. Both the political right and left are animated by this religion. Whether it is proposing the maintenance and protection of what is as it is for the privileged, or changing the structures and injustices of society, the hope is still placed in technology and the control of nature. Even criticisms of technology are made within the assumptions of modern technological society. The movement of progress toward the universal and homogenous state is too dependent on technology to judge it. Moreover, the whole language of 'values' is based on something human beings have created, rather than grounded in an objective standard that transcends our making and doing. It is exceedingly difficult to think about technology from a perspective transcending it.

This difficulty is rooted in the North American primal itself. The Protestant theology of our ancestors was a conscious rejection of the tradition of contemplation as founded by the Greeks. We have already considered the reasons for this. It was in the name of a charity which was unable to reconcile the evils of the world with the love of God. But, without a tradition of contemplation, it was also left vulnerable to the influence of modern science. In the early stages, modern science was put in the service of charity through the struggle to overcome scarcity, disease, and overwork. Later, it also shaped the thought of Protestants by cutting them off from apprehending the world as anything beyond a field of objects, or responding to the whole not simply in terror, anguish, or in doing, but in 'wondering or marvelling at what is, being amazed and astonished by it, or perhaps best, ... admiring it; and that such a stance, as beyond all bargains and conveniences, is the only source from which purposes may be manifest to us for our necessary calculating.'[78] In the best traditions of Western Europe, contemplation was not discarded but made subservient to revelation and put into the service of charity. It was under the necessity of contemplating the meaning of revelation and the whole that Christianity sought in philosophy a handmaid and discovered the best foundation for this in the Greeks. Grant has in mind the patristic period. But under the influence of Aristotle in medieval theology, some were led to contemplation that was not subservient to revelation, nor in the service of charity (natural theology). The Protestant reaction, however, was at the opposite extreme. It rejected contemplation altogether, although this is more true of Calvinism than of Lutheranism or even Anglicanism.

As a North American, Grant grew up within a Calvinist orientation. Yet his study and life in Europe gave him the unique privilege of tasting something of a pre-modern Christianity which incorporated the best traditions of Greek contemplation: 'Public and private virtues having their point beyond what can in any sense be called socially useful; commitments to love and to friendship which lie rooted in a realm outside the calculable; a partaking in the beautiful not seen as the product of human creativity; amusements and ecstasies not seen as the enemies of reason.'[79] In North America one cannot say such things are totally absent. They are, however, much more distant. This distance from or absence of contemplation has perhaps spared North Americans from the massive nihilism that has spread throughout Europe. But it has also cut them off from the depth and richness of life that has been experienced there also. Whatever nihilism North Americans have come to experience is quite shallow. This also means that the technological drive faces less impediment in asserting itself. There is less resistance to the growing violence and passion of freedom in the service of mastery and control outside any restraints or purposes transcending them. There is, in short, less capacity to think and exist outside technology.

In 'A Platitude,' Grant is in search of 'intimations' of our deprivation of the good as North Americans. The difficulty is that our technological society has, at one and the same time, deprived us of any sense of a good outside itself and asserted itself as the unique and universal good. Thus, any knowledge of the good that is outside technological society must come by intimation of deprival – that is, negatively. When we experience the absence of something, we experience indirectly the thing itself. What Grant has in mind by 'the good' is only too obvious: systems of meaning which 'mitigated both our freedom and the indifference of the world, and in so doing put limits of one kind or another on our interference with chance and the possibilities of conquest.'[80] But conquest today is freed from any purpose, even the purpose of building a universal and homogeneous state. Grant cites once again the example of the space program. We are moving into 'an unlimited freedom to make the world as we want in a universe indifferent to what purposes we choose.'

But Grant also calls us to 'listen' critically for intimations of deprival in our society. This is difficult because we find it an incredible challenge to articulate even to ourselves what has been lost in our technological society. This is because we are so pervaded by it in every way. It is also difficult because we must separate the deprival of the good as good for humanity as a whole, from the deprival of our own particular psychic and social histories (the absence of the good in terms of faith and philosophy as distinguished from the loss of a particular tradition and culture). But Grant does believe such listening is possible. Indeed, the fact that we can even speak of deprival reveals that we have already experienced the good indirectly. The recollection and articulation of what has been lost must be within a world in which it appears only a catastrophe will slow down the pace of technological expansion. In spite of this, Grant calls for courage in resisting the temptation to 'turn one's face to the wall' (Henry James) or simply to live within the present drive toward mastery, working and celebrating in it. We are called, rather, to cultivate an openness to 'listening or watching or simply waiting for intimations of deprival which might lead us to see the beautiful as the image, in the world, of the good.'[81]

In the 1960s, Grant makes further advances in clarifying how a theology of the cross comprehends the evil and suffering in the world as the absence of God, but also as the gateway into the genuine presence of God in the world in the form of love of the beauty and goodness in all that is. Moreover, he clarifies further what for him are the genuine forms of philosophy and Christianity as opposed to the inauthentic ones.

Although he continues to make distinctions within the Western tradition – Augustine and Luther versus Calvinism and liberal Protestantism – he rejects this tradition for the most part in favour of the

Eastern one, wherein belongs Plato, the mystics, and Weil. The Eastern tradition he identifies with a cluster of ideas which go together: the transcendence of God; openness to divine revelation, illumination, and grace; and self-denial and self-restraint, which are conducive to love defined as consent to otherness and openness to the beauty of the world beyond a desire to change it. The Western tradition, by contrast, he identifies with human freedom and will, the divine will joined to the human will, the human mind as capable of grasping God and, therefore, denying the mystery and transcendence of God, the desire to change otherness to suit one's own purposes, and the focus on mastery, conquest, manipulation, and control.

With Weil, Grant also relates these differences to the problem of evil, human excellence, and fulfilment. Weil, like Plato, perceives a great distance between the necessary and the good, a distance which, given the overwhelming fact of evil and suffering in the world, can only be bridged by God. Moreover, excellence and fulfilment, according to this understanding of Christianity, are not simply a matter of eliminating all suffering in the world, but of being opened to the good through it. It is a matter of learning self-denial and self-restraint, which are the negative prerequisites to genuine love (the positive being openness and attention to otherness), and recognizing the beauty of what is without desiring to change it to suit one's own purposes. This understanding of Christianity stands in contrast to the type that has dominated in the West, which is more inclined to changing the world in a way that does not recognize the beauty of otherness as a limit on oneself. Rather, otherness is seen as something to be shaped according to one's own image of the good, which is, finally, idolatry and insensitivity.

Given Grant's wholesale denunciation of Western Christianity, it is interesting how he continues to make implicit, as well as explicit, references to Luther. He refers again to Luther's Heidelberg theses 19–21 as illuminating most profoundly the distance between necessity and the good, the evil in the world that prevents us from thinking the purpose of the whole and the good hidden within it. How can this be explained? We have already encountered the manner in which Grant related the theology of the cross as expressed in Luther's theses to the thought of Weil and Plato, as early as the 1950s. This continued in the 1960s, for in 1975 Grant wrote to Simone Petrement (Weil's biographer) expressing the same conviction. He was asking her about Weil's understanding of the resurrection and offered his own understanding based on Luther's teaching in the Heidelberg theses, although read in a

'Platonic sense.' He then quotes theses 19–21. Petrement wrote back to Grant in astonishment over these theses, which she had never seen before, and assured Grant that they expressed what Weil believed.[82] Luther's teaching about the 'illumination of that mystery' in 'the crucifixion apprehended in faith as a divine humiliation,' was about the crucified Christ revealing the fullness of divine love in his openness to God and his consent to love God through affliction and through the annihilation of his being. What Luther and Weil were able to teach Grant was that the affirmation of divine purpose in a world which includes evil and suffering does not have to be blasphemous – denying the distance between necessity and the good, or denying divine transcendence, absence, or hiddenness, and thus trivializing evil. But in order for this to be genuine in the soul, one had to come to this purpose through the cross of affliction, rather than by escaping its brutal reality or minimizing its capacity to destroy everything in oneself – morality, joy, recognition, etc. – except openness to God through it all.

In the 1960s, Grant also continues to struggle with the relationship between faith and philosophy, revelation and reason, or, as he now calls them, charity and contemplation. Again, it is important for him that the two are interrelated and interdependent. What he clarifies further is the type of contemplation that is irreconcilable with charity and the type of charity that is irreconcilable with contemplation. The type of charity which 'scorns' contemplation is represented by liberal Protestantism, in particular, with its roots in Calvinist Puritanism. In its naïve optimism about human possibilities in the world, and without an emphasis on critical thought necessitated by the depths of human evil and suffering, it serves a theology of glory. At times, he broadens this characterization to neo-orthodox theology, although he is on less solid ground here. The type of contemplation which operates independently of charity is also associated with a theology of glory, be it in Aristotle, medieval natural theology, or modern forms of philosophy which offer concrete political and historical visions of redemption at the expense of facing the depth of evil and suffering in the world (e.g., Hegel).

The attempt to relate charity and contemplation, however, is not without tension. This tension is at the heart of a theology of the cross. It is the tension between consenting to love God and the world by submitting to its limitations and sufferings (contemplation), and seeking to overcome evil and suffering which keeps life from being human (love). It is the tension between suffering as an evil to be overcome and as a gateway into spiritual purification through the love of God and the world. Maintaining the fragile balance between the two, as Grant attempts to do, is possibly best reflected in the prayer of serenity by Reinhold Niebuhr: 'God, give me the serenity to accept what cannot be changed; the courage to change what can be changed; and the wisdom to distinguish one from the other.'[83] Perhaps, Grant would express it slightly differently, following Luther and Weil: give me the joy to consent freely to what cannot be changed and the self-restraint to refrain from changing what I want to change; the courage to change what can be changed for the sake of alleviating the suffering of another; and the wisdom to know what to do in a given situation. Finally, however, although contemplation gives voice to charity, it is also subservient to charity, the way reason is to revelation, and philosophy to faith. It is this affirmation at the centre of Grant's thought which kept him from embracing Strauss fully.

In his final reflections of the 1960s, Grant calls us to listening and waiting for intimations of the good within a society in which we have been deprived of it. We have been so deprived because technological thinking has invaded every aspect of our lives, choking out any alternative conception of the good in the face of its monolithic assertion of it. But it can never eliminate the good completely from the human soul. The task, therefore, is twofold. First, we can know that whatever the benefits of living in the technological society, we experience the deprival of something more fundamental. To experience this is to experience the good indirectly. The good may be absent or hidden in the face of the evils that surround us. But the experience of absence or hiddenness (deprival) already implies an intuition of the good of which we are deprived. We need to give voice to this deprival without veiling or escaping it.

Second, the fact that we are deprived of the good must make us listen and wait for it that much more openly and faithfully. We must search for signs of it in the world. We must be open to see its image in the beauty which can never, finally, be completely banished from the world. The image of the good in beauty or love is the hidden, secret presence or revelation of the good in the world.[84] The task of listening and waiting for intimations of the good of which we are deprived is, therefore, to discover how technological society deprives us of it. It is also to open ourselves to the beautiful in the world, which inspires us to know, love, and experience the good in the world. Here Grant has in mind Weil's *metaxu* (mediators of friendship and love, art and commu-

nity, tradition and country), the love of which brings us into the presence of the good/God in the world. This is no easy task, according to
Grant, and, indeed, for most of us practically impossible. This is why
Grant was labelled so frequently a pessimist. Yet he believed, following Weil and Luther, that the bridges linking the human to the divine
are only possible through divine revelation, grace, and illumination,
rather than through human thought, will, or creativity. This is also why
it is in listening and waiting (openness) rather than through active
doing that we come to know, experience, and grow in the good/God.

In spite of the charges of pessimism, there are some who have perceived Grant's method more profoundly. P. Hanson has described
Grant's method as a 'negative theology' which is consistent with the
methods of Plato and Luther. This method does not speak directly
about the good/God, but indirectly. Its aim is to destroy all the illusions in thought and practice which stand in the way of seeing the distance between the necessary and the good, the true nature and depth
of evil in the world, and the utter transcendence of the good in the
world as it is. In Luther's language, it is to counter the method of a theology of glory, which says 'evil is good and good evil,' with a theology
of the cross, which says 'the thing is as it is.'[85] For D. Duffy, this
method is also consistent with a Protestant understanding of salvation
as an unmerited gift in human thought and practice, coming to one
beyond one's moral and intellectual possibilities.[86] For David R. and
Edwin B. Heaven, Grant's hesitation in speaking directly about the
good of which we are deprived in modern technological society has to
do with his consciousness that he is far from the 'saints' in his thought
and practice. If theoretical clarity is intimately related to morality, as he
claims Plato and Weil believed, then he must consign himself to
destroying inadequate sources of hope which stand in the way of experiencing the good in the world, rather than speaking about the good
directly as one who has consented to it through the afflictions of the
world.[87] Be that as it may, it is Weil, Luther, and Plato who are Grant's
teachers about the good, as well as about the nature of evil in the world
which deprives us from being in communion with the good in the concrete reality of our existence.

With the help of Ellul and Strauss, Grant came to realize how deeply
necessity was separated from the good in practical life and thought.
Through Sherrard and Weil, he came to realize how deeply the animat-
ing thought and life of Western civilization as a whole was caught

within the web of necessity. Through Weil and the theology of the cross, he also came to see images of the good in the world via a more Eastern Platonic reading of the Bible (especially the Gospels) as well as his particular relationships, loyalties, commitments, and traditions in the world, by which he was opened to the more universal, eternal good. These ideas will develop further in Grant's later thought.

Chapter Five

Faith and Justice in the Technological Era

It is in the 1970s and '80s that Grant's thought reaches its greatest depth. From his earliest writing of this period, *Time As History*, to his last major essay, 'Faith and the Multiversity,' he struggles to understand the technological era as it is, bring to light its darkness as darkness, and witness to the light that continues to shine in the darkness. Stimulated by Friedrich Nietzsche, Martin Heidegger, and Louis-Ferdinand Céline, Grant achieves further depth of understanding about the human condition and its affliction in the technological era. With the continuing inspiration of Simone Weil and her understanding of Plato and the Gospels, Grant achieves further clarity about the truth of the good/God. Finally, and perhaps most significantly, Grant makes some bold attempts at expressing how the good/God can be manifested and experienced positively (as presence as well as absence) in a world dominated by the technological paradigm. In this attempt, the theology of the cross as formulated by Luther and expressed by Weil continues to inspire Grant's deepest insights.

5.1. Understanding the Technological Era 'As It Is': Nietzsche, Heidegger, and Céline

Nietzsche, Heidegger, and Céline play the same role in Grant's thought that Ellul and Strauss did in the 1960s. Grant's struggle with their thought brings him to a deeper understanding about the way things are in the technological era. Nietzsche and Heidegger provide the philosophical stimulation, and Céline, an experiential one. In addition, the limitations and weaknesses of Ellul and Strauss are overcome by the two thinkers and the artist. While Ellul was able to unfold the all-embracing nature of technology in society, he failed to understand sufficiently the thinking or 'ontology' behind it. Heidegger would overcome this failure. Moreover, both Ellul and Strauss failed to appreciate the influence of Christianity in the coming to be of modern secularism and technology. Here again, Heidegger, and especially Nietzsche, would unfold this influence in profound ways. Finally, Strauss failed to clarify the relationship between biblical Christianity and Greek philosophy. While he seemed to hold them together when opposing ancient thought to the modern, he also seemed to deny the truth of biblical religion and to prefer an Aristotelian emphasis in Greek philosophy over a Platonic one. Nietzsche as well as Heidegger (insofar as he serves as interpreter of Nietzsche) think of Christianity and Platonism together and confront them as the most serious moral tradition of the Western world. While they and Grant stand on diametrically opposite sides vis-à-vis the truth of Platonism and Christianity, Grant admires the seriousness with which they engage this tradition. This is not to suggest that Grant turned away from Sherrard's distinction between Western and Eastern Christianity, and his preference for an interpretation of Plato and the Gospels within the latter tradition. Rather, Grant saw in Nietzsche and Heidegger the greatest exponents of the essence of the technological era because they understood the need to overcome the deepest criticism of this essence: namely, the teachings of Plato and the Gospels. Céline's contribution as an artist is to express fundamental experiences of human affliction in the technological era with a sensitivity and tragic beauty that Ellul as a social scientist could never do.

5.1.1. Early Encounters with Nietzsche

Grant's lengthiest writing devoted to one thinker is his 1969 Massey lectures published under the title *Time As History*. Although the title is based on a phrase Grant found in Heidegger's writing, he applies it to Nietzsche, who is the main subject of the lectures.[1] Grant had encountered Nietzsche earlier in life but had never struggled with his thought in any depth. The occasion for his renewed engagement arose as a result of Nietzsche's popular appeal among many university students in the late 1960s, who were taken by his bold attack on tradition and the celebration of life lived beyond the narrow horizons of good and evil. The struggle with Nietzsche's thought would now continue to the end of Grant's life.

In *Time As History* Grant portrays Nietzsche as the greatest herald of the modern world. Grant is also conscious, however, that he approaches Nietzsche as an English-speaking Westerner and a North American living in the spearhead of the technological era. He isolates one key word that captures how English-speakers think of themselves and their world: 'history.' This word has particular significance because it is not a word that was known or used in the same way in pre-modern times. Neither the Bible nor ancient philosophy knew words that are synonymous with 'history' as we understand it today. In the technological era, however, history has come to dominate thought not only about human existence but about nature as well. Today, everything has a history. Human beings, nonetheless, are no mere products of history. They are also capable of transcending history by their very consciousness of it, and through such consciousness, able to direct it. Human beings are part of nature and, therefore, determined, contingent creatures. But they are also free to determine themselves and exercise control over their world.

The modern concept of history, then, is related to the growing consciousness of human beings as free to make themselves and their world. This sense of history also gave rise to the focus on doing, which led further still toward the development of modern science and technology in the service of human freedom. The originators of this era in thought and action were not, as was mentioned earlier, 'value-free' in their passion for determining the course of history. The very concept of history was future-oriented and directed toward very concrete purposes. These purposes are evident in words such as 'progress' or 'evolution.' This applies to Marxists as well as capitalists, both of whom believed in and sought to serve these 'higher' purposes, however much they differed in the means by which they thought these purposes could be achieved.[2]

Yet Grant questions how stable these purposes could remain in the face of the major shift in human self-consciousness indicated by the word 'history.' This shift is also evident when one considers the change of meaning in the word 'will.' According to ancient thinking, the meaning of 'will' was tied to feeling, thinking, and desiring. The language of desire was the language of dependence on something loved and needed. Thought was linked to openness to otherness, seeking to understand and appreciate in order to know. Any action that proceeded from thinking so conceived was done 'for the sake of bringing into immediacy the beauty of a trusted order, always there to be appropriated through whatever perils.' According to modern thinking, however, the will is related to resoluteness and determination to carry out one's purposes and desires, outside any restraints or limitations arising from reverence for an order transcending one's freedom. To will is to be serious about actualizing one's purposes in the world. To think is to apply one's rational powers to manipulate and control in order to shape and change the existing human or natural order according to one's determinations. The result is the advent of modern science, with its rationality of objective experimentation carried out by a creative thinking subject-ego standing over an objective, faceless world of data to be used by the individual or collective will. Can such a way of thinking and willing be limited and directed by purposes which are not planted firmly in a transcendent order of meaning beyond human determination? Grant bids us consider Marxism and capitalism. Are not such purposes going to be transgressed by the passion for free creative mastery for the sake of nothing but novelty?

Although Grant had discussed such ideas in earlier work, his study of Nietzsche gave him new clarity as to the essence of the technological era and how it came to be. He emphasizes again the distinction of both Greek philosophy and biblical Christianity from the modern way of thinking designated by the word 'history.' In both traditions, 'thought and reverence are sustained together.' At the same time, however, he also states the basic truism that 'the modern conception of progress may be characterized as secular Christianity.' Time as history in 'its first optimistic and liberal formulation was at one and the same time a critical turning away from our origins and also a carrying along of some essential aspects of them.'[3] Nietzsche's contribution is to unfold what the concept of time as history means with brilliant clarity and honesty, as well as to recognize the profound crisis to which such meaning has led.

The problem with all previous philosophy, according to Nietzsche, is a failure to think historically. Historical thinking means that all thought is subject to the limitations of the context and perspective of the thinker. Thought can never transcend the historical, the sphere of becoming, the constantly changing, evolving reality of existence. Any ideas of permanence or moral 'values' transcending the historical are rooted in wishful thinking unrelated to reality. The historical way of thinking knows only a relativity of value. At the same time that Nietzsche makes these statements, he also recognizes the terrible implications of their meaning. The historical way of thinking destroys any transcendent hopes or principles which functioned in the past to mitigate the chaos of living in a world without purpose or meaning. To

reject any transcendence above the historical is to admit human soli-
tariness in the universe; to admit that 'God is dead.'[4]

This last statement, which is commonplace in Nietzsche, is shorthand for what he perceives to have happened in the modern world. In
pre-modern Western thought, beginning in Plato and continuing in
Christianity (which is 'Platonism for the people'),[5] thought about
human existence was abstracted from reality. The assertion of a good
or God taught a transcendent purpose and meaning to existence which
obscured reality for human beings and imposed moral restraints and
obligations on them. Such ways of thinking were nothing but human
inventions meant, at the most superficial level, to protect human
beings from the chaos of reality and, on a deeper level, to give power to
the weak against the strong through the imposition of moral valua-
tions.[6] But because both Platonic rationality and Christianity asserted
the primacy of truth as the goal of faith and thought, such abstract and
contrived fabrications could not withstand the test of reality constantly
intruding itself into human experience. Both Platonism and Christianity produced their own 'grave-diggers'[7] in the form of modern science
and historical thinking. Christianity, nonetheless, also produced some
bastard offspring. Belief in historical progress and the values of democratic equality and fairness are based on Christian principles, which
have been secularized by modern liberalism. But Nietzsche calls liberalism's bluff. What basis is there for an absolute commitment to equality and fairness, or a belief in an overriding purpose and direction in
history, without a belief in the good/God or a transcendent order
behind the universe? With God declared dead, such ideas and values
cannot be sustained very deeply.

At the same time that Nietzsche makes these bold criticisms, he is
also aware of how fearful it is to give up transcendent horizons of
meaning. To live without a larger purpose or meaning is to admit that
we live in a meaningless universe as lumps of matter, driven by pure
instinct and will, or not at all. In the past, be it through contemplation
or charity, human purpose was rooted in a transcendent order.
Whether it was in loving or in rational contemplation, human beings
knew what were the highest purposes for human life. But how does
one live without transcendent horizons of meaning and purpose and
not fall into complete despair? Nietzsche's early work was aimed at
destroying these horizons and bringing to light the implications of
time as history. His later work was an attempt to provide positive ways
for human beings to affirm life within the finality of becoming.

This attempt was made even more urgent by Nietzsche's realization that the historical way of thinking had emerged at the same time as the heightened capacity of human beings to master the world. For earlier generations, such mastery was guided by freedom and rationality rooted in the values of social equality and fairness. This secularized Christianity was also combined with a belief that history itself was serving these values progressively in science, economics, and politics. With the growing awareness that 'God is dead,' there was little basis for continuing to hold liberal values and their guiding principles. Without these principles there was nothing to direct or limit human mastery. Science could not provide the human intellect and will with purposes beyond the human ego.

The destruction of all horizons in the modern world has produced two kinds of people. Nietzsche calls them 'last men' and 'nihilists.' Last men are those who inoculate themselves from reality by setting their sights on trivial goals. Comfort, entertainment, and a cozy existence allow them to escape into an illusion of happiness and contentment. The price for such escape, however, is an inability to feel and experience the depths of life: its suffering and its joy. Nihilists, on the other hand, realize that all values are relative human creations and there is nothing beyond the human will to guide the passions. Nonetheless, they 'would rather will nothing than have nothing to will'[8] and are resolute and courageous in the face of such willing. These are the honest and strong, for whom Nietzsche has obvious sympathy. But he also realizes that nihilists are dangerous and destructive, for they know no limits and respect no bounds in their meaningless quest for mastery. Until recently, claims Grant, North Americans were kept from the purely historical way of thinking by a dominant liberalism, which also protected them from the more virile manifestations of nihilism in Europe. Yet increasingly, the nihilists and last men are making their appearance in North America as well. The question is whether there is a way of existing beyond the alternatives of the last men or the nihilists that is not simply a return to the transcendent horizons of the past?[9]

Nietzsche discovered in the tragedic tradition of Greece a vision of existence which inspired him. Greek tragedy presented human beings in a noble encounter with the chaos of existence, with resolute courage even in the face of profound suffering. For human beings such as these, suffering produced greater strength of character and resolve. In them there was also a positive love of life and the earth that did not turn rancid and bitter. While mastery in the hands of the last men is directed to their own pleasure and in the nihilists for its own sake, the noble human being – the superman – wills and creates in joy. He alone deserves to be master of the earth, and in the emergence of the superman Nietzsche places his hope.[10] It is only he who, albeit a creator of his own values, creates in joy and, therefore, out of a positive love and acceptance of reality. This means that he resists the temptation to act out of hatred or revenge – the curse of the nihilists, on the one hand, and the creators of transcendent horizons, on the other. Revenge against the strong, against time, and against life or the earth is an escape from and a revenge on existence. Those who will out of revenge are a curse on the earth.

Grant agrees with Nietzsche in some fundamental ways. He agrees that any horizons of meaning or 'nets of inevitability,' be they in God, nature, evolution, or progress, which serve as comfortable illusions about or escapes from reality, must be rejected. Against such illusions the radical contingency of existence must be asserted, for 'the absence of all nets is a truth that those of us who trust in God must affirm.' Moreover, he agrees that the spirit of revenge is a major curse on the earth, be it the revenge of the religious, the secularized, the weak, or the nihilists. Grant also agrees with Nietzsche's psychological analysis of the root causes of revenge in human life. The more our wills are broken in the chaos of existence, the more we are humiliated and trampled upon from our earliest years, the more 'botched and bungled our instincts become in the vicissitudes of existing,' the more the will to revenge is activated in us. Finally, Grant sympathizes with Nietzsche's hope for the emergence of those who will overcome the spirit of hatred or revenge in their existing. Nietzsche speaks of himself as a convalescent, letting go of the spirit of revenge and growing toward a positive love of the earth. Such love Nietzsche calls *amor fati*, a term borrowed from the Stoics. It is only by loving our fate – that is, positively accepting all that has happened and will happen in life and the world – that we can overcome the spirit of revenge. This must also include a consciousness of all the suffering and misery in the world. Without such love, Nietzsche argues, we cannot will and create in joy and, therefore, do not deserve to be masters of the earth. The love of fate in Nietzsche's thought is also related to his doctrine of the 'eternal recurrence of the same.' This doctrine asserts that all that has been, will be again in an endless cycle of repetition. To love our fate is to consent to this endless repetition of events and circumstances throughout time. With this doctrine, Nietzsche transferred the eternal completely into the realm of history and becoming.[11]

Nietzsche's immense contribution as a thinker, for Grant, is to bring to light the essence of modernity – namely, the historical way of thinking and existing – with brilliant clarity. His purpose in so doing is not to turn away from the modern, but to help overcome its contradictions and fulfil its potential. In the affirmations of mastery over human and non-human nature, the primacy of the will, human beings as creators of their own values, becoming over being, movement and change over rest and restraint, and the coming to be of modern science and technology, modernity has revealed its potential heights. In the revolt of many of the young against established authorities and middle-class values, one can also detect the influence of Nietzsche. And yet, some have questioned his affirmation of the love of fate as too ready an acceptance of or passivity before history, rather than an active will to master it. Grant, however, stresses that Nietzsche's affirmation of this doctrine was not a call to passive acceptance of the world as it is (which includes much suffering and misery). Rather, against those whom he perceived to be engaged in manipulation and change out of a spirit of revenge, Nietzsche asserted that only those who are able to love and create in joy, in spite of and in full consciousness of the miseries and afflictions of existence, deserve to have freedom and power to change and determine the world.

In the end, however, Grant must reject Nietzsche's counsels about redemption in human life and the world, and this rejection is based on his 'suspicion of the assumptions of the modern project.' Indeed, Grant cannot understand how one can love fate and at the same time assert the eternity of becoming, 'unless within the details of our fates there could appear, however rarely, intimations that they are illumined; intimations that is, of perfection (call it if you will God) in which our desires for good find their rest and their fulfilment.'[12] Grant believes that human beings are not 'beyond good and evil' (i.e., creators of their own values), and that the desire for good in the human soul is one that cannot find its final fulfilment in history, however distant or absent such good may be.

The points at which Grant agrees with Nietzsche, as well as those at which he turns away from him, clearly reveal the influence of Weil. His radical assertion of contingency and suffering in existence against all horizons or nets that obscure this reality is also emphasized by Weil. This is also an attack on all attempts, be they religious or secular (natural theology or liberal progressive doctrines of glory), to escape from reality as it is and to trivialize the suffering and fragility within it. His perception of the reality of revenge as a prime motive of the instinct tortured and broken by the necessities of life, and the need to overcome such revenge, is also emphasized by Weil. Both religious and modern secularized ideologies fail to understand with adequate depth the kind of humiliation and affliction suffered in the soul, which then acts with ruthless force when in power. Finally, the doctrine of *amor fati* is also affirmed by Weil, though she comes to it from a completely different orientation. Nietzsche had not known what Grant came to know through Weil and the theology of the cross: namely, a revelation of the good/God that did not obscure or trivialize reality and which alone could redeem human life in the face of the afflictions of reality. Grant could not see how Nietzsche or anyone could live in and out of love without this revelation and inspiration of God. The distance between Grant/Weil and Nietzsche is reflected in how they understood the crucifixion of Christ. For Nietzsche, the crucifixion is the supreme act of revenge on humanity. Through it, God imposes an eternal debt which only God can redeem through forgiveness. Such a debt keeps human beings subservient and enslaved.[13] For Grant/Weil, the crucifixion is the supreme act of *amor fati* on the human side and the supreme act of liberation from the divine side, revealing the transcendence of the good in the very midst of the reality of affliction.

The challenge for Grant, as for anyone who affirms a Christianity illuminated by Platonism, is to incorporate into his love of fate a love for the world which includes the Nietzschean rejection of any horizons of transcendence outside human valuation and free creation in history. This does not mean passive acceptance of the world as it is but, rather, a rising above the spirit of revenge in engaging the evil within it. In order to accomplish this, human beings of faith are called 'to remembering and to loving and to thinking.' Remembering is related to receiving inspiration from a tradition – namely, Christianity or philosophy. Such tradition may be absent in the technological era, but remembering it can keep one in touch with primordial foundations of reverence, nobility, and trust. Thinking and loving have to do with thinking an ancient tradition and living its counsels in the modern context. Such a challenge is an immense one for Grant, for the technological era has eclipsed any language or way of thinking outside its historicist and liberal assumptions. Yet confronting this challenge is a responsibility Grant will not shirk, admitting at the same time that 'for myself, as probably for most others, remembering only occasionally can pass over into thinking and loving what is good. It is for the great thinkers and the saints to do more.'[14]

In another paper written during this period, Grant spells out the political implications of Nietzsche's teaching. In the past, those who followed the traditions of Jerusalem and Athens affirmed an absolute reverence for life. Such reverence, however, is seriously compromised in the technological era, 'when the most respected scientists have for generations shown absurd imprudence about putting nature to the question ... when our own respected leaders have been willing to use defoliant and atomic weapons ... when oil and pulp and mining businessmen have been free to rape the earth and wipe out many species ...'[15] Yet most continue to believe that revolution and change, which has marked the political aspirations of this era, are proceeding toward greater and greater good. How can such good arise when all change is further encased within a greater technological determinacy which imposes its own routinization and necessity on all human endeavour. The deeper problem is that the whole question of good has been darkened in the technological era, since all horizons above the human have been discarded. Grant's purpose in speaking about the darkness of our era is not to discourage anyone but, rather, to offer clarity about our situation in order to prevent people from falling into deceptions and illusions about the way things are. To use the language of good is already to speak in language outside the modern. Nietzsche's claim is that the modern consciousness at its height is one in which the language of good is destroyed and human beings are confronted with the challenge of living beyond the horizons of good and evil. Redemption in the modern era consists in accepting this challenge and living without moral limits. But Grant, following the traditions of Athens and Jerusalem, asserts that human beings are made to live within the limits of good and evil and that such language belongs to the very nature of human existence.

Nonetheless, Grant also acknowledges how difficult it is to think in this language when the technological era has so completely cut itself off from it. How can one maintain any tradition when the dominant ideology is oriented toward novelty and the future? How can any reverence be sustained when the dominant religion is one of greater progress beyond what has been and is presently? Both Marxists and capitalists shared a naïve view of human nature, and they believed in a net of historical and social inevitability that functioned as an opiate from reality. They mistakenly identified the order of historical, political, and economic necessity with the order of the good and, in the process, left a void for the violent and all-embracing force of technological necessity to undermine and subsume all revolution and change toward its own universalization. Any hope of revolution today only serves the mechanical recurrence of the same, not the interests of the good.

In spite of all this, however, an honest confrontation with the way things are in modernity must not lead to passive despair or cynicism but, rather, to a continuing commitment to struggle against pollution and war within cities and universities, and for Canadian sovereignty (whatever is left of it). On a theoretical level, we are challenged to think about the whole outside modern assumptions, and to think about what it means that human beings are not beyond good and evil and not intended to be masters of the earth. To think and act in this way requires that we nurture ourselves in traditions outside the dominant Western ones culminating in the technological paradigm.[16]

In later class lectures on Nietzsche, Grant offers further clarification about Nietzsche's political recommendations and his critique of liberal politics in the technological era.[17] Although both Marxism and liberalism rejected earlier horizons of faith in the name of human freedom and mastery over nature and history, Nietzsche suggests their brand of atheism is worse than the theism they revolted against. At least, theism was honest and open about its faith horizon, and at its best (e.g., the Old Testament) offered its own vitality and vigour, even though it never overcame its fundamental revenge against the strong who lived beyond good and evil. Liberalism and Marxism, however, have claimed to be atheistic while upholding the basic Christian values of democratic equality, liberty, and fairness. This illusion is furthered with the transference of faith from the vertical to the horizontal plane in the form of evolution or progress in history. Underlying this form of atheism is not only a revenge against past theism but also against the past and present structure of reality in which the weak feel impotent, as well as against the natural inequality of the weak and the strong.[18] Such 'left-wing' atheism is afraid of confronting reality as it is, and it also obscures the fragmentary and contingent nature of all existence in a world indifferent to any purposes other than the will to power and mastery by human beings courageous enough to accept reality as it is. Nietzsche's 'right-wing' atheism rejects these liberal values as secularized Christianity in an era when 'God is dead.' He asserts that the fragmentariness and affliction of human existence is not overcome by conquering it, but by redeeming it. This is done through the consent, will, or love of all that was, that is, and that will be – the eternal recurrence of the same.

Grant, as we have already stated, has sympathy for Nietzsche's courageous honesty to name things as they are in a way that liberalism and Marxism, for all the Christianity hidden in them, do not. Following Weil and the theology of the cross, Grant seeks to articulate a faith in God and thought about the good that is honest about things as they are and, yet, has been opened and illumined by the good/God in the very midst of the darkness of reality. Nietzsche affirms the complete finitude of human existence without seeking for the consolations of transcendent hopes in open or concealed forms. Grant suggests that philosophy in the Platonic mode is also focused on death and finitude, as is Christianity with the cross at its centre. Yet the consent to death and finitude, be it in spirit or flesh, is preparation for genuine life rather than a prelude into nothingness. Although Grant admires Nietzsche's honesty about modernity and his challenge to modern liberalism in all its forms, he is repulsed by the assertion of the free, creative will to power which Nietzsche proposes as the path to redemption for humanity in the void of existence. Creativity is the prerogative of a creator God, and it is for humans to open themselves, contemplate, and consent to the divine re-creation even in the face of the void or absence of the good/God in an afflicted world.[19]

5.1.2. Nietzsche and Heidegger

Many of the issues Grant wrestled with in his confrontation with Nietzsche are deepened in later years. This deepening is linked to his encounter with Heidegger's interpretation of Nietzsche.[20] What he appreciated, in particular, was how Nietzsche was unfolded as the last great metaphysician of the West. Nietzsche brought metaphysics to its final resting place by completely inverting and, ultimately, subverting the metaphysics of Plato. Although Grant was hostile to such a movement, he appreciated how seriously Plato was taken by Heidegger and Nietzsche as the father of Western metaphysics, how Christianity was perceived as a popularized version of Platonism, and how the whole Western tradition, with its roots in Plato and Christianity, was perceived as a unified whole. Moreover, he appreciated how the rise of modern science and technology was related to Western metaphysics.

The combined will to power and commitment to truth in Platonism and Christianity eventually broke through the abstracting limitations of metaphysics to assert itself as the free mastery of the earth by the human will, without any power or truth transcending it. In Heidegger and Nietzsche, Grant recognized the heights of the modern vision brilliantly illuminated, as well as the thinking he had to overcome in order to bring the light of Platonism and Christianity into the modern darkness.[21] To do this successfully, Grant realized that he had to address the criticism of Plato and Christianity in Heidegger and Nietzsche. His greatest writing of this period was an attempt to offer a positive response to their vision, a response based on Platonism and Christianity as unfolded by Weil and the theology of the cross.

Some have criticized Grant's understanding of Nietzsche as too dependent on Strauss's image of him as 'a radical historicist' and Heidegger's image of him as 'the arch-philosopher of technological mastery.'[22] Even if this is true, it only demonstrates further how dependent Grant's interpretation of Nietzsche was on that of Heidegger, and how Nietzsche and Heidegger were perceived as offering a common vision of the modern world.

Grant's response to Heidegger and Nietzsche was shaped by their criticism of ancient metaphysics in two key areas. First, Heidegger and Nietzsche criticized Platonism for obscuring reality and rationalizing it away through metaphysical speculation. In Grant's words: 'Socrates, Nietzsche says, couldn't face the fact that the world is an abyss of chaos, and therefore he turned away in fear from this abyss of chaos and pretended it was rational.' Reason, according to Nietzsche, is simply the capacity in human beings to calculate what their will to power desires to achieve. Human beings are not rational animals, but creatures of instinct living in a chaotic universe. In class lectures on Plato's *Symposium*, Grant presents the position of Heidegger and Nietzsche against Plato thus:

... the condition of the highest human excellence is that human beings remain fully loyal to the earth. That is, that the condition of the highest human excellence is that there should be nothing beyond the world which is our first concern. Biblical faith in God, or the ideas as the good in the world, lead us to other-worldliness and asceticism, which alienates men from this world and is only pursued as an art – an escape – because we are unwilling to face the terrifying and perplexing character of the world by positing the Beautiful itself – beyond the world. But this turning of life as it is in the world is an escape, and an escape which holds us from the highest human excellence.[23]

Secondly, Grant is alarmed by the ethical implications of their definition of the essence of human life and the universe. If there is no purpose or good above the human will in a meaningless universe, what then becomes of the concept of justice in human relations? If human beings are completely explainable in terms of historical necessity and chance, what does this imply for the possibility of a humane politics, or for human equality and worth in terms of the idea of inalienable rights? Indeed, the whole language of 'values,' 'artistic creativity,' 'quality of life,' and 'human engineering,' which has its origins in Nietzsche, contradicts such ideas. According to Nietzsche, any concept of justice must rise above the perspectives of good and evil – traditional metaphysics – and be defined according to the human creating of the quality of life through free willing, manipulating, and changing the world and its inhabitants according to one's own measure or passion.[24] Grant finds a direct connection between Nietzsche's teaching about justice (which includes a criticism of the liberal values of equality, fairness, and inalienable human rights as foundationless) and the increase in abortion and eugenic experimentation, as well as other scientific, technological manipulations of human and non-human nature. In pointing out the meaninglessness of liberal values in a post-Christian world, Nietzsche is also questioning the very basis of human rights. What stands in the way of the human free creating of the quality of life? Nietzsche even admits that for some human beings nothing is due but slavery and extinction – the law of nature and evolution. Grant must conclude that even though Nietzsche is a brilliant expositor of the modern, in the end, he is a 'teacher of evil.'[25] All of Grant's writing during the last period of his thought is aimed, in one form or another, at responding to the criticism of Plato and Christianity by Heidegger and Nietzsche, along with their concept of justice manifesting itself increasingly in the modern world.

Grant makes some preliminary criticisms of Heidegger and Nietzsche which provide a clue to some of his broader responses to their vision of life and the world. Heidegger, Grant claims, interprets Plato within historicist assumptions. That is, even though Heidegger can speak about Plato's doctrine of justice, this is done in a formal way. He fails to give proper content to what justice means to Plato; what it means that it is the due of every human being and that its substance is reflected in the proposition 'It is better to suffer injustice than to inflict it.'[26] Heidegger can appreciate neither the concept of a good beyond being as it is, nor the pain and suffering involved in ascending to that good through self-mortification and openness toward it. While Heidegger asserts that the abyss or nothingness is primary, Plato declares that the good is primary and that evil is not simply the opposite but the absence of good (since all that is, insofar as it exists, is good).[27] The doctrine of the absence as opposed to the nothingness of the good in the face of evil is central to Grant's thought and his response to Heidegger and Nietzsche (as we shall see further below). Elsewhere he refers to the good as 'darkened' in our world. In speaking of absence or darkening, Grant is acknowledging that in a world of evil and suffering it is not easy to experience or know the good directly. Hence, any philosophy or theology (i.e., Western Christianity or modern liberalism) that asserts the good/God or absolute purpose and meaning as easily accessible through human thought or experience, fails to account for the darkness of reality which obscures any such good and meaning in human life. At least the scientific, technological paradigm of necessity and chance recognizes the radical contingency of life and the radical indifference of the universe to any discernible purpose imposed or believed by human beings.

At the same time, however, while the experience of the good/God may be darkened or absent in the world, it can never be extinguished. One has to be opened within to see it even in the midst of the darkness. One must be opened to see it on the cross. Grant appreciates Heidegger and Nietzsche insofar as they break through the superficial and optimistic liberal hopes to present a tragic world indifferent to whatever meaning human beings want to impose on it. Yet, whereas they counsel a mastery of the world and a will to create purposes in manipulating and controlling it, Grant, following Weil and the theology of the cross, counsels an openness emptied of false illusions about the way things are, yet receptive to the revelation of the beauty of the world. Grant cannot accept that human beings are beyond good and evil. Even though he knows he is one of the 'botched and bungled,' he does not want to live Nietzsche's instinctive will. Rather, he desires to give himself to the forces of the world and take part in them out of a love of the earth, a love inspired and grounded in the transcendent love of God.[28]

Grant accepts Nietzsche's and Heidegger's analysis of modernity as it is. But, whereas Nietzsche counsels a 'wilful self-making'[29] as the means to redemption in a meaningless, tragic universe, Grant offers a more ancient vision of open trust in and self-denying waiting upon the good/God. Although, in later years, Heidegger moved further away from Nietzsche toward this more ancient type of language, the content of Being is not identified with a transcendent good, but with the constantly changing, historical becoming of being in the world. Grant learned much from Heidegger's analysis of technology, but he could never accept Heidegger's 'ontology' as he perceived it. Human beings are not made to live beyond good and evil, and to say that the world is 'as it is' is also not to confuse evil with good and good with evil. Although Heidegger and Nietzsche are not theologians of glory in the same way modern optimistic progressive liberals are, by asserting that human beings are beyond good and evil, they fail, finally, to say 'the thing is as it is' in its heights as well as its depths.

5.1.3. Céline

It is in the French, in particular, that Grant saw the 'tendency to say the thing is as it is.'[30] Whether it was Weil, Sartre, Ellul, and now Céline, the French had a tremendous sensitivity to the tragedy and affliction of life in the world. Céline's contribution was not as a thinker but, rather, as an artist expressing the truth about the chaos and abyss of reality. Grant was especially moved by Céline's trilogy.[31] Although Grant was aware of Céline's anti-Semitism, he refused to allow this to detract from the power of Céline's account of the ravages and afflictions of war. This is not to say that Grant did not believe that anti-Semitism should be opposed vigorously, and that insofar as Céline was anti-Semitic he should be denounced. Rather, Grant criticized those who would use Céline's anti-Semitism as an excuse for avoiding a serious consideration of his art. Indeed, Céline's capacity to 'chronicle' the collapse of Europe in the mid-1940s, and to capture this chaos to its very depths with such intensity and 'tenderness,' moved Grant as no other art had done (except for that of Mozart).[32]

Others claimed Céline was insane and used this as an excuse to dismiss him. Grant argued, in contrast, that anyone who was able to survive what Céline had survived and recount it in such a comprehensive way, could not do it justice without being a little insane. And yet, on a deeper level, this was not insanity but, rather, the art of being present in the narration as 'storyteller and participant.' To recount reality with sensitivity as a participant, and to see it as a whole in a time of immense chaos and destruction, was not something that could be done steadily or rationally. It was said that saints in prayer 'can at moments touch that love wherein "the tears, the agony, the bloody sweat" can be loved.' Céline was certainly no saint, but he was afflicted. His hopes had been 'burnt out of him by prison and persecution, by poverty and by age.' The depth of Céline's account was not simply a result of his talent as an artist, but a consequence of the fact that he was himself afflicted.[33]

In an unpublished manuscript on Céline's trilogy, Grant goes into more detail. He offers a tentative characterization of the trilogy as 'an epic of the afflicted.'[34] It depicts a German-dominated Europe in the final throes of its collapse. It is about the violence and extremity of a technological war and how its consequences penetrate and destroy the lives of people. All this is recounted in relation to what was happening to Céline, his wife, Lili, and their cat, Bebert. *Castle to Castle* is about the fall of the pro-German French leadership, who know they have backed the losing side and are trying to escape the violent revenge they anticipate at the hands of the French left and the Allies. *North* recounts the destruction of Germany and the desperate, pathetic attempt of the German leadership to save their lives. *Rigadoon* offers a witness from the inside to the massive bombing and collapse of Germany, the wounded and disoriented civilians, and the disorder and despair of spirit. In all three there is a stark, yet tender, portrayal of the humiliation of a recently strong and triumphant society. Céline himself knew about humiliation, a loss of any belief in goodness, integrity, and dignity, from his impoverished circumstances as a child.[35] He grew up within the poorer middle-class, which was forced to serve the richer class in order to survive. This bred deep resentment and hatred within him, and this certainly came out later in his life as is so well documented. Yet the question for Grant is whether this hatred finally corrupted Céline's art. Grant's answer is no. With all his hates and loves, his prejudices and his resentments, Céline was a compassionate doctor who never compromised the care of his patients and loyalty to his wife and cat. And this is the case even in the face of constant slander, persecution, vilification, and poverty that he endured till his dying day.

The essence of great art, according to Grant, is to reveal the truth about reality without 'prettying it up.' Céline's genius is in portraying reality as it truly is.[36] In the face of such massive destruction and devastation made possible by technology, the fragility and insignificance of human life is revealed. Céline is a tormented soul, but never one who says good is evil or evil good. To be so tormented and so clear-headed seems too difficult to imagine. But only those, such as modern liberals, who think of 'charity without the cross,' can think Céline insane. Great art is that which brings one into greater truth about reality. Much modern art, however, simply wants to portray reality as more pleasant and ordered than it is.

In the final section of the manuscript, Grant asks himself why he is so 'enraptured' with Céline's art? Céline can show us how the world is ruled by brutal necessity and chance, and yet do this very beautifully. He gives the reader a sense of being present in the events being narrated, and he portrays human beings honestly, with their purposes and passions 'doomed to a kind of incompleteness in this life.' Seeing life as incomplete or 'broken' is not being pessimistic, nor is it harbouring a morbid preoccupation with finitude and mortality. Rather, it points to a basic recognition of the vulnerability and fragility of life, which is easily twisted and mangled in the face of the brutal necessities of the world.

The truth about the vulnerability and limitations of human life in the world is one of the truths at the centre of such religions as Buddhism and Christianity. Yet Christianity in its Western form increasingly lost sight of this truth. Grant believes this development to have begun with no less a figure than Saint Augustine, who started to emphasize the power of God above the weakness of God. This Western theological emphasis found its way into modern liberalism through the secular doctrine of progress, encouraging a triumphalist belief in human power to shape the world. Insofar as Céline is aware of the brokenness in himself and others, 'he is a witness to the weakness of God and the fragility of the flesh.' In a world of broken hopes and pain-filled lives, he finds little meaning. If there is a God, Céline witnesses 'the absence.' The mixture of cynicism and love in his art pushes him to the truth of what is. He is neither a nihilist, for he knows love, nor a liberal, for he knows the evil and suffering of human beings. One can never know at what point a vision of the good/God can emerge from the very depths of God's hiddenness or absence in suffering. Céline may not have had such a vision, and for this reason his art is incomplete. He refuses, nonetheless, to portray things better than they are. 'The thing is as it is.'[37] For this portrayal, in the splendid beauty of his art, Grant is profoundly grateful to him.

5.2. Bringing to Light the Darkness as Darkness: The Fate of Liberalism in the Technological Era

From what has been written in the foregoing about Nietzsche, Heidegger, and Céline, it may seem that Grant had little sympathy for modern liberalism, given its triumphal optimism about human nature and history, and its naïvety about the dangers of the modern science and technology which it was instrumental in bringing forth. Could mastery serve humane purposes, or would it eventually twist itself free from liberal ideals to follow a path more in keeping with human passions as unfolded by Nietzsche? In the 1970s and '80s, Grant increasingly saw the latter taking place. His writing of this period, then, is an attempt to explain why it is that liberalism was unable to discipline technological development according to its secularized Christian 'values,' and why, as a result, it was declining as a moral force in the technological era. Grant's deepest criticisms and insights continue to be inspired by a theology of the cross in the form of 'negative theology' or, in his words, 'bringing to light the darkness as darkness.'[38]

5.2.1. The Essence of Technology

In order to understand the fate of liberalism in the technological era, it is necessary to understand the essence of technology itself. Certainly Grant had written about this subject before, and since the 1960s, under the influence of Ellul and Strauss, he had come to understand its increasingly all-pervasive influence in society. Writing on technology in the 1970s and '80s, he came, under the influence of Heidegger, to reflect more deeply about its essence.

Technology is something new in civilization, and its novelty is related to the unique union or 'copenetration' of science and art, knowing and making. This copenetration is indicated in the very word 'technology,' which combines the two Greek words *techne* and *logos*. *Logos* is the word for reason or thought, and *techne*, the word for art or production. For the Greeks, these two sets of activities were kept apart. Reasoning had as its end a knowledge of the world, not in order to act upon it or change it, but to contemplate its order and beauty. Art had as its end the 'leading forth' of something into existence. The word to designate this leading forth was *poesis*. But the making of something like a desk is very different than the leading forth or *poesis* of an osprey. The latter is a production beyond the human, to be contemplated and loved. In the technological era, however, we have the capability to unmake an osprey or to believe that we can make it better than it is. Grant uses this illustration to reveal how different thinking about reality is in the technological era. In this era, knowing (science) has been put in the service of making, and making in turn has been put in the service of mastery and control over human and non-human nature.[39]

The crisis of our era is that along with these new powers for making and unmaking there is also an inability to think about what 'should' be made or unmade. The scientific account of nature understands it as a field of objects summoned for questioning to give its reasons for being the way it is, and subject to human determination of what it should be. While the ancients held a concept of the good which defined what everything in creation was fitted for, modern science does not understand nature in these teleological terms. It replaces the concept of 'good' with that of 'value' – the evaluation of things according to human standards.

Grant's discussion is not intended to offer a singularly negative judgment on modern science. Insofar as it tells us the truth about the way things are, modern science is good. But Grant does not hold the tragic vision of life to be the highest. That is, the world as ruled by necessity and chance is not the highest truth. In the end, Grant is a 'rationalist.' He believes that there is an order of the good/God that provides a *telos* for human life and the world. His concern about the scientific, technological vision of life is its capacity and determination to make and unmake outside any *telos* other than human passion and will. One's passion is the oppression of another, and the passions let loose cannot easily be contained or disciplined by any human being. Our era offers the uniquely fearful possibility of the making of tyrannies and monstrosities unheard of in previous eras. While ancient civilization was held by a concept of the good which provided a basis for knowing the proper purposes for all human doing in the world, any such overriding concept or claim is absent today. What, then, will limit the technological will to making in relation to humanity or the earth? We can already see the results of such making in the steady destruction of the earth and the objectification of human beings as data for experimentation and manipulation.[40]

The problem is that the only response to the growing crisis which technology is causing in our era is even greater technology. The reason for this is that we have great difficulty thinking outside technological thinking. Once we have conquered nature, what prevents us from conquering human nature, which is also a part of it? According to Grant, Heidegger became convinced that technology is increasingly focused on 'cybernetics' – the mastery of human nature in conformity to technological necessity. Even the language of values and ideals, quality and ascent of life, arises out of the same technological 'ontology.' To think outside technology is to think outside this language.

The first step in this regard may be thinking about what has been lost – the negative task – in this ontology. To bring this out, Grant uses the illustration of a statement made by a computer scientist about the computer – 'The computer does not impose on us the ways it should be used.'[41] Such a statement, claims Grant, obscures what computers are and the purposes for which they have been made. The making of computers arises out of the same ontology that has combined *techne* and *logos*. The two false assumptions of the computer scientist is that human beings are free to determine how computers are to be used and that computers are neutral instruments. The truth is that the ways computers are to be used are built into them. Their coming to be in existence entails purposes beyond those of their users. Such purposes are to store and classify information. Storing and classifying already implies reduction and homogenization. This serves the greater destiny of the universal and homogenous state made increasingly possible through technology. To achieve this, the conquest and control of human and non-human nature is necessary. It is within this larger technological destiny that the computer exists. To think that one is free to determine its use is to be blind to this greater reality undermining genuine freedom.

Modern liberalism thought that in discarding the concepts of the good/God, human beings would be free to be masters of their own fate. The truth is, human beings are now being determined by a much greater necessity because it is so impersonal and all-encompassing. Only a 'hunger and thirst' for an absolute justice could place some checks and balances on such a force, although Grant is not sure whether even that could make much difference at this point. As ever new crises arise as a consequence of technology, greater and greater technology is needed to meet them. As a result, ever new forms of mastery are coming to be, even over the most intimate aspects of human life.[42]

All of these insights are woven together in Grant's last major essay on technology. He begins by reiterating the all-embracing impact of technology on our lives. This includes our private as well as public pursuits and activities. Grant acknowledges once again that the liberal originators of technology were moved by their determination as secular Christians to overcome hunger and disease, heavy labour, and the curse of war, and no one can deny the many real benefits technology has brought to humanity. Nonetheless, technology has also introduced unprecedented crises into human civilization. As Grant puts it: 'where Plato warned clearly against the dirtying of the waters, he did not face their pollution as a possibility in the immediate future.' Moreover, the coming to be of technological instruments of control and manipulation permits certain forms of community and excludes others. As individual communities and nations disappear, we move into a global, corporate, impersonal world where large masses of people are determined by forces they cannot see or know. Any attempt to limit or direct this development is hindered by the lack of any standards of value or justice beyond the human will (which is itself subsumed within the larger technological destiny). Whereas the original Western conception of justice was rooted in an absolute good, the modern technological conception is rooted in the free human creating of the quality of life which has no reference point beyond itself. There are no absolute 'shoulds' or 'musts.' There is no absolute justice beyond all bargains and without alternative. There is no good that transcends the relativity of perspective. In adopting technology, we have bought into a 'package deal.' Technology has become the ontology of our age. Even political alternatives are simply predicates of the same technological destiny.[43]

Grant's aim in writing about the essence of technology and its practical implications is not to be pessimistic. Rather, it is an attempt 'to bring to light the darkness as darkness' in the spirit of negative theology.[44] In order to do this, he must attempt to destroy all the 'inadequate sources of hope,' so that people are opened to the way things are as they are. He also admits, however, that in order to see things as they are and not to despair to the point of madness, one needs to be acquainted with a joy that transcends the chaos. For the Christian there is the intimation, based on faith, that thought and practice are not all. Even though God may at times be more absent than present (as Grant confessed was most often the case for him),[45] the Christian is always open to the revelation of God's fullness. As Weil indicated, to know God's absence is already to know indirectly God's presence, for how can we know God is absent if we do not have an intimation of God's hidden presence? This is also why Weil and Luther speak of God's presence in a world governed by a brutal necessity and chance (the cross). The cross is the revelation of God's absence and, paradoxically, also the revelation of God's deeper presence. The Christian must wait patiently at the foot of the cross with open desire (love) and trust (faith). Bringing to light the darkness as darkness is a way of bringing people to the foot of the cross, for it destroys any possibility of absolute meaning in human terms and within the possibilities of this world.

5.2.2. Liberal Justice in the Technological Era

Grant continues to engage in negative theology as he focuses on the theme of 'English-speaking justice' in a series of lectures he delivered in the early 1970s and later published as a book. Although in one letter he speaks about wanting his future work to be devoted to what can be said positively about the good/God in our time, in another letter he speaks about the purpose of *English-Speaking Justice* to be the clearing away of 'the junk of the modern era and to say how difficult it is to make positive affirmations.'[46] This difficulty does not simply arise because the modern technological ontology makes it difficult to think positively outside its assumptions, but also because of Grant's personal sense of moral failure and imperfection compared to a Simone Weil, who could speak positively. We have already noted this issue in Grant earlier, but we shall also encounter it further below as Grant struggles, in spite of this, to say something positive. To prepare the ground for these positive affirmations, however, Grant's negative work remains to be completed. He has spoken clearly about the technological era as it is. Now he must address the liberal ideology which has served as its 'theology.'

The goal of *English-Speaking Justice*, according to Grant, is to move through a discussion of the close relation between 'the development of technology and political liberalism' toward an analysis of each of the terms. We have already begun to consider this with the previous discussion on the essence of technology. Grant's concern is to defend English-speaking liberalism at a time when technological development is undermining its moral ideals. This is crucial not only because liberalism is the only moral language to sound a convincing note in the secular public sphere today, but also because, at its best, liberalism was much more than a justification of progressive mastery of human and non-human nature. It also affirmed that 'any regime to be called good, and any progress to be called good, must include liberty and consent.' Such an affirmation is essential at a time when our tradition of good has 'degenerated into an ideology the purpose of which is to justify the uninhibited progress of cybernetics' – that is, human mastery. In an era when technology has permitted the use of massive force around the globe and massive development of public and private corporations, can the free politics of equality and the protection of individual rights be maintained? Grant would begin to answer this question by seeking to bring to light the modern assumptions 'which at one and the same time exalted human freedom and encouraged that cybernetic mastery which now threatens freedom.' He wants to address the modern liberal idea that justice is neither a natural nor supernatural virtue, but the result of calculated self-interest in terms of a social contract agreed upon by the majority. The question for Grant is whether the idea of a social contract can, indeed, support a political order based on justice.[47]

In order to address this question, Grant engages in a criticism of modern liberal contract theory at its best, as represented by the English-speaking political philosopher John Rawls.[48] Rawls's basic question is: why is it that human beings must consent to a minimum measure of social cooperation? The answer lies in the self-interest of the individual. It is to the advantage of each individual to cooperate with other individuals (which also implies accepting certain limits) in order that society comes to exist. A society of free calculating individuals, who have contracted together to meet their interests, can provide a better service of those interests collectively in terms of greater protection from harm and greater power to acquire primary goods. Primary goods, according to Rawls, have to do with those things which promote comfortable self-preservation. Here he depends heavily on the thought of Locke. But he differs from Locke in one fundamental area. While Locke rejected the traditional understanding of nature as providing us with a conception of the highest good, he did look to nature to provide knowledge about the greatest evil, namely, death. In order to preserve ourselves, and preferably in comfort, we have to cooperate with others. Justice is nothing other than the convenient rules and arrangements to secure our protection from death and our preservation, with the greatest measure of comfort possible within the limitations of necessity. Rawls, in contrast, cannot build his theory of justice on a metaphysical proposition about nature (the 'naturalistic fallacy') which derives an understanding of how humans ought to act on the basis of a common sense about the way things are in nature. As a contemporary thinker within the scientific paradigm, Rawls must base his theory of justice on a more objective foundation. He does this by suggesting the concept of an 'original position,' wherein principles of justice are determined by individuals abstracted from their immediate (subjective) situation. Under this 'veil of ignorance,' principles of justice can be posited which can be agreed upon by the majority, for these principles transcend the immediate interests of any one calculating individual.[49]

Rawls then appeals to Kant in order to provide a positive basis for social fairness and equality. We can overcome nature not only with our technological ability to correct its deficiencies (i.e., painful death), but also with our moral will, which asserts that they ought to be corrected. Human beings are able to determine freely and rationally their moral laws. This leads to equality in basic legal rights, as well as in goods and powers, which are to be distributed fairly by the rational will of the community. Nonetheless, even though Kant taught the autonomous will of the individual as determining justice and realizing it in history and society, he also asserted the categorical imperative and the 'Good will' as a good without restriction and beyond all bargaining. Even though human beings determine the content of morality, the fact that human beings are morally oriented is a universal given of reason. Rawls, however, cannot accept Kant's metaphysical position either. Reason can only be instrumental, and human beings can be nothing but calculators of self-interest. Freedom consists simply in human preferences. But Grant confronts Rawls with several questions:

> Why is it good that all human beings should live in a society to which they can give consent and in which they are guaranteed an equality of political liberties? Why is it good that human beings should have political rights of a quite different order from members of other species? Why should equality in legal rights stand above and not be influenced by the obvious inequalities in contribution to progress whether in production, in the arts or in the sciences?[50]

For Kant, human beings are equal in what is essential – their moral choice for good – and unequal only in lesser things. But why, according to Rawls, are those who can calculate and cannot avoid choices worthy of inalienable rights? Why ought they to be treated as 'persons' as opposed to something else? The term 'person' itself, which Rawls slips in, is not scientific and merely covers up his inability to state clearly what it is about human beings that makes them worthy of the highest political respect.

Justice, according to Rawls, cannot escape basic self-interest. In the pluralism of opinions and interests within society, a compromise and agreement (contract) must be reached, and this constitutes justice. The principles of justice that Rawls advances as a result are not as disinterested or abstracted as he may think. They represent basic bourgeois common-sense values. These can be summed up in two principles. First, 'each person is to have an equal right to the most extensive basic liberty compatible with a similar liberty of others.' Second, 'social and economic inequalities are to be arranged so that they are both: a) to the greatest benefit of the least advantaged, and b) attached to offices and positions open to all under conditions of fair equality of opportunity.' Grant's criticism, however, is that the difficulty and tension between liberty (1) and equality (2) have not been addressed. In the technological era, does the massive liberty of some not undermine the equality of others? How can liberty and equality be maintained at a time when massive public and private corporations interfere with the liberty of every individual? Can the calculating individual put forth a principle of the common good strong enough to withstand the ambitions of the powerful and the increasingly unequal use of the world's resources? Rawls's theory of justice is written in abstraction from the realities of the technological era: an era of war and imperialism, individual consumption and entertainment. Grant is not rejecting Rawls's principles of justice. Rather, he is suggesting that justice as self-interest cannot establish those principles. Self-interest, according to Rawls, is acquiring those things that would make life cozy. Self-interest, according to Socrates, is reflected in his statement 'It is better to suffer injustice than to inflict it.' It is always in our interest to be just. Justice is not a set of external political arrangements which serve as useful means to the realization of our self-interest in terms of cozy goods. Rather, it is the inward harmony of human beings with a good that transcends them and defines their nature. Justice inspired by the self-interest of human convenience cannot possibly support the pursuit of liberty and equality in an era when technological convenience is increasingly unfavourable toward them.[51]

But why is it, asks Grant, that the liberal understanding of justice, which is not sustained by any foundational affirmations, is still the dominant political morality in the English-speaking world? He posits two reasons. First, the concept of justice in the English-speaking world never developed significantly beyond the contractual theories of Hobbes and Locke. Comfortable self-preservation and self-interested calculation were never transcended by the more extreme expressions of contractual freedom in Rousseau, and later transposed into revolutionary equality and historical progress in Kant, Hegel, and Marx. Nor did the Nietzschean counter-response to this Continental liberalism –

absolute contingency of human existence and nihilistic historicism in a post-Christian world – ever take root. The price for having bypassed these Continental philosophies was a superficiality in thought, but one that allowed enough social moderation and tolerance to prevent the secular/religious ideological extremity witnessed in the rest of Europe – namely, Marxist socialism, on the one hand (revolutionary, progressive liberalism), and National Socialism, on the other (Promethean will to power). Moreover, the necessities of pioneering expansion brought a greater egalitarian shape to English liberalism in North America, albeit never one that hindered the growing development of industrial capitalism.

Second, the fact that contractual liberalism was intertwined with Calvinist Protestantism in North America infused greater meaning into the concept of justice than mere comfortable self-preservation could have done. Whereas the more profound and more extreme forms of philosophy and art in Europe had more in common with the Lutheran spirit, the English-speaking tradition of thought was well suited to a more practical and less reflective Calvinist Protestantism, particularly in North America. This provided liberal justice with a greater moral foundation than mere contractualism could offer, and a greater motive for sacrifice and cooperation than mere comfortable self-preservation.[52]

The price for this more moderate, less profound copenetration of philosophy and faith, however, was a fundamental incapacity to engage the deeper forces being unleashed by modern science and technology. Not only was this type of liberal justice unable to anticipate the deeper passion or will to mastery driving the technological imperative, but as the religious tones of liberal justice were being stripped away under the growing secularism of modernity, liberalism actually served to fuel technological development in North America as nowhere else. This was because, contrary to more Eastern Platonic expressions of biblical Christianity, Western Christianity of the type most fully realized in North American Calvinism was dominated by the idea of 'Will.' Will implied dynamism, change, and activity. As the divine will lost its power to elicit the obedience and subservience of the human will in a teleologically defined universe, the human will was left free to deify its own passions and apply dynamism, change, and activity toward its own purposes. Yet because the Calvinist heritage is still retained in the collective memory of North American culture, it is still possible to hold the illusion that liberal justice is sustained by foundations beyond the conventional agreement of contract and the self-interested calculation of comfortable self-preservation. The problem, however, is that the growing technological will to will, combined with the historicist ontology of an indifferent universe devoid of meaning outside human passion, cannot be checked, disciplined, or restrained by liberal principles of fairness, equality, and the rights of the individual.

The Continental forms of liberalism represented by Rousseau, Kant, Hegel, and Marx were much more libertarian and revolutionary in the hope of achieving an ideal order. They represented a secularized Christianity which transferred the transcendent into the sphere of the imminent in terms of the kingdom of humanity as opposed to the kingdom of God, the human will as opposed to the divine will, and the human progressive transformation of history as opposed to the divine redemption of the world beyond human possibilities. The Continental form of liberalism assaulted Christianity directly by adopting its ideals, while stripping it of its ordering principle – God. English-speaking liberalism, by contrast, simply admitted that the Christian ideals were too difficult to achieve and, therefore, 'lowered the horizons' (Strauss) to make an ordering of society possible. This meant less extremity and more civility, but also at the price of superficiality. Grant is arguing that with the new power being unleashed by modern science and technology, English-speaking liberalism cannot engage, order, or restrain human passions. Nor are these passions under the control of a Continental version of liberalism, which, albeit deifying the human passions, was also driven by the goal of an ideal order of liberty and equality for all.

What liberalism was unable to come to terms with, finally, was the depth of the potentiality for evil in the human soul. At least English-speaking liberalism recognized human self-interest and put some checks on it in order to manage it. Continental liberalism, however, saw evil as external to human nature and hoped optimistically for its overcoming with the human liberty being realized progressively in history. In this way, liberalism was a theology of glory, underestimating the distance between necessity and the good, obscuring the transcendence of the good and the depth of evil and suffering in the world. The power of a Nietzsche was in confronting liberalism with the emptiness of speaking of any good or evil when God had been crucified. Now human beings were forced to muster up courage to define their own good and master their own destiny outside any supports provided by social or metaphysical ordering. Neither the universe nor the human soul was morally structured or directed. Freedom was the knowledge and power to create and will in the midst of a chaotic mass of forces. But would the movement from a conservative English-speaking liberalism, to a more revolutionary Continental liberalism, to a historicist, nihilistic will to will, not spell disaster for the liberal values of liberty, equality, and individual rights, especially in an era of unprecedented capacities for mastering, controlling, and manipulating human and non-human nature?

5.2.3. Test Case: Abortion and Euthanasia

Grant came to see exactly this happening. Justice as liberty, equality, and the inalienable rights of the individual could not be sustained by a contractual liberalism in the face of the technological will to power in the modern era. Grant saw this happening in a number of ways. He saw it in education and politics. He also saw it in the new possibilities opened up with medical technologies – abortion and euthanasia. Grant was especially awakened to these latter issues through his wife, Sheila, with whom, implicitly and explicitly, he co-authored all of his writing on the subject. For Grant, modern developments in abortion and euthanasia made clear the destiny of English-speaking justice in the technological era.

This became particularly evident in the majority decision of the American Supreme Court in the case of Roe vs Wade. This decision reflects the inherent contradiction between contractualism and liberal justice. The decision itself was a compromise one. It declared that foetuses under six months old were not considered 'persons,' permitting abortion within the first six months of a woman's pregnancy. The modern contractualism in this decision was reflected in the statement that 'the allocation of rights from within the constitution cannot be decided in terms of any knowledge of what is good.'[53] Modern North American society is morally pluralistic, and hence any legal decisions must claim a moral agnosticism about good and evil. Legal decisions about what can or cannot be done in society must be decided by convention and agreement among its members. This also implies compromise between competing interests. At the same time, however, the Supreme Court declaration also uses the term 'persons' to distinguish those who have the right to life from those who do not. Not only is this term unscientific, but its content is not clearly spelled out. It reflects the 'unthought ontology' of modern liberalism, which asserts, at one and the same time, a relativity with regard to all moral valuation and a uniqueness about human beings that makes them 'persons' and, therefore, worthy of rights. But, asks Grant, what is it about human beings that makes them persons worthy of justice and rights? If a foetus who is of the same species as a human being is deprived of rights, what is it about any human being that makes rights his or her due? If the definition of rights is based on convention, what prevents society from deciding that a two-year-old, an eighty-year-old, the criminal, or the mentally ill are not persons 'in a whole sense'? If what makes individuals possessors of rights is their ability to calculate and assent to contracts, what is it about the weak and inarticulate that makes equal rights their due?[54]

In asking these questions, Grant is conscious of the implications of Nietzsche's understanding of justice – namely, that quality of life is a human creation and there is a natural inequality between the powerful and the weak which makes the weak subject to the creative and annihilating justice of the strong. Nietzsche affirms this conception of justice as the only honest one in a world that is understood according to the modern scientific, technological paradigm of the universe (i.e., governed by necessity and chance). But there is a fundamental contradiction in trying to hold together what is affirmed about reality in the modern scientific view and the ancient conception of justice. According to the ancient view, 'justice is the overriding order which we do not measure and define, but in terms of which we are measured and defined.' According to the modern view, justice is whatever we will to choose and create in freedom once we have taken our fate into our own hands.

In using the term 'persons,' liberal justice is attempting to retain the ancient view within a context which recognizes only the modern understanding of reality and justice. According to the ancient view, to call someone a 'person' was to recognize a quality about them that transcended human convention and, therefore, imposed restraints and obligations on human action in relation to them. In Greek philosophy, justice was embedded in the order of reality, which was morally structured and rationally discernible. In biblical Christianity, justice was due to every human being because creation was an act of a loving God who made human creatures to find their ultimate purpose in giving and receiving love. Moreover, the language of personhood was applied to relations within God as Trinity, which, in turn, provided an inviolable sacredness and dignity to human beings when applied to them.

Modern liberalism retained the principles of justice and personhood but rejected the Christian affirmations undergirding them, affirmations derived in dialogue with Greek philosophy. Nietzsche attacked liberalism because it was dishonest about what it had done and was afraid of following through on the implications of its crucifixion of God. With God 'dead' there was no foundation for justice beyond human convention and convenience. Moreover, there was no foundation for equal rights when human beings were unequal in their capacity for negotiating and enforcing their rights.[55] Grant recognized the truth in Nietzsche's understanding of modernity, but he was fearful of Nietzsche's prescriptions for justice. Although he affirmed liberal principles of justice as consistent with the content of justice according to Christianity, he also perceived the weakness of the foundations for those principles in a post-Christian technological era, an era when God was 'dead' and human beings held new powers for making and unmaking human and non-human nature. The challenge, for Grant, was to offer the possibility of a justice that was based on fundamental Christian principles, but also one that recognized the truth of necessity and chance in the world (as taught by modern science). Addressing this contradiction in positive terms, with the help of Weil and the theology of the cross, would be Grant's last major contribution. In the meantime, however, he continued to write and comment about abortion and euthanasia.

Grant writes about the precariousness of human rights in a society where human beings are thought of as 'accidental conglomerations of matter,'[56] and human life as measured in terms of 'potential life' or 'quality of life.' Not only are these measurements subject to human calculation but also to human freedom, which may become inconvenienced by the claims of the weaker members of society. Indeed, suggests Grant, is not the language of potential life or quality of life a way of 'sugar-coating' the elimination of the rights of some for the convenience of others. Although abortion may be an important option in cases of rape, danger to a mother's life, or even teenage pregnancy, the vast majority of abortions are performed for the sake of convenience.[57] This, argues Grant, is also the case with euthanasia, and particularly in cases of the 'benign neglect' of the mentally disabled. Grant argues that it is a slippery slope from the desire to take life in order to relieve suffering, to eliminating life because it interferes in the interests and conveniences of the able. He points to the developments in Nazi Germany. Euthanasia began with the insane and incurable, and then it was extended to children orphaned by the war. Eventually, the techniques of the gas chambers and crematoria were applied to Jews, Gypsies, and political opponents. Although North America is far from this reality, the modern conception of justice is moving into ways of thinking that could well justify this type of action.[58]

Indeed, argues Grant, the language of North American liberalism is increasingly that of the 'triumph of the will.' This triumph is realized when the individual will is liberated to its full power. This also means that nothing can interfere with it, whether it be other life or even the state. Fascism at its is core is based on the belief in the triumph of the will. In the late twentieth century, it manifests itself in terms of faith in the mastery of ourselves and our world. The language of the triumph of the will is the language of Nietzsche. In a meaningless world of indifferent chaotic forces, human beings are called to assert themselves and subdue nature – human and non-human. This also implies the subjugation of the weak by the strong. Grant sees precisely this happening in abortion and euthanasia. Those who have the power to calculate and enforce the conventional contracts that define rights in society are deciding who has the right to live. Talk of women's freedom, or sexual freedom from ancient religious and cultural slavery, obscures the implications of such freedom for those who stand in its way. Not only are foetuses in the way of sexual freedom and a woman's freedom over her body, but they are also in the way of a corporate technological world which demands the absolute obedience and efficiency of the individual (male or female) in its expanding mechanism of necessity.[59]

The Grants were also horrified to see modern justifications of abortion and euthanasia coming from, of all places, the church. What was particularly disturbing was how the biblical language of 'sacrifice' was being utilized to rationalize the elimination of the life of the foetus and the 'severely retarded' for the sake of the mother's well-being. This was nothing less than the taking of God-given life for the sake of convenience. The language of sacrifice was also intended to facilitate the acceptance of social and economic considerations for abortion. But what did the church's scriptures have to say about the 'quality of life'?

> Poverty and unhappiness are obviously evils to be fought but did Jesus ever imply that they necessarily diminished sanctity? The beatitudes are not about quality of life. He did not say 'blessed are the comfortable, the

successful and the well adjusted.' But he did ask, 'What will it profit a man if he gain the whole world and suffer the loss of his own soul?'[60]

Moreover, does freedom in Christ have anything to do with the freedom afforded the individual through technological advance? What does our calling to be stewards of all created life have to teach us about true freedom in relation to obedience to God? Are we to use the reasoning of technological progress to believe that we can 'evolve' beyond Christ's summation of the law and the prophets as self-denying love, or his prescription for the highest quality of life in the sermon on the mount?

Such ideas are deepened even further by the Grants' reflections on euthanasia proper. Again, euthanasia was of particular concern to them as it was being applied increasingly to cases of benign neglect, and this, just as in the majority of abortions being carried out, had more to do with convenience than with anything else. In these reflections, they bring out even further the contradiction between the Christian perspective on human personhood and the modern one. In the modern context, one's personhood is measured above all by one's intelligence. One's capacity to calculate and articulate one's interests is the measure of the quality of life. The Christian understanding of personhood is one in which the value of life is a God-given absolute and, thus, unnegotiable in terms of its quality. In addition, it is love and not intelligence that defines human life as made in the divine image. The mentally disabled can in many cases be better persons than those with greater intelligence, because they are better able to love. Indeed, because Christianity proclaims love as the divine standard for personhood, it also calls human beings to treat those who are unable to 'realize their full personhood' with special care.

Finally, underlying the modern language of quality or 'dignity' of life is the desire for self-sufficiency and autonomy. This is not necessarily an evil. Yet when it obscures the reality of our fundamental vulnerability and fragility as human beings, as well as the truth that we cannot die 'in control,' it becomes a vehicle for evil. Life's value or worth becomes measured by one's ability to be autonomous, and without it life is considered not truly worth living. But, argue the Grants, are autonomy and self-sufficiency the highest goals of life, and is the value and quality of life and death to be measured by how much one may be in control of them? If this were the case, then the death of Socrates would have been better than that of Christ, and suicide would

be better than both. According to the modern understanding, it is precisely the latter approach which is increasingly being encouraged.
According to the Christian understanding, our lives are completely
dependent on the grace of God in life and in death. Autonomy may be
far from Gethsemane, but a human being cannot be more dignified
than when she or he can say, through whatever agony, 'not my will but
thine be done.'[61]

5.2.4. Continuing Evidence: Politics and Education

Although politics never held Grant's interest in later years as it had
done earlier in life, he continued to reflect and comment on political
issues and particularly those surrounding the question of Canadian
nationalism. Grant had written extensively about this theme earlier,
and he recognized the impossibility of maintaining a genuine nationalism in the face of the expanding globalization of the world according
to technological necessities. The demands of corporate and technological structures in public and private life left little room for loyalties to
traditions, cultures, or principles outside the technological will to will
made palatable by the opiate of material consumption, sexual exploration, and entertainment. Moreover, the Vietnam war revealed to Grant
the degree of coercion technological necessity would exercise through
its principal enforcer – the United States – in order to maintain humanity's allegiance to its purposes. In the 1970s and '80s, Grant continues
to perceive this trend in the particularities of Canadian political developments. The liberals continue to be seen as those who ease Canadians
into the process of globalization, while true conservatives are those
who resist it out of loyalty to Canadian independence.[62]

Grant saw in Pierre Trudeau the quintessential liberal. His response
to the 'October Crisis' in Quebec – that is, the War Measures Act –
was another instance of the degree of force modern liberalism was
prepared to use to overcome nationalist resistance to universalization. In trying to 'put Quebec in its place,' Trudeau was destroying
the best model for and aid to Canadian nationalism. His openness to
Canadian integration with the United States, combined with English
Canada's acquiescence and French Quebec's conflicting commitment
to French culture, on the one hand, and American technology, on the
other, advanced Canada's integration into the global technological
society that much further. At the same time, Grant continued to
defend the aspirations of French Quebeckers as represented by the

separatists and believed that there was room for a distinct Quebec within Canada. The Parti Québécois government, which came into power in 1976, was not ideologically separatist and could, Grant believed, be persuaded to stay within Canada if they came to realize that this was the best safeguard for their distinctiveness. What this would require above all else, however, was moderation. Moderation was not weakness. It was the opposite of intemperance and confrontation. But Grant also realized that moderation was incredibly difficult in a highly immoderate era.[63]

In later years, Grant saw the threat to Canadian nationalism coming from the free-trade agreement between Canada and the United States. This was another step in the process of universal integration according to the technological corporate imperative. Grant was aware that this was simply part of the larger fate of any nationalism in the technological era and that 'fate leads the willing and drags the unwilling.' Yet he was moved by those who were unwilling to be dragged and committed to going down with 'flags flying' and 'guns blazing.' Indeed, argues Grant elsewhere, it is out of such commitments and loyalties that genuine nobility arises in public life. The tragedy is that such loyalty and nobility are seen as outdated in this era and, consequently, there is little place for a genuine conservative approach to political issues in public life.[64]

The truth, according to Grant, is that contemporary politics is increasingly preoccupied with basic administration. Even though there is the appearance of political disagreements among parties and groups, there is no conflict about the larger purposes of society or the question of good. The highest good is agreed to be 'the building of the technological society by the overcoming of chance, through the application of the natural and social sciences.' Political disagreements have to do merely with the better means to this end, not the questioning of this end itself. Moreover, social science's distinction of fact from value and the banishment of value to the realm of the subjective, has opened up a large vacuum for the imposition of the values of the ruling class riding on the top of the technological, corporate wave. Academics in the universities of our era are blind and naïve about the purposes for which their natural and social sciences are being applied, or else they are complicit in this development. Protests by students in the 1960s were based on the recognition that in giving up the question of ends, social scientists had given themselves over to serving the ends of global capitalism at the expense of providing a critical education for students.

They were serving nothing less than the technological 'ideology.' An ideology is either a surrogate religion pretending to be a philosophy (i.e., capitalism or Marxism) or a surrogate philosophy trying to fulfil the role of a religion (i.e., liberalism). As philosophies, ideologies deny that 'reverence is the matrix of human nobility.' As surrogate religions, they try to 'slip reverence in.' At that point, however, reverence is directed at 'something not worthy of reverence, such as the state, the race, the multitude, the nation.' For the Christian or Jew, such misplaced reverence is idolatry and, therefore, destructive of genuine human community. Nonetheless, the question of good can never be eliminated from the human soul, even in the modern darkness of the technological era when it is incredibly difficult to think it. The question, for Grant, is whether one must respect the necessity for public order even in the face of an 'unspontaneous administration, backed by all the growing powers of physiological and psychological technique', or whether one must 'sympathize with the manifold, if impotent, revolts against this order, as expressing a fumbling towards human good, and yet be fearful as they are expressed in the form of illicit and even mad ideologies'?[65]

In spite of these disturbing questions, Grant does not consider himself a pessimist: 'Anyone who believes in God ... cannot be a pessimist. ... I think we live in an atrocious political era. But it is God's world and if you assert that, you cannot be a pessimist.' As a Christian, Grant affirms that it matters absolutely what happens in the world, but at the same time, whatever happens is 'seen in the light of eternity.' Elsewhere, Grant states that the end of life is not politics but 'loving the good,' or God. This also implies that the precious things which give life its joys are not destroyed by political failures, because life's goodness transcends politics.[66]

Grant's love of the good/God was also tested in the university life of which he was a part. He witnessed the progressive shift in the priorities of modern universities from teaching to research. Particularly painful was the application of the research model in the area of the humanities. Grant came into conflict with members of his own department over how religion and the Bible were to be taught. With the arrival of 'Americans' such as E.P. Sanders, Grant witnessed the Bible being treated as an object of research rather than as a sacred treasure housing the living word of truth. The research model was based on the scientific method of knowing, in which things were summoned before the court of human reason in order to give their reasons for being the way they were as objects. The achievements of modern scientific research could not be denied, particularly in the field of medicine. Yet there were also fundamental questions about human existence which could not be engaged or answered through scientific research: questions about justice, beauty, the divine, or morality. What was required for such questioning was a type of teaching and learning that was more 'erotic,' basing what was to be known about justice, God, or beauty on an openness to loving them.

Such teaching, learning, and questioning, however, were increasingly being driven out of the university. The scholarship that should have served as a means to thought had become the end in itself in terms of research. Even the study of the past, which had become especially important in the humanities, had become objectified. The past was no longer studied as a means to knowing ourselves in our present but, rather, as a relic which had been surpassed. Indeed, research in the humanities had produced nothing less than a 'museum culture.' One can learn about the past but not from the past. One can stand over the past and study it as an object, but not stand under it and wait upon it in order to discover truths to help one live in the present. Although Grant was pessimistic about the modern university, he was not pessimistic about the human soul. Eternal questions would continue to be asked by human beings because they were human beings. Whether these questions would continue to be asked within universities or outside them in the future was an unknown. What was known was that by holding the scientific model of research as the only means to knowledge, universities were manifesting themselves to be servants of the larger technological, corporate will to power and mastery over human and non-human nature. They were no longer places for serious questioning about the whole.[67]

Bringing to light the darkness as darkness was a central task for Grant. It was necessary preparation in order to be turned toward a good that transcended the world as it was. There was no inherent *telos* in the world which was accessible in any immediate way. The scientific, technological account of the world as an indifferent play of forces governed by necessity and chance was more true to reality than a liberalism which detected signs of progress and evolution in human nature and history. The Christian affirmation of the world as marked indelibly by evil and suffering (the cross) was sensitive to the impossibility of discerning meaning and purpose in the world as it was. Grant had sympathy for liberalism nonetheless. This sympathy was in response to the Christian motivations of liberalism's reforming emphasis and the Christian principles of its ethics. Through technological development, liberalism envisioned a means to overcoming much of the affliction in the world. In its ethical principles of equal rights and liberty for all, liberalism was concerned to protect the weak from the strong and uphold the absolute dignity and worth of all human life. Yet with the ejection of God from its theoretical foundations, liberalism undermined the chief cornerstone of those foundations. It had no solid ground from which to mount a resistance to the expanding will to power being realized through the necessities of the technological era. Liberalism's naïve optimism about this era, and its incapacity to see how its own foundations were being undermined, served to obscure the darkness of this era. Grant's efforts were an attempt to bring this darkness to light, as well as to express his lament at the decline of liberalism as the last theoretical and political means of resistance against the technological will to power.

At this point, however, Grant's work had to move beyond the negative task. He had to find a way to think the truth of the good/God that also recognized the truth about the world as taught by modern science and technology – the truth about good/God, the world as governed by necessity and chance, and the way in which good/God could illuminate thought and shape life in the world as it was. In other words, Grant was now called to witness to the light that continued to shine in the darkness.

5.3. The Light That Continues to Shine in the Darkness: Faith, Love, and Justice in an Afflicted World

In thinking about the positive task of theology and philosophy, Grant depends on the theology of the cross as appropriated through Weil as never before. Weil offers Grant a way of thinking and existing in the world that is rooted in the transcendent good/God but also sensitive to human affliction in a world governed by necessity and chance. If meaning and purpose are to be perceived, a transformation is required in the human soul, a transformation activated and directed by the good/God. Such a transformation can open the soul to experience the good/God in the world (faith), think according to the good/God in relation to the world (love), and act in obedience to and love of the good/God in the world (justice). Much of what Grant has to say in this regard is not altogether new. Many of his insights are based on ideas he had already written about earlier. Yet he does arrive at a clarity and coherence that is unprecedented, and, therefore, when seen as a whole, to a new point in his thought.

5.3.1. Reason and Revelation: Plato and the Gospels

We have already seen how the relationship between reason and revelation was one that preoccupied Grant from the earliest years of his study of theology and philosophy. We have also seen how Grant subscribed to Augustine's approach to this relationship captured in the phrase *Credo ut intelligam* (faith seeking understanding). Grant understood this phrase to mean that the role of reason or philosophy is to make intelligible the truth of revelation or faith – that is, God and God's relation to the world. Grant applies this approach consistently throughout his thought. What changes for him is the content of each of the terms.

In the early years, Grant was struggling to find clarity about the nature of reason and revelation. First, he recognized the capacity of ancient philosophy to speak about morality, justice, and the good in rational and meaningful ways. At the same time, he was wary of philosophy when it was not sensitive to its limits. By arguing for these truths outside revelation – on the basis of the way things were in nature and the world – philosophy was denying the truths of revelation, which were beyond human intellectual and moral abilities to derive. It also obscured the good and mistook it for something of human making. In so doing, it also trivialized the depth of evil and suffering, which prevented any direct intellectual and moral ascent from the human to the divine.

Second, Grant recognized the ultimate truth in divine revelation and the experience of that revelation through faith. From his first experience of faith in the midst of the war, Grant was graciously opened to trust that all that is, is grounded and sustained by an absolute good/God in spite of the vast evil and suffering that darkens this truth in the human soul. This experience was a primal for Grant. His study of theology and philosophy could only help in making intelligible what this experience meant and how it could be applied to his thinking and existing in the world. At the same time, however, Grant became sensitized to how theology has often tried to bypass or sidestep philosophy in its attempt to make intelligible the truths of revelation. According to Grant, the Gospels were not philosophy, and when theologians rejected philosophy in making intelligible the truth of Christ and the cross, the results were rather poor if not superficial. Philosophy at its best was a handmaid to revelation, making its truths meaningful and relevant in the varying historical and geographical contexts of human existence in the world.

Grant's understanding of reason and revelation also matures over the years. From the earliest years, Grant preferred ancient to modern philosophy, although he was open to the contributions of Kant, Hegel, and other modern philosophers who attempted in one form or another to synthesize ancient and modern thought. Moreover, when thinking of ancient philosophy in his earlier years, Grant did not make a clear distinction between Plato and Aristotle. With his reading of Weil and others, Grant begins to distinguish altogether ancient from modern philosophy and Plato from Aristotle. Although Grant continues to have deep reverence for Aristotle, and even for some modern philosophers, by the late 1960s he sees Aristotle's philosophy and much of modern Western philosophy as theologies of glory. Such theologies undermine revelation and deify human thought and moral ability. They reject the transcendence of the good, trivialize the evil in the world, and worship some aspect of human individual or communal existence in history, whether in present manifestation or future hope. Plato alone stands out – and Plato as interpreted by Weil – as the only philosopher who can serve as a genuine handmaid to revelation as understood and appropriated through a theology of the cross. From the earliest years, Grant offered many reasons for Plato's superiority as a philosopher, and he continues to do so in the 1970s and '80s (as we shall see further below).

Grant's understanding of revelation also matures over the years. Although the person and crucifixion of Christ as the fullest revelation of God was always the centre of Grant's faith, this revelation was also linked to the 'Western' interpretation of the Bible and Christian faith. Grant begins to move away from this interpretation in the 1950s, when he distinguishes between a Platonic, Augustinian, Lutheran theological strand and an Aristotelian, natural theological, Calvinist, Puritan strand within the Western Christian tradition. In the 1960s, under the influence of Sherrard and Weil, Grant rejects the Western Christian tradition altogether in favour of a more 'eastern' Platonic interpretation of the Bible and Christian doctrine. Moreover, he distinguishes the Gospels, and especially the accounts of Jesus at Gethsemane and Golgotha, from other parts of the Bible where God is portrayed in terms of will to power, vengeance, exclusivism, and interventionism in human history.

Although Augustine too falls within the Western tradition, Grant's relationship to his thought is more nuanced. He believes that Augustine may have been the originator of the will-centred understanding of God, humanity, and their relationships with the world. But Augustine was also a Platonist in his understanding of the nature of God and evil in the world. Moreover, Grant continues to appeal to Luther's theology of the cross and to distinguish Lutheranism as more open to contemplation and mysticism than Calvinism. In the 1970s and '80s, these developments continue to the point where Weil's thought and Luther's formulation of the theology of the cross are joined completely and the Western theological, philosophical tradition is rejected as a whole, minus certain Platonic elements in Augustine. These developments are all related to the increasingly central influence of Weil on Grant concerning what constitutes genuine philosophy, revelation, and their proper relationship. Grant's faith becomes centred in Christ as manifesting the divine essence at Gethsemane and Golgotha, and in Plato as giving rational, intelligible voice to this faith.

Plato and the Gospel accounts support one another in some fundamental ways. In earlier writing, Grant distinguished between charity and contemplation (see chap. 4). Over the years, he came to see Plato's philosophy as the supreme expression of contemplation, and the accounts of Christ at Gethsemane and Golgotha as the deepest expressions of charity. Through Weil, however, he also came to see Plato as making an implicit place for charity within his philosophy, placing him that much closer to Christianity so conceived. Plato made room for sanctity in his philosophy, love in his thought, grace in his doctrine of the good, and praxis in his understanding of justice. Let us consider each of these.

The relationship between sanctity and philosophy was one that preoccupied Grant from early on. What Weil did for him was to show him how sanctity brings illumination and clarity to philosophy and raises it to a higher level. In doing this, Weil also showed Grant how much this was true of Plato's philosophy. We have already seen how Grant felt inadequate before the purity of Weil's sanctity and how this prevented him from speaking positively about the good, recognizing that only a 'saint' had the credibility and insight to do this. He, like most others, could reach the level of nobility through inner struggle and discipline, but not the level of sanctity. Yet he also came to realize that by the grace of God activated through Weil and Plato, he was granted some measure of the vision of the good in his own thought. This vision was manifested to him, as it was to most people who were not saints, in mediated forms – that is, through human love, the beauty of the world, just actions, or, for the Christian, through the revelation of the good in Christ and the cross.[68] The vision of the good was dependent on one's desire for it. According to Plato, thought was not a human-centred activity but one of openness and receptivity to the truth of the goodness in all things, a goodness which was a reflection of the good transcending the world as it was. The desire for this good was basic to human nature, yet the human condition was one of ignorance and confusion, mistaking lesser goods for the ultimate good and realizing human desire in more carnal, idolatrous ways. Sanctity was essential as a means of purifying one's desire for the ultimate good. Such purification had to move through the negation of false, misdirected desires for good. This process Weil, and Grant also, understood in Christian terms, be it as moral self-renunciation, mystical self-annihilation, dying to self, or being crucified with Christ. The classic illustration of this journey toward sanctity was Plato's allegory of the cave. On this journey, the struggle for sanctity and for knowledge of the whole are brought together, since one's purity before the good also brings clarity of vision.[69]

Grant speaks about this unity of sanctity and philosophy in Plato in several ways. He speaks, for instance, about the unity between the 'cosmological' and 'ethical-religious' approaches. The cosmological approach asks questions about reality and the nature of the universe. How does one gain knowledge about the whole? The ethical-religious approach asks about the meaning and purpose of life. How ought one to live? The danger of the cosmological approach without the ethical-religious one is philosophy as an abstract discipline, one cut off from the good and from existence as it is. This turns philosophy into a ready instrument for the will to power manifesting itself in the technological era. Existentialism, according to Grant, was an important protest against such a philosophical approach. Abstract philosophy was also the approach of Aristotle, who cut reason off from the life of sanctity. But the ethical-religious approach without the cosmological one is also inadequate, for it fails to provide understanding about the way things are in the world and, therefore, fails to guide morality and charity in the complex contexts of time and place in history. In Plato the two approaches are combined.[70]

Grant also speaks about the unity of love and knowledge in Plato. True knowledge is related to being opened to the goodness and beauty in all that is. Only out of such knowledge does one have the right to change the world. But such knowledge is impossible without love. Love is not something one can will, but rather something that has to be brought to life in the soul. Plato's understanding of love as *eros* or desire implies a longing in the soul for the good, but one that is frustrated in a world where the good is absent. Evil, according to Plato, is the absence of good. By stating this doctrine, Plato was also stating that all that is, insofar as it is, is good because it has come forth from the absolute good. Evil has no independent existence. It exists as a negation of the goodness of created things. Evil can be so terrible that it can darken any reflection of the good in the world. To be opened to the good, therefore, the soul must be changed. To be changed, the soul needs grace. Weil and Grant interchange Christian and Platonic language to suggest that obedience to the good requires the power of the good or the Holy Spirit. Only through such power can the soul be awakened and directed to the good, which is beyond the world but also manifest in the hidden beauty of all that is. The good is not only the object of love, but inspires love as well. Only as we are opened and receptive to divine love can we then love created things fully, and only then can we truly know them. This, of course, contradicts completely the scientific, technological approach to the world.[71]

Plato also asserts that the good/God is beyond being. The good transcends the world as it is.[72] We have seen why this affirmation was important to Grant. The more one was confronted by the evil and suffering in the world, the more one had to assert the absence or hiddenness of good in the world. Grant refers to the *Deus absconditus* of Reformation theology,[73] or the absence of God on the cross. Plato speaks of the good outside the world. For Plato, one was moved toward this truth by coming to the realization, through a process of transformation, that nothing in this world could satisfy the longing of the soul for good. This understanding was also consistent with a theology of the cross, which arrived at this conclusion negatively from the side of the experience of affliction. This world was the cross or the absence of God. But being aware of God's absence, having this unsatisfied longing and hunger in the soul, was also indirect knowledge of the transcendent good/God. The transcendence of the good was also an essential affirmation against all human attempts at identifying the good with human projects, history, or thought in the present or future.

The error of liberalism was precisely in eliminating the transcendence of the good and deifying some aspect of human thought and potentiality. The mystery and inscrutability of divine providence stood against ecclesiastical and secular theologies of glory which denied the transcendence of the good, the absence of good in the world (evil and affliction), and the points of redemptive contact within this distance.

Finally, Plato's teaching about justice is consistent with the justice spoken about in the Gospels. In a paper entitled 'Justice and Technology,' Grant spells out this consistency beginning with two quotes:

> Christ said: Happy are those who are hungry and thirsty for justice (Matthew 5:6). Socrates said that it is better to suffer injustice than to inflict it (Crito 49b–e; Gorgias 474bff).[74]

In order to know about justice, one must be prepared to love it. But how can one love something that can be costly to oneself? Grant points to the fact that for both Plato and the Gospels, justice is not visibly attractive or desirable. This is because justice that is obedient to the good/God, absent in a world of injustice, is bound to entail profound suffering. Such an orientation is foreign to the modern technological will to power, which pays allegiance to nothing above the human will. But, outside obedience to the good in one's actions, the human will is enslaved to corrosive necessities. Only in such obedience is true freedom to be found. Plato speaks about the beauty of justice which appeals to and awakens the longing for the good within the human soul, but also about its unattractiveness. Justice is a crucified slave in the world. It stands against human convenience and calculation for comfortable self-preservation. It also goes against the technological imperative because it demands that we submit our doing to the necessities of absolute good, in obedience to which alone human beings can find their felicity.

Such a doctrine of freedom in obedience to justice also contradicts Grant's earlier understanding of freedom (i.e., in 'Two Theological Languages'). Under the influence of existentialism, Grant thought of biblical freedom as a freedom prior to good and evil. Later, as we have seen, Grant comes to understand freedom as finding fulfilment in obedience to the good, which reason can contemplate but not derive. This major shift in Grant's thinking over the years reveals how Weil and Plato came to define his reading of the Gospels and his understanding of biblical faith. Moreover, his understanding of Greek thought also shifts according to the influence of Weilian Platonism. The illumination of the intellect through reason and the desire for obedience to the good are both the fruit of divine grace. The affirmation of divine grace implies that 'the great things of our existing are given us, not made by us ... our making takes place within an ultimate givenness.'[75] This is central teaching for both Christianity and Platonism. This understanding of grace and freedom is also related to the Platonic doctrine of evil, in which evil can exist only as the absence, and not the opposite, of good. This in no way lessens the horror and intensity of evil in the world. Rather, it is a way of defining the existence of evil as the negation of good, a good hidden in all things insofar as they have come into existence through a loving creator.

But even though Grant wrote considerably about the unity of Plato and the Gospels during the 1970s and '80s, he never, finally, equated the two. Indeed, the point of distinction between the two was as important as were the grounds for their unity. The distinction is evident in Grant's shorthand definition of his faith as 'Plato plus the cross.'[76] It was the cross at the heart of the Gospels that distinguished and elevated the Gospels above Plato and established the primacy and truth of revelation above reason. To explain this difference, Grant frequently compared the deaths of Socrates and Christ. As he puts it in one place:

> Whatever must be said about the consummate serenity and beauty of Socrates at his execution, that scene is not as comprehensively close to the heart of being as are Gethsemane and Golgotha. The appalling admonition 'take up your cross and follow me' cuts to the heart of our existing and indeed to the heart of both being and goodness.[77]

For Grant, like Weil, the uniqueness of the Gospels was not in their revelation of the purity of Christ's goodness or love, but how this love was revealed from out of the depths of affliction. The fear, the sweating of blood, and the cry of dereliction represented a more 'archetypal' death because it was closer to the truth about the human condition in the world as well as the truth of the transcendent love of God revealing its power in the very midst of this condition.[78] The cross was a deeper testimony of the experience of divine absence as well as the fullness of divine presence to the eyes of trusting and open faith.

Grant explains the importance in the distinction between the two deaths more personally in an interview. He refers to the brutality and anguish of the deaths he witnessed during the war, and how the anguish and affliction of Christ is closer to that reality than the death of Socrates. Socrates died in calm control, while Jesus died in violent anguish and intense pain outside his control at the hands of others and with the feeling of God's absence.[79] It is this reality to which all human life is vulnerable, a reality which modern technology and optimistic liberalism want to veil, which is the reality Grant wants to engage through faith. If faith is real and if divine love is sovereign even through the evil and suffering in the world, then it must be experienced and thought at this level and within this reality. It is to experience and contemplate the 'perfection' of God in a world governed by brutal necessity and chance.

5.3.2. Being and Acting in the World: The Theology of the Cross, Weil, and Western Christianity

To be and to act positively in the world, then, one must be forever sensitive to the affliction of life in the world as possibility and actuality, as well as the transcendence/absence from or hiddenness of the good/God in relation to this reality. The cross is the central symbol of this reality and the gateway to redemption within and beyond it. Grant continues to be preoccupied with the concrete cases of affliction in the technological era, the tragedy of how good is crucified in this era, and how the purity of this good continues to shine miraculously even in the midst of the darkness of this era.[80] In order to bring these aspects together, Grant asserts the importance of faith, which, as we have seen, is a gift of God to those humbled and opened to receive it. But what is it that faith believes or sees positively? Here Grant's dependence on Weil and the theology of the cross come together most profoundly. In appealing to Weil for positive content for the meaning of faith, he places her thinking within the 'reformed'[81] tradition of Christianity in spite of her formal ignorance of that tradition, and he states that 'she is essentially a theologian of the cross.' Why this is so, according to Grant, is that she speaks about the distance of the world from God (the cross) as well as the commitment of God to the world which bridges this distance. The biblical statement 'God is love' means that God is always in relationship because 'love is always a relation.'[82] This also means that a God who is love must manifest this love in relation to all the afflicted in the world. God's love for the world God has created must be revealed to souls within the world, and it must transform these souls so that they see the world as God's world and, therefore, as beautiful and worthy to be loved.

In order for this to take place, several affirmations are essential. First, the love of God and the suffering of God, the creation and the passion, must be brought together. Following Weil, Grant believes that the suffering of God was denied in Western Christianity, and, as a result, the definition of God as love took on a different meaning. For Weil, the creation of the world was an act of self-renunciation on the part of God. Self-renunciation involves suffering, and a consent to suffering is essential for love. To love means to deny one's self and one's power to determine or define another according to one's own standard. It is to consent to the freedom and the right of another to exist freely. God's act of creation, which finds its culmination on the cross, is a perpetual act of self-renunciation. It reveals God's infinite consent to life lived outside God, even at the cost of being 'pushed out of the world' (Bonhoeffer). The act of reciprocation on the part of human creatures must be one of free consent, a consent to give one's self back to God in order to live in and out of God in relation to the world.[83]

According to the Western tradition of Christianity, however, creation was an act of self-expansion on the part of God. It was an exercise of power to determine and shape the world in a way that denies its beauty as it is. For Western Christianity, this has meant a commitment to change the world according to human determination. Human beings were co-creators with God, and the human will was in union with the divine will in the shaping of history. Such an understanding could only lead to a negative view of suffering, perceiving it as manifesting weakness and impotence before a world of evil. According to a theology of the cross, however, the divine response to human suffering is the suffering of God. Human suffering is taken up into God. On the cross, the distance between a God who is love and an afflicted, God-forsaken world is borne by God through God's suffering of this distance. On the cross, the distance between God and the creation is bridged. On the cross, the love of God unites the afflicted creation and the loving creator in Christ. Christ reveals the love of God active in him even in his agony and abandonment. Opening one's soul to this witness and power in the form of repentance, forgiveness, and purification is the means to salvation and to the illumination of the divine standard of justice in relation to the world. This also means that suffering is not only an evil to be overcome but a means to salvation for those who consent to their human fragility, and to the humbling and openness such consent can bring.[84]

The differing perspectives on the suffering of God according to a theology of the cross and the dominant Western tradition also find their corollary in their perspectives on the resurrection. Grant always confessed a difficulty in speaking about the resurrection. He preferred to point to artistic expressions of it rather than engaging in rational discourse about it. Nonetheless, he asserted that the way to understand the resurrection properly was with reference to the cross. He also referred to the twenty-first thesis of the Heidelberg disputation as providing the proper perspective for its understanding. The resurrection could never be asserted in a way that escaped or obscured the reality of affliction in the world. The true miracle of the resurrection was revealed on the cross. It was revealed as the divine love hidden, yet visible and active to the eyes of faith, a love that was not diminished nor corrupted even in the depths of suffering and abandonment. It was a love that was creative in the soul and through the soul, toward all living things. Such a love experienced, lived, and thought is consistent with an understanding of the resurrection as informed by a theology of the cross.[85]

The rejection of suffering in God and the 'triumphalist' interpretation of the resurrection also find their reference in the Western church. Grant attributes the beginnings of this movement, with hesitation, to Augustine. Even though he continues to hold the deepest reverence for Augustine and to recognize his Platonism in essential matters – namely, in his doctrine of evil as the absence of good – he also holds Augustine responsible for encouraging certain elements in the Western church to which its official status in the Roman Empire made it especially susceptible. The Western understanding of revelation and the cross was exclusive, rather than inclusive, and historical and particularistic, rather than universal. This criticism follows the teaching of Weil.[86] To argue against an exclusive understanding of revelation is not to suggest that the Hebrews or the early Christians did not receive a unique revelation of God. Both Grant and Weil recognized the uniqueness of the crucifixion of Christ as divine revelation. Rather, the concern was that divine revelation was not something that could be fenced in by human institutions. There was a mystery about the depths of revelation that could not be comprehended by human thought or attained by human sanctity. This also meant that the cross was not simply a historical event that happened some two thousand years ago, but a symbol of human reality as a whole – its affliction as well as the divine possibilities of redemption hidden within it.

Moreover, the particularistic, historical focus of Western Christianity also encouraged an idolatrous understanding of divine providence in the world. Here again, the cross revealed the working of divine providence beyond human understanding and human control, even the control of the church. This was not to deny the truth of divine providence in the world. Grant always affirmed the sovereignty of the divine in the world. The reality of evil (the cross), however, made such an affirmation one of faith rather than of sight. One was called to trust in and be open to the divine working in the world even though one was confronted more immediately by the divine absence – evil and suffering within a world indifferent to God's love. To declare the scrutability of providence, then, was to lower one's vision of God, on the one hand (idolatry), and to trivialize the evil and suffering in the world, on the other (insensitivity). It was to call evil good and good evil, rather than to say the thing is as it is.[87]

This criticism of Western Christianity was not meant to deny the importance of history. As was stated earlier, a God who is love had to be in concrete relationship with real people, and real people existed in history. Moreover, it was the task of serious thought to relate God's love to the particular contexts of time and place in history. Yet the language of love stood in contrast to the language of will, and the language of contemplation to that of rational speculation. Even though the Western tradition of Christianity debated intensely the doctrine of the human will in relation to God and the world, the language of will in a progressively secularizing civilization could not but deify the human will vis-à-vis all life in the world. This is why Grant preferred the language of love to that of will when speaking about God. This is also why he felt that mysticism was better able to convey the experience of God than philosophy. Without a denial of human self-centredness, God could not be experienced let alone thought authentically, nor could human beings be opened within for transformation in their relationships in the world. Indeed, the philosophy of the will in Christianity eventually led to the modern progressivism of liberalism and, finally, to the will to will of the technological era, which holds no principles above the human will for being and acting in the world.[88]

And yet Grant also came to see the redemptive side of history in relation to Christianity and the technological era. The end of Christianity as the official religion of the West in the technological era was not necessarily the end of Christianity itself. Rather, it was the end of the Western expression of it in terms of human speculation and will, the scrutability of divine providence, triumphalism, and optimistic hopes about human nature and community. The understanding of the world according to modern science as governed by necessity and chance was more consistent with a theology of the cross and a Platonic philosophy than it was with a theology of glory and an Aristotelian philosophy. The latter believes that the good is attainable through human intellectual and moral possibilities in the world. The former believes that the world is a 'kind of nothingness.' Consequently, one must be opened to a good outside the world as it is without at the same time negating the beauty and goodness of the world. Grant also speaks about two traditions within Christian theology: the positive and the negative. 'The positive tradition moves to God through the world; the negative tradition moves to God by negating the world. The negative tradition is in essence Platonism, and the positive tradition is, in its essence Aristotelianism ...'[89] Following Weil, Grant associates necessity and chance with evil and suffering in the world. It follows, then, that one must either be insensitive to this reality or underestimate its destructive impact on life in order to argue for some good purpose according to the evidence of human history, morality, or insight. Rather, one must depend on a revelation of the good/God which comes upon one as 'an entire surprise,' opening one up to a truth outside the world or deeply hidden within it (hidden because of the brutal facts of reality). This also implies that thinking about the good is 'darkened' in our world. To say it is darkened is not to say, like Nietzsche, that it is extinguished. Nor is it to say, like Ellul and Barth, that it shines forth clearly for the believer.[90] To say it is darkened is to affirm the good through faith (which includes doubt) rather than through sight, and in open faithful waiting rather than in cynicism or despair.

But how does such an orientation in faith and thought affect one's practice in the world? When one consents to a good that is beyond one's moral and intellectual possibilities, as well as the possibilities within history, one also finds fulfilment in surrender and obedience to this good and not in one's own definition or standard of good. According to the theology of the cross, then, the first step to practice is a denial of self and will, and an openness to a good that transcends oneself. The power of movement toward the good is a gift of grace arising from the good itself – that is, the Holy Spirit. This good is defined by Grant and Weil as love, and it is love that must be obeyed and become the source of transformation in the soul. Of course, it is Christ crucified who is the supreme revelation of divine love: pure, unconditional, and uncompromising. But what is the form that love must take concretely in the world? For Grant and Weil, it is justice. Justice, too, is revealed and defined most supremely on the cross. It is the highest form of justice to act in obedience to love in all one's relations in the world, even in a world governed by brutal necessity and chance. The supreme act of justice is Christ's forgiveness of his torturers and the thief beside him, who of all people may have deserved the cross but receives unconditional mercy.[91] This understanding of justice in no way denies the critical, judgmental side of justice. Love demands that justice include judgment. Yet judgment must always serve the greater requirements of love. To love one's enemies does not mean one must not recognize and address the evil in their thoughts and actions. Love demands that judgment serve the reintegration of criminals back to wholeness by sensitizing them to the weight of their evil and its consequences. Weil and Grant understood the importance of penal justice if carried out with the greatest respect for the dignity and humanity of the criminal.

Such an understanding of love and justice, however, also offers a unique understanding of suffering. Suffering is both an evil to be alleviated and a good to be consented to. Consenting to suffering is not being passive toward it. Rather, it is consenting to one's limits, moral and physical, in the face of a greater necessity. The value of such consent is that it sensitizes one to the reality of evil and suffering, in one's self and one's world. It humbles one into recognizing that evil and suffering cannot, finally, be overcome completely through human capacities, since humanity is corrupt and fallen. Such humility and sensitivity can then also open one up to the appreciation of the existence and beauty of otherness. This, of course, is always a struggle for human beings living in the world. In Weil's terminology, it is the struggle between divine grace seeking to enter the human soul and the pull of gravity corrupting the soul with evil. Grant refers to the struggle between grace and gravity within his own soul. He speaks about his difficulty in dealing with other professors who have given themselves over to the scientific, technological spirit of the age by treating religion as data for scientific research and objective analysis. Even though Grant has a difficult time consenting to this necessity, he is also able, through Weil's insight and an understanding of necessity, to deny himself and his ego, and give up the spirit of revenge and hatred that poisons his soul and prevents love from rising within him.[92]

Grant also speaks about how the language and ideas of self-renunciation and consent to suffering are so foreign to the technological era. In an age when comfort and entertainment are considered the measure of happiness, the idea of a higher justice which makes stringent demands on being and acting in the world is far from attractive.[93] The idea that one must find one's happiness by denying oneself and one's conveniences for the sake of loving another, and loving another in a brutal world where everyone is vulnerable to evil and suffering, turns on its head the thinking of this era. Yet at a time when the only alternative to the last men so described are the nihilists who will for the sake of willing and out of a hatred for the earth, the demands of justice according to a theology of the cross have never been more relevant or necessary.

Throughout his writing, Grant offered many directives and examples of what type of acting in the world would be faithful to being according to a theology of the cross. This continues in the 1970s and '80s. Whereas Nietzsche and Marx counsel the importance of changing the world as the greatest imperative, Plato and Weil speak of consenting to the world and to the life within it. Only then do we have the right and obligation to change it.[94] We have already considered Grant's difficulty in consenting to the world as it is. This difficulty was related to the evil and suffering which so pervade the world in the technological era. The focus on change can be motivated by love in the form of a desire for justice and the alleviation of suffering. But consent is essential for gaining wisdom about human possibilities and limitations, as well as the reality and goodness of the other one is seeking to change. Liberalism may serve as a secularized Christianity insofar as its reformism is motivated by love, but its naïve optimism also tends to arrogant pride, on the one hand, and insensitivity toward otherness, on the other. Changing the world can become self-centred and destructive. This is all too evident in an era when change has become idolized as an end in itself beyond the recognition of otherness as sacred. Such a recognition immediately places a limit on one's right to change the world for the sake of convenience or comfort.

Grant's hesitation in emphasizing change over consent vis-à-vis the world gave many, as we have seen, the impression that he was a pessimist and an anti-liberal. In a letter, he writes about how much this saddens him. Although he admits that he is, at times, guilty of the sin of despair, as a Christian he knows this sin must be overcome. At the same time, however, the virtue of hope, which is an obligation for the Christian, must not make one pretend the world is better than it is.

Grant then quotes Luther's 'great phrase' (The thing is as it is). Furthermore, Grant also wants to resist the temptation within certain forms of Christianity to insist too strongly on accepting the world as it is. This can induce an indifference to the evil and suffering in the world which can and should be changed.[95] To participate in changing the world without entertaining grand hopes outside reality as it is, and with a reverence for and consent to all that is, is a difficult theoretical and practical stance to maintain. But it is possible!

Grant makes repeated reference to specific types of action and to specific people who act in the spirit of a theology of the cross – Weil being the most obvious example. Grant also writes about one of his students killed in an automobile accident. This student represented the necessary balance between contemplation and charity, being and acting in the world, to the highest degree. He was, on the one hand, enraptured with his studies of Weil, Plato, and the Bible, along with the music of Bach and Mozart, and, on the other hand, was deeply concerned about the environmental degradation of the earth in the technological era. Human beings had lost sight of their place in the universe. Even though he did not believe that enough people would be awakened to this growing problem in order to avert eventual disaster, he did not 'withdraw into pessimism.' He believed in the meaning of life beyond human determination and that 'it is sometimes necessary and good to fight in a lost cause in order to assert that meaning.' Because of his obedience to a justice above him, he was prepared to deny himself and to die. But such a dying was rooted in a commitment to the world and to life. This meant that he 'could not rest in negation even in a time of negation.' A vision of the particular evil and suffering of the technological era was 'only valuable when it is the occasion for searching through to the noble roots of human existing.' In leaving his studies for the life of action, he was not deluded by a false optimism about the possibility of success in his cause. 'He was not touched by the modern blasphemy [calling good evil and evil good] about being on the side of history (that is, the side of worldly success).' He did know, however, that it is always 'necessary to keep certain flags flying even when it is likely that flag will finally go down before the superior forces of unreason.'[96] It was an immeasurable tragedy that such a man was taken from the world, a man who truly reflected the beauty of the divine image hidden in the world as it was. Yet it was the possibility of such being and acting in the world that kept Grant from being a pessimist.

The positive relationship between Plato and the Gospels, as well as the thinking and acting in the world consistent with a theology of the cross, are taken up and brought together most powerfully in Grant's last major essay, 'Faith and the Multiversity.'

5.3.3. 'Faith and the Multiversity': The Culmination of the Search for Clarity of Vision

This essay, Grant once declared, contains the reasons why he is a Christian.[97] It focuses on the challenge of faith in the technological era, and especially where this touches Grant personally – life in the modern university. The purpose of the essay is to establish grounds for knowing which are faithful to reality as it is in the technological era, but also informed by a revelation of the good apprehended through faith and experienced as love. Grant's discussion proceeds in the manner of an exegesis of a statement made by Weil about faith: 'Faith is the experience that the intelligence is enlightened by love.'[98] In an earlier version of the essay, Grant defines love as 'attention to otherness, receptivity of otherness, consent to otherness.'[99] To love another, one must have paid attention to them and received something of who they are and the goodness of their being. The human instincts for survival and self-centredness make the reality of otherness almost disappear for us. According to Plato, the tyrant is the worst human being because his self-centredness has caused otherness to disappear for him.

But why is it that we ought to love otherness? The love of otherness is rooted in the experience of apprehending otherness as beautiful. Such apprehension is an experience open to everyone, but it depends on one's openness to receive it and be shaped by it. Those whom we name 'saints' are those who have been enlightened by the beauty of otherness even when otherness appears to be ugly and brutal. This is incomprehensible in an era when beauty is thought to be in the eye of the beholder, or simply something subjective determined by the variety of necessities and chances that have marked our desires. According to this view, beauty is a value determined by the human agent and dependent on her or his loves. It is not an affirmation which we trust because we have been touched by a love beyond us, a love which opens us up to the beauty of otherness. Otherness is simply viewed as an object to be known, not something which must be loved in order to be known properly. In both the Platonic and biblical languages, however, love and beauty are linked to the knowledge of otherness. Love and beauty are images of a transcendent good/God above the human knower which enlightens the knower in his or her quest for knowledge. The assumption of trust is one that must carry the knower through the darkness of reality into the hidden beauty of all things, marred as they are by evil and suffering. The uniqueness of biblical revelation is not its assertion of the ultimate goodness of all things, but 'the fact that Christ declares the price of goodness in the face of evil.'[100] This is also consistent with the Platonic language which affirms the ultimate cause of being to be beneficence. And this affirmation has been made by people who have been marked by war, torture, disease, starvation, and the cruel accidents of existing. They recognized that these evils were best understood as deprivations of good, and they often had to affirm this teaching in trust rather than in sight. The doubts arising in their souls as a consequence of the experience of the absence of good were addressed within a larger framework of trust in the goodness of life and the world in spite of reality as it appeared to be.

Grant then considers the reasons why modern science rejected the affirmation of the goodness of all that is as the basis for knowing. This affirmation was made in the West primarily through an Aristotelian science, which argued for a teleological understanding of the universe based on the workings of nature. It was also supported by the church, which went on to identify this *telos* with its own quest for power. Many, however, eventually rejected this understanding of science 'so triumphally used': 'The more representable the purpose of the whole was said to be, the more this natural theology became a trivializing, a blasphemy against the cross.'[101]

For modern science, this implied that in order for the whole to be understood as it is, it had to be understood outside the idea of an overriding purpose or *telos*. It had to be understood as determined by necessity and chance. Faith, however, could not rest on this understanding of the whole as sufficient. Faith was rooted in an experience that the intellect was enlightened by love and, therefore, was open to apprehend the whole, which includes otherness, as beautiful. But does such an affirmation of beauty rooted in faith not lead knowledge into the kind of blasphemous assertions of purpose condemned by modern science and the theology of the cross? Are we not 'led to assert that evil is good and good is evil, and so lose what is essential in any love of truth – namely the continual recognition that the world is as it is'? What Grant wants to develop, then, is a way of speaking about the good/God and about purpose (providence) which recognizes the experience of love in relation to the world without, at the same time, trivializing the evil and suffering within it. In so doing, he would offer an alternative way of being and acting in the world than that offered by the scientific, technological paradigm.

Following Weil and Kant, Grant argues that beauty provides us with a sense of purposiveness, but its good transcends us. To explain this, he compares the modern understanding of art with art as understood by Mozart. The purpose of modern art is entertainment. It has been given this purpose by human beings, and thus it has little power to transform. Art understood according to Mozart, however, provides us with an experience of beauty whose goodness we can affirm unqualifiedly, but whose purpose transcends human determination. Grant relates Mozart's own account of inspiration when writing music. The music comes to him as a revelation, mystically, and he opens himself to receive it and express it. What is it that he is receiving? Certainly it is music. But with the music comes love, a love which fills the one open to receive it. This same love then inspires the artist or knower, who can now see beauty more clearly, in her or his vision of the world. Ideas of spiritual receptivity and intellectual intuition are foreign to modern forms of thought, rooted as they are in a Kantian affirmation of human autonomy and freedom. If the human being alone is the determining agent, how can there be a place for openness to something beyond one's intellect and understanding?[102]

The difficulty with 'partaking' in the beauty of the world is 'the misery, the hardness, the sadness of so much of our lives, which is caused not only by the ugliness in ourselves, but by the very conditions of the non-human world.' Scientific, technological mastery of nature was intended to overcome this evil and suffering. But to do this, it also had to contemplate the world with a desire to change it, rather than with open love, ready to receive a vision of its beauty. If the world is seen simply as necessity, or worse, as a resource, it cannot be apprehended as beautiful. The beauty of the world manifests itself to us most concretely in the beauty of other people. Grant points to the modern preoccupation with sexuality, in which the other is seen as an instrument for our calculated self-engrossment and pleasure. In the past, however, sexual relations with another human being were considered so sacred that restraints and obligations were placed upon them in order to protect their sacredness. Moreover, loving and knowing were considered interdependent. Loving was necessary to knowing the other, and therefore it could not be self-centred. In the modern era, however, love is associated with the emotions and is thought of as 'blind.'

The classic teachings about the interdependence of loving and knowing are found in Plato and the Gospels. Plato's definition of justice as a rendering to each his/her due is a classic example of how loving is linked to knowing. In order to know justice, one has to desire it, and as desire for it grows, so does one's knowledge of it. The Gospels' contribution to this teaching is in the revelation of what is due to human beings and its ultimate fulfilment. On the cross, 'a tortured being says of his torturers that their due is to be forgiven.'[103]

This also means that knowing is linked to one's being and acting in the world. One's openness to divine love – which opens one up to the beauty of the world one seeks to know – is also a call to love the world in one's actions. As Weil declared, 'matter is our infallible judge.' This, of course, is not easy. The demands of justice in relation to the necessities of the world can lead to great suffering. It is an incredible challenge for one to open oneself and one's intelligence to be enlightened by love in all its concrete implications. Grant asks us to 'contemplate what happens to those who have been deeply illuminated by love.'[104] For some, the desire for justice (the good due to others) has possessed them so deeply that they have become completely 'transparent to justice.' Most of us, however, are far from that level of commitment to love. Love of the good becomes little more than love of our own, and sometimes nothing more than love of ourselves and our own interests. Thus, justice appears to us and to the majority of people as extremely unattractive. It is not easy to know justice because it is not easy to love it. But those who have come to love justice have also been enlightened in their knowledge of justice in relation to the necessities of the world. And, in knowing and loving justice, they have come to a vision of its beauty. The apparent ugliness of justice arises from our own discomfort with, if not fear of, its demands. Justice demands the giving up of our own conveniences, comforts, and self-centred preoccupations. These are painful to give up. Yet the process of self-renunciation is an aspect of love and essential to knowing.

Such an understanding of love, however, is completely foreign to the modern consciousness. Any truth which transcends one and makes demands of one beyond one's determination and interests requires a faith in something beyond oneself – a knowledge of good that we do not measure or define but by which we are measured and defined. It demands an affirmation that 'we are not our own.' Thus, the idea of receptivity, reverence, openness, and trust before a greater good which reveals itself to us as love and transforms us in our relations with otherness, is unthinkable today. The idea that the beauty of otherness can somehow humble and inspire us to contemplate otherness and the universe as a whole without desiring to change it, is also unthinkable. Again, this is not to deny the good things modern technology has brought us. Nor is it a denial of liberal principles, which arose as a revolt against the false basis of transcendence established in the hierarchies of church and society in pre-modern times. Nonetheless, the destitution of spirit in our era is evident when beauty can be thought of as little more than entertainment and justice as nothing but the result of self-interested calculation.[105]

Grant's more particular concern in this essay is with those people in the university who, like himself, have been enlightened in their intellect by love and beauty, however poorly. How can people of faith live intellectually serious lives in the university? In modern science and technology, which dominate the priorities and focus of the university, a separation is made between beauty and truth. Truth is an objective reality cut off from the subjective realm where value judgments and emotions reside. The problem is that it is very difficult to maintain this separation altogether. Grant points to the example of contemporary biologists who argue for the preservation of endangered species. If otherness is not beautiful and if the world is simply a resource, why is it worth preserving the life within it, and particularly life that does not touch one in any immediate way? The scientific, technological vision of the world may have brought us many benefits, but its barrenness is pressing in upon us in ever increasing intensity. How can a person of faith be opened to the truth of the goodness and beauty of all that is in an era that denies this truth in thought and practice?

Grant concludes by offering two possible responses to this reality for a believer whose intellect has been enlightened by love. The first is based on a statement by Dostoevsky:

> I believe that there is nothing finer, deeper, more lovable, more reasonable, braver, and more perfect than Christ ... More than that; if anyone told me that Christ is outside truth, and if it had been really established that truth is outside Christ, I would prefer to stay with Christ than the truth.[106]

Grant qualifies this statement by stating that Dostoevsky was one who knew the truth about the cross and about human evil and suffering firsthand. Yet he also affirmed the priority of faith in the truth of Christ even when that truth was contradicted in the world. This is important for so many in the modern university for whom the truth of the good is killed by their exposure to the scientific, technological paradigm. The second possible response is offered by Weil, who states:

> One can never wrestle enough with God if one does so out of pure regard for the truth. Christ likes us to prefer truth to him because, before being Christ, he is truth. If one turns aside from him to go towards the truth, one will not go far before falling into his arms.[107]

Weil was one who could focus on the truth without being diverted or distracted. She had a capacity of intellect and a purity of spirit that made her uniquely gifted in this regard. But how possible is this for most people, asks Grant? How can one reach through the modern paradigm into the truth that the world proceeds from the good/God through love? Dostoevsky's response is more accessible for the believer. But Weil's level of commitment to the truth, even through the darkness of the modern paradigm of necessity and chance without the consolations of faith, is the standard toward which every believer must strive.

Grant concludes the essay with an appendix in which he asks two questions. Why use philosophy, and the philosophy of Plato in particular, in order to describe the essence of Christianity when Christianity appears to have little concern with philosophy? And why, if he must use philosophy, does he not use the philosophy of a more contemporary thinker than Plato? To answer these questions, one must consider how close Plato's teaching is to that of the Gospels. In spite of the difference between the deaths of Christ and Socrates, both Platonism and Christianity call human beings to self-renunciation. Both agree that knowledge of otherness depends on our love of otherness. Platonic *eros* and Christian *agape* are very close in meaning. Consent to otherness also involves a need in so doing. Human obligation and fulfilment are rooted in the same good/God. The language of receptivity in Platonism is consistent with the concept of divine grace in Christianity. Our capacity to fulfil love's demands and the satisfaction such fulfilment offers us are both gifts of grace. Openness to receive and trust that we will receive are also gifts of divine grace. Both teach that freedom is not our essence, but rather, the liberty of being indifferent to the good/God. Both teach that existence is a gift rather than a self-propelled reality. Finally, both affirm the ultimate unknowability and mystery of goodness. The good/God may be experienced personally, but its larger purposes transcend our comprehension. Without this agnosticism, we 'move to the great lie that evil is good and good evil. In Christian language this great lie is to say that providence is scrutable.'[108]

But why depend on Plato and not on a more contemporary philosopher? Grant compares Plato to Heidegger, the greatest of modern philosophers. Heidegger, however, is a follower of Nietzsche in excluding Christianity from his quest for truth and in declaring that God is dead. This can only mean that faith and morality are also dead since they are based on an unreality. Again, Grant is concerned with those in the modern universities who are believers. How can one think the faith (with its implications for justice in the world) in a way that is intelligible and meaningful within the technological era, and without losing the truth of faith altogether?

Here, again, Grant's concern is reflected in the modern methodological debate in Protestant theology between Kerygmatic and Apologetic approaches.[109] Does one simply unfold revelation positively without engaging in conscious dialogue with modern thinking and existing, or does one try to find points of contact for such a dialogue? In affirming the importance of philosophy for making intelligible the truths of the faith experience, Grant is certainly more an apologist than Barth. In finding it difficult to find any positive point of contact with modern thinking at its best, he is less of an apologist than Tillich. There is, however, a negative point of contact which may offer a gateway into a movement forward. Grant comes together with Nietzsche and Heidegger in their rejection of Western Christianity. According to Grant,

western Christianity simplified the divine love by identifying it too closely with immanent power in the world. Both Protestants and Catholics became triumphalist by failing to recognize the distance between the order of good and the order of necessity. So they became exclusivist and imperialist, arrogant and dynamic. They now face the results of that failure.

And further,

modern scientists, by placing before us the seamless web of necessity and chance, which excludes the lovable, may help reteach us the truth about the distance which separates the orders of good and necessity.

However, whereas Nietzsche and Heidegger think this truth to have negated Christianity in essence, Grant sees it to be the means to Christianity's salvation:

> The web of necessity which the modern paradigm lays before us does not tell us that God is dead, but reminds us of what Western Christianity seemed to forget in its moment of pride: how powerful is the necessity that love must cross. Christianity did not produce its own gravediggers, but the means to its own purification.[110]

This is Grant's response to Nietzsche and Heidegger, and to the technological era unfolded at its height through them.

Dialogue with the world is possible, and there is a point of contact between faith and the modern scientific, technological understanding of the world as governed by necessity and chance. Grant, following Weil and the theology of the cross, believes this understanding is more faithful to reality as it is than the teleological understanding of the universe of pre-modern Western thought as influenced by Aristotle. But this is only a partial truth, resting on a negation. The negation is important as preparation for the positive experience of the good/God, but a good/God which transcends our thoughts and wills and comes to us when we are humbled and opened to receive it. Only then are we enlightened in our intellects and wills, and only then are we opened to see the world not merely as necessity and chance – that is, life as meaningless and vulnerable before evil and suffering (the visible side of the cross) – but as made in the image of the good/God and, therefore, beautiful and worthy to be loved (the good/God hidden beneath the cross).

The possibility of a more genuine faith opened up by the truth about the universe taught by modern science does not only have implications for Christianity in the technological era, but for Western civilization as a whole. Even though we cannot portend the future, as modern liberalism has tried to do, we can be open to see the space created for a more redemptive relationship of human beings with the world. The response of the technological era to the modern scientific paradigm has been to reject any place for love of otherness (human and non-human) in its quest for knowledge. The dead end of the theoretical and practical implications of this response are becoming all too evident, and it has been a major part of Grant's work to bring this out. But the understanding of Christianity through the cross offers an alternative response: consenting to the world as it is, not as we dream that it is or that it should be (liberalism), nor merely as necessity and chance (Nietzsche and Heidegger), but as beautiful and, therefore, an image of the absolute good/God out of which it has come forth. It is on the basis of such thinking that one is then opened to redemptive avenues for being and acting in the world.

Conclusion

In this book, we have argued that George Grant's thought is best understood and appreciated in the light of a particular theological orientation/tradition which animates and illuminates the critical and constructive dimensions of his thought. We have argued that the context of Grant's formation and education, combined with his war experience and 'conversion,' fuelled a crisis in his thinking and existing to which the theological tradition known as the 'theology of the cross' offered an answer. Grant discovered this tradition through his studies at Oxford and, particularly, in his struggle with the thought of John Oman. The points at which he affirms Oman's thought, as well as those at which he finds him wanting, push Grant further toward this theological tradition. We have also argued that Grant associated this tradition with Luther, and even though he did not study Luther in any depth, he understood the meaning of this tradition in Luther's sense. He also used Luther's words from the Heidelberg theses to express the critical and constructive tasks of his thought.

The critical task forms the bulk of Grant's writing, and he understood it to be necessary preparation for the positive task. It involved 'bringing to light the darkness as darkness' of the modern technological civilization spearheaded by the North American empire and spreading throughout the globe. This also involved describing this civilization 'as it is.' In this regard, Grant would be illuminated by Weil and existentialism in the 1950s, Ellul, Strauss, and Sherrard in the 1960s, and Nietzsche, Heidegger, and Céline in the 1970s and '80s. The limitations of these thinkers (Weil excluded) were located, not in their critical reflection on modern civilization, but rather in their constructive proposals for overcoming the crisis of the modern. It was their

critical rather than constructive contributions which were most significant in shaping Grant's thought.

At the same time, the critical task of bringing to light the darkness,
as darkness and describing the thing as it is, involved a criticism of all
forms of thought that obscured the truth about technological civilization, made it seem better than it was, and/or fuelled its expansion. In
this camp, Grant would place modern liberalism in all its religious and
secular forms, characterizing it essentially as a theology of glory. Liberalism was characterized as such, not because of its principles of justice,
founded as they were on Christianity, but because of its optimism
about human nature and destiny in the world without God as transcendent ground. In later years, Grant perceived the 'glory' of liberalism to be fading rapidly in Western society. The expanding historicist
and nihilist technological forces had a diminishing need for liberalism's theoretical support, while finding its moral principles burden-
some and limiting. Grant's preference for liberalism over the newer
historicism brings out his sympathy for it and his lament over its
decline in the West in a way not displayed in his earlier work.

The standard for Grant's sympathy for and criticism of modern liberalism, and the technological civilization it was instrumental in bringing forth, was based on ancient philosophy, particularly that of Plato,
combined with pre-modern affirmations of Christianity, especially the
'Eastern' Christian understanding of the Gospels. Plato's philosophy
stood opposed to that of Aristotle, who was associated with the Western tradition and the theology of glory. Eastern Christianity was linked
to Platonic influences in Christian doctrine, mysticism, and the 'negative' theological, philosophical tradition. Grant's attitude toward
Augustine and Luther was ambivalent; he saw them as within the
Western tradition, and yet as affirming theological, philosophical
truths which are of the essence of the Eastern tradition. Grant's standard of truth and authenticity in both philosophy and Christianity was
shaped, above all, by Simone Weil. Her thought combined with her life
represented the highest standard for truth in philosophy and Christianity. She unfolded for him the meaning of the Gospels and the Platonic philosophical tradition at its best. She also provided the negative
(critical) and positive (constructive) voice for what the theology of the
cross meant to Grant in relation to modern technological civilization.

Under the guidance of Weil and the inspiration of the theology of the
cross, Grant proceeded in later years to articulate the constructive task
of his thought, a task which he also expressed earlier, albeit in more

concealed forms. This task was complicated because of Grant's difficulty in consenting to love God, and the world through God, even in
the face of the technological necessity that had so engulfed it. Grant
struggled to open himself to the good hidden beneath the evil and suffering brought on by this necessity. He saw that a world which, according to modern science, was understood to be governed by necessity
and chance, also confronted human beings with the truth about their
fragile and finite physical and moral condition in the world. This,
Grant came to realize, was also necessary (negative) preparation for a
more genuine openness to the good/God which transcended the
world as it was. Such an openness had been hindered in the West by
the predominance of various theologies of glory which portrayed reality better than it was. Only as people were brought to the end of their
false assumptions about their intellectual, moral, and physical capacities; only as they were brought face to face with their failures and
imperfections – in particular, the technological civilization and their
deluded hopes about this civilization; only then was there room for
genuine hope to arise. Only then was there hope that people would be
humbled and opened to see the world from another perspective – that
is, as proceeding from the good/God – and seek to understand the
world by loving it and treading reverently within it. Grant, nonetheless, never mistook his hopes for divine providence. His task was to
bring out the truth and sow the seeds of openness: openness before a
good/God whose witness was revealed in mediated form in the world,
and particularly in the cross of Christ, but also one which transcended
the world and human comprehension. Grant's hope was based on faith
(trust), not on sight. His faith was rooted in a knowledge of the good/
God based on love seeking to understand, and not on empirical certainty seeking to dominate, manipulate, and control.

Of the numerous critics of Grant's thought, it is important to distinguish those who have misunderstood his thought or failed to grasp the
theological, philosophical orientation behind it, from those who have
appreciated his insights but remain unsatisfied. Many have characterized Grant as a 'pessimist' and criticize his 'negativity' about the
world. For some, it is Grant's damning indictment of technological globalization that is difficult to accept. Far from being a development
destructive of human freedom and meaning, technological necessity
could help these flourish in ever new and broader ways. Others have
taken stock of Grant's message of warning but cannot agree with his
analysis completely. Human beings are still sufficiently free to reject or

reverse technological expansion. Some liberal critics go even further by pointing to positive signs of hope in movements of resistance and community-building. It is not that Grant was unable to see these signs or affirm the possibilities of human freedom. Rather, it was the fact that he was too deeply marked by the fragility and vulnerability of all life in the face of evil and suffering in the world, and particularly as these resulted from technological globalization. Grant could not bear to fall into the category of those who called good evil and evil good, failing to declare the thing as it is and, consequently, trivializing the affliction in the world.

But was this pessimism? For liberal critics whose hopes were limited or reduced to the horizontal plane of history, Grant's systematic criticism could not but be pessimistic. For those who saw hope in broader terms, however, Grant's criticism was necessary preparation for the birth of genuine hope.[1] Such hope was not based on a particular historical outcome, although it was not afraid of taking sides and fighting for justice even when it was a losing proposition. Rather, it was based on a denial of self and an openness to a good/God which measured and defined the purpose of life by a standard that transcended the particular and historical, while illuminating thought and practice within them. If history was too often a chronicle of the crucifixion of justice, this was not a matter of perceiving reality pessimistically, but truthfully.

Others have suggested a tendency for otherworldly escapism in Grant. Although Grant may not, finally, have capitulated to this tendency, the influence of Weil tempted him in this direction. She, it is said, weakened his commitment to this world.[2] The whole argument of this book, however, would counter this view in the strongest possible terms. Weil was not only a mystic but an activist who finally died in the name of her concrete commitments to the oppressed of her people. This truth about her inspired Grant as much as her mysticism and Platonism. Being a 'saint' was not about consenting to the world by escaping it, but by living in it and embracing it with all its suffering and affliction. Consenting to or loving the world also meant loving all those precious things vulnerable to destruction. It was also being confronted by the impossibility of this task on the purely human and historical plane of purpose and meaning without calling good evil and evil good. It was only out of this broken, suffering love, and a confrontation with oneself and one's world as they were, that there was any hope for human redemption. This also required the giving up of illusions based on human personality or history and the acceptance of human finitude, vulnerability, and fragility in the world.

But Grant also knew of the possibility of the experience of a good/ God which transcended the horizontal plane and opened one up to a vertical plane of inspiration and illumination. He knew of the possibility of an openness to loving the world based on humility, honesty, and self-denial, without false hopes and illusions which prevented one from being genuinely attentive to otherness. Only then would it also be possible to change the world without abusing it or using it to serve one's own self-centred ends. The paradoxical teaching of the theology of the cross is that only by taking stock of the critical truth about humanity and the world, and being broken by it, is it then possible to be opened to the good hidden within the world. Only then does one come to realize that one needs to be broken and changed to see reality differently – from God's perspective. The cross of Christ is that point of contact. The cross is the lens through which one must look at the world as it is, as well as the divine possibilities which reveal themselves in the very midst of it.

Against those who suggest that Grant did not make clear what the theology of the cross meant to him, or the relationship of Plato, Weil, and the Gospels through which it was expressed,[3] we have argued the contrary. We have argued that Grant did express the meaning of the theology of the cross, and he expressed it through the influence of Weil's understanding of Plato and the Gospels combined with his own experiences of faith and life in the world. But could Grant have done this better? Here, we will suggest, there is room for critical reflection. Grant's singular condemnation of Western Christianity, his ambivalence about Augustine and Luther, and his limited understanding of contemporary Protestant theology, may have weakened the clarity and coherence of his positive message.

First, Grant failed to appreciate fully the dissenting voices within the Western church which attacked its tendency toward a theology of glory in theory and practice. Moreover, even though Grant preferred a theology and philosophy based on the language of love rather than will, and perceived the language of will to be at the centre of Western thinking, he did not, at the same time, appreciate to what degree the theologies of Augustine, Luther, and even Calvin agreed with him in this regard. Their teachings were rooted in a complete denial of the autonomous human will and a complete affirmation of divine grace as the basis for human salvation. The human will could only find its expression in subservience and obedience to God. Whether these theologians could avoid speaking in the language of will altogether in a context where this was the spoken language, is another matter.[4]

Finally, and perhaps most critically, Grant's few references to contemporary Protestant theology, and to neo-orthodox theology in particular, reveal a significant lack of understanding. Indeed, neo-orthodox theology can be credited with reintroducing Luther's theology of the cross into the modern context of global war, and the evil and suffering it fuelled. Moreover, neo-orthodox theologians such as Barth and Brunner, as well as theologians within its broader stream such as Bonhoeffer, Tillich, and Niebuhr, were all united in their rejection of nineteenth-century liberalism in philosophy and theology for reasons similar to those of Grant. In speaking about Christian hope, they did not see it as a human possibility or an inevitable outcome of history, nor did they subscribe to the progressive doctrine of providence. Rather, the kingdom of heaven on earth was a divine possibility and one of infinite distance from and radical discontinuity with the world as it was. They, too, understood the distance separating the necessary from the good, although they used biblical language to express it. They, too, came to experience salvation as rooted in the cross. They understood salvation as being opened to the truth of things as they are, but also as they could be through a union with the crucified one who spoke the eternal word of forgiveness and compassion from the cross. But being biblical theologians, they also spoke about hope. Their understanding of hope was one rooted in a commitment to this world without calling good evil and evil good but the thing as it is, one that embraced the light that could never be extinguished even in the darkness of the technological era.

Such an understanding of biblical hope is expressed in more contemporary and contextual terms by Douglas John Hall. In explicit dialogue with Grant, he writes about the possibilities for an alternative vision of faith and life in the technological era. First, he speaks of the possibility of an 'indigenous theology of the cross' for North America which would offer a 'paradigm' or 'frame of reference' for the 'prolonged and intense experience of negation.' Second, such a theology would develop 'foundations for raising and meeting the question of limits' and an ethical sensitivity for the limits within which human beings should live. Finally, such a theology would 'call into being a community whose most conspicuous mark would be the frustration of its every attempt to have a theology of glory' and one 'which is prepared to suffer.'[5] As a theologian of the cross, Hall is not predicting such an outcome as either inevitable or even probable, and every struggle to think and act positively must also have the courage to face failure. Nonetheless, he is also open to signs of hope in the emergence of ways of thinking and existing within the faith community which are consciously post-Christian (at the end of Western Christianity). He is encouraged by the rise of critical minorities within this community who are also leading the process of rethinking the faith, as well as by the growing ecumenical nature of the church which brings poorer Christians from more oppressed contexts into dialogue with those in the West, whose context is the legacy of global oppression.[6] For all his brilliant insight and penetrating analysis of technological civilization under the critical scrutiny of a theology of the cross, Grant could only have been further enriched by dialogue with contemporary theologians of the cross. For all his openness to the good/God which transcends this world as it is and yet illuminates one's being and acting in the world through faith, Grant's thought would have reflected greater theological clarity if it had been developed in partnership with contemporary theologians struggling to affirm similar ideas. Grant could have found support among those theologians who struggle to express a theology of the cross which names things as they are and as they ought to be in the world without calling good evil and evil good, and who speak of a hope that does not ignore the reality of despair.[7]

What can account for this failure in Grant? Perhaps we can find the clue in several references Grant makes to Protestant theology where he is disturbed by its affirmation of the 'tradition of Jerusalem' to the neglect, if not rejection, of the 'tradition of Athens.'[8] This, of course, would be more true of Barth and Niebuhr than it would be of Tillich.[9] Yet is Grant's failure to see the truths expressed in Protestant theology as inspired by the tradition of Jerusalem any worse than the denigration of the tradition of Athens in Protestant theology? Through Weil and Sherrard, Grant came to see the truth in Plato as opposed to Aristotle, and the truth in Plato as distinguished from more popular forms of Platonism which were dualistic and anti-materialistic. Platonic ideas of the good, justice, and love were transcendent vis-à-vis the reality of the world, but also real and true in the soul only when appropriated through and realized in one's concrete commitments in the world. For both Weil and Grant, 'matter is our infallible judge.' Plato's allegory of the cave,[10] one that was pivotal for the thought of both Weil and Grant, relates how the soul is awakened by divine grace toward the good. It makes the painful journey (in the language of dying) out of the cave of shadows and illusions, which is the reality of life in the world, into the sunlight of the knowledge of and union with the good. But then this same soul is constrained by an inner necessity, also inspired by the good, to make the descent back into the cave to help open the eyes of those still bound by the chains of illusion and blindness. Liberation by the transcendent is not an end in itself, nor is it an escape from the world. Rather, its *telos* is an active commitment to participate in the liberation of the world, a world loved into being by the good. The apparent denigration of history by the Greeks has little to do with an aversion to things particular and material. The Greeks were more concerned about the temptation to treat history and the particular as absolute and final (idolatry), as opposed to perceiving in them a means through which one could access a deeper universal truth. Moreover, Weil and Grant were especially conscious of historical time and place, and their struggle in thought and practice was very contextual. Evidently they did not see any contradiction between their Platonism and their Christianity. Whether one can agree with them or not, one is at the least constrained to pause in wonder.

Grant's aversion to a theology that failed to appreciate the wisdom and truth of the Greeks was also compounded by his attitude toward the Old Testament. Here, the influence of Weil is also obvious. The criticism of Weil by Emmanuel Levinas in this regard can also be applied to Grant: namely, that Weil's interpretation of the Old Testament was based on its worst tendencies, while her interpretation of the Greeks was based on their best insights.[11] Even if this is true, it is also a criticism that may be levelled at much of Protestant theology, which has tended to the opposite extreme. It has too often interpreted Greek thought according to its worst tendencies (e.g., anti-materialistic, dualistic, otherworldly), rather than its more profound insights into reality divine and human. Indeed, can it not be said that traditions which have exercised such a profound influence on individuals and civilizations for so long may appear to be distant from one another on the surface level, and yet on the deepest level share a common ground? It is a gift to be opened to the truth through either one of our primal traditions in the West. But our choice for either one must not then lead us into thinking that the other, which we have not known and loved in the same way, is any less proximate to the truth. We must attribute to human limitation, rather than to the limitation of either tradition, our inability to appreciate the fullness of truth in them.

Whether one is inspired by the God who calls a particular people, a people whose grand failures and modest successes in history would be the divine means of redeeming the world, or the good which reveals the 'perfection' of love in the concrete matter of an afflicted world bound to tragic cycles and yearning for transcendent freedom, no one, and least of all one who lives in this world, can afford to discard either one of these foundational traditions. Indeed, as we have seen in Weil and in Luther, both traditions can be vehicles for arriving at the profound insights about reality, human and divine, consistent with that 'thin tradition' known as the theology of the cross. Open dialogue in the light of the 'realism' which is an indispensable mark of the theology of the cross, is our only hope as we move into a technological future which portends a tyranny of unprecedented proportions in the possibility of monstrous inhumanity toward human and non-human creation.

Notes

All the unpublished papers and lecture notes by Grant that I have cited in this work were found in his study at his home in Halifax. These unpublished materials are indicated in the Notes by the designation 'home.'

1: The Great Discovery

1 William Christian, *George Grant: A Biography* (Toronto: University of Toronto Press, 1994), 9.
2 Carl Berger, *The Sense of Power: Studies in the Canadian Ideas of Imperialism 1867–1914* (Toronto: University of Toronto Press, 1970), 36.
3 For a more complete account of G.M. Grant's life and thought, see William L. Grant and Frederick Hamilton, *Principal Grant* (Toronto: Morang & Co. Ltd, 1905).
4 Berger, 171.
5 Donald B. Mack, 'George Munro Grant: Evangelical Prophet' (Ph.D. diss., Queen's University, 1992), 73–6, 205.
6 A term used by A. Kojeve and L. Strauss, quoted frequently by Grant. See especially chapter 4 below.
7 Berger, 218.
8 David Cayley, *George Grant in Conversation* (Toronto: Anansi, 1995), 46; and *The Moving Image of Eternity* (Toronto: CBC, 1986), 4.
9 George Grant, 'Canadian Universities and the Protestant Churches' [1955], home, n. pag.
10 Grant, 'Canadian Universities.'
11 Christian, *Biography*, 23.
12 Christian, *Biography*, 7.
13 Christian, *Biography*, 29.

14 Christian, *Biography*, 30.
15 George Grant, *Selected Letters*, ed. William Christian (Toronto: University of Toronto Press, 1996), 36–7.
16 George Grant, rev. of *Grey of Fallodon*, by George M. Trevelyan, *Queen's University Journal*, 16 Nov. 1937, p. 3.
17 George Grant, rev. of *Searchlight on Spain*, by the Duchess of Atholl, *Queen's University Journal*, 11 Nov. 1938, p. 8.
18 George Grant, rev. of *The Higher Learning in America*, by Robert M. Hutchins, *Queen's University Journal*, 18 June 1938, p. 3.
19 George Grant, 'Art and Propaganda,' *Queen's University Journal, Literary Supplement*, March 1938, pp. 6–7.
20 Grant, *Letters*, 26.
21 Larry Schmidt, ed., *George Grant in Process: Essays and Conversations* (Toronto: Anansi, 1978), 62.
22 Christian, *Biography*, 62.
23 George Grant, 'George Grant and Religion: A Conversation Prepared and Edited by William Christian,' *Journal of Canadian Studies* 26, no. 1 (Spring 1991): 52, 60.
24 Christian, *Biography*, 64.
25 Christian, *Biography*, 62–8.
26 Grant, *Letters*, 70–1.
27 Grant, *Letters*, 75.
28 Grant, *Letters*, 88.
29 Christian, *Biography*, 81.
30 Grant, *Letters*, 91.
31 Christian, *Biography*, 84.
32 George Grant, 'The Owl and the Dynamo: The Vision of George Grant,' interview, *CBC-TV Arts, Music, and Science*, 13 Feb. 1980.
33 Cayley, *Moving Image*, 4; Schmidt, ed., *George Grant in Process*, 63.
34 Grant, *Letters*, 92.
35 Grant, *Letters*, 95.
36 Grant, *Letters*, 98, 100.
37 Grant, *Letters*, 85, 94.
38 Grant, *Letters*, 114.
39 Grant, *Letters*, 105. Grant was very moved by Tolstoy's short story 'God Sees the Truth but Waits.'
40 Grant, *Letters*, 107.
41 George Grant, *Canada – an Introduction to a Nation* (Toronto: Canadian Institute of International Affairs, 1943); *The Empire, Yes or No?* (Toronto: Ryerson Press, 1945); 'Have We a Canadian Nation?' *Public Affairs* 8, no. 3 (1945): 161–6.

42 Grant, *The Empire*, 15.
43 George Grant, 'Citizen's Forum,' column in *Food for Thought*, 1943–5.
44 George Grant, 'Integration through Education,' rev. of *The Universities Look for Unity*, by John U. Nef, *Food for Thought* 4, no. 1 (1943): 19–20.
45 George Grant, rev. of *The Machiavellians*, by James Burnham, *Food for Thought* 4, no. 3 (1943): 23.
46 George Grant, rev. of *The Philosophy of Francis Bacon*, by Fulton Anderson, *Dalhousie Review* 28, no. 3 (1948): 312–13.
47 George Grant, rev. of *The Pickersgill Letters: 1934–1943*, ed. George Ford, *Dalhousie Review* 28, no. 3 (1948): 313–14.
48 Grant, *Letters*, 116.
49 Grant, *Letters*, 121.
50 Grant, *Letters*, 119, 122.
51 Grant, *Letters*, 129.
52 Grant, *Letters*, 127, 135, 151.
53 Grant, *Letters*, 130.
54 Grant, *Letters*, 164.
55 Paul Tillich, *A History of Christian Thought: From Its Judaic and Hellenistic Origins to Existentialism* (New York: Simon and Schuster, 1967), 360–6.
56 Immanuel Kant, *Critique of Practical Reason*, trans. L.W. Beck (Indianapolis: Bobbs-Merrill Educational Publishing, 1956); W.T. Jones, *Kant and the Nineteenth Century* (New York: Harcourt Brace Jovanovich, 1975), 55–99.
57 An excellent example of this is found in the work of Albrecht Ritschl and his student Adolf von Harnack. See Hendrikus Berkhof, *Two Hundred Years of Theology: Report of a Personal Journey*, trans. J. Vriend (Grand Rapids, MI: William B. Eerdman's Publishing Company, 1989), 115–30; Adolph von Harnack, *What Is Christianity?* trans. T.B. Saunders (Philadelphia: Fortress Press, 1957).
58 Karl Barth, *The Epistle to the Romans*, trans. Edwyn C. Hoskyns (London: Oxford University Press, 1933).
59 Grant, *Letters*, 352; John Baillie, *Our Knowledge of God* (London: Oxford University Press, 1939); Donald M. Baillie, *God Was in Christ: An Essay on Incarnation and Atonement* (New York: Charles Scribner's Sons, 1948).
60 Austin Farrer, *Finite and Infinite: A Philosophical Essay* (New York: The Seabury Press, 1979).
61 Cayley, *Moving Image*, 4; Christian, *Biography*, 121.
62 Grant, *Letters*, 138.
63 Augustine of Hippo, *The City of God*, trans. G.G. Walsh et al. (New York: Image Books, 1958); *The Confessions of St. Augustine*, trans. R. Warner (Toronto: New American Library, 1963); 'The Trinity,' in *Augustine: Later*

Works, trans. J. Burnaby, Library of Christian Classics, vol. 8 (Philadelphia: Westminster Press, 1955), 37–181.

64 Charles N. Cochrane, *Christianity and Classical Culture: A Study of Thought and Action from Augustus to Augustine* (Oxford: Clarendon Press, 1940).

65 Grant, *Letters*, 126, 127.

66 Grant, *Letters*, 119, 125.

67 John Oman, *The Natural and the Supernatural* (Cambridge: Cambridge University Press, 1931).

68 George Grant, 'The Concept of Nature and Supernature in the Theology of John Oman' (D.Phil. thesis, Oxford, Balliol, 1950), 1, 11, 174.

69 Baillie, *Our Knowledge of God*, 189–98.

70 Grant, 'The Concept of Nature and Supernature,' 1.

71 Grant, 'The Concept of Nature and Supernature,' 193.

72 Grant, 'The Concept of Nature and Supernature,' 7, 196–8.

73 Grant, 'The Concept of Nature and Supernature,' 195.

74 John Oman, *The War and Its Issues: An Attempt at a Christian Judgement* (Cambridge: Cambridge University Press, 1915).

75 Grant, 'The Concept of Nature and Supernature,' 90, 205, 233.

76 Grant, 'The Concept of Nature and Supernature,' 8, 163, 167, 186–7.

77 Romans 8:28.

2: The Theology of the Cross

1 Walther von Loewenich, *Martin Luther: The Man and His Work*, trans. L.W. Denef (Minneapolis: Augsburg Publishing House, 1986), 72–90; Heiko A. Oberman, *Luther: Man between God and the Devil*, trans. E. Walliser-Schwarzbart (New York: Image Books Doubleday, 1989), 175–85.

2 Martin Luther, *Luther's Works*, vol. 31 (Saint Louis: Concordia Publishing House, 1958), 40; *D.M. Luther's Werke*, Kritische Gesamtausgabe, vol. 1 (Weimar: 1883–), 354.

3 Our discussion will follow, but not repeat, the excellent studies that have been done on Luther's theology of the cross by Walther von Loewenich and Alister McGrath.

4 Luther, *Works*, 31:10.

5 Luther *Works*, 31:40, 101.

6 Luther, *Works*, 34:336–7.

7 Luther, *Works*, 34:337. See also 25:30.

8 Luther, *Works*, 31:50–1, 55; 44:28.

9 Luther, *Works*, 32:40, 44.

10 Luther, *Werke*, 1:354, 362.
11 Luther, *Werke*, 1:613–14; *Works*, 17:131–2; 31:53, 225.
12 Luther, *Werke*, 18:663; *Works*, 33:62.
13 Luther, *Works*, 42:11; 35:243; Loewenich, *Luther*, 95.
14 Luther, *Works*, 34:336–7.
15 Luther, *Works*, 31:53; 33:62.
16 Luther, *Works*, 31:44; 42:72–4.
17 Luther, *Works*, 12:373–4; 7:175; 31:44, 101; 32:226; 35:252.
18 Luther, *Works*, 33.
19 Ian D.K. Siggins, *Martin Luther's Doctrine of Christ* (New Haven: Yale University Press, 1970), 80–1; Alister McGrath, *Luther's Theology of the Cross: Martin Luther's Theological Breakthrough* (Oxford: Basil Blackwell, 1985), 165–6.
20 Karl Holl, *What Did Luther Understand by Religion?* trans. F.W. Meuser and W.R. Wietzke (Philadelphia: Fortress Press, 1977), 58.
21 Luther, *Works*, 10:404; 22:306; Paul Althaus, *The Theology of Martin Luther*, trans. R.C. Schultz (Philadelphia: Fortress Press, 1966), 280–6; Loewenich, 38–49.
22 Eberhard Jungel, *The Freedom of a Christian: Luther's Significance for Contemporary Theology*, trans. R.A. Harrisville (Minneapolis: Augsburg Publishing House, 1988), 33–4; Regin Prenter, *Luther's Theology of the Cross* (Philadelphia: Fortress Press, 1971), 4; Burnell F. Eckardt, Jr, 'Luther and Moltmann: The Theology of the Cross,' *Concordia Theological Quarterly* 49 (1985): 20.
23 Luther, *Works*, 31:53; 42:8–9.
24 Luther, *Works*, 26:276ff; 42:8ff. See also Althaus, 203–8. Different metaphors have been used to express the same reality. For example: distance, judgment/crisis (Dillenberger and Barth); absence (Jungel, Weil, Grant); forsakenness, wrath, hiddenness (Luther).
25 Luther, *Werke*, 45:370ff.
26 See Gustaf Aulen, *Christus Victor: An Historical Study of the Three Main Types of the Idea of the Atonement*, trans. A.G. Herbert (London: S.P.C.K., 1961), 117–38; Burnell F. Eckardt, Jr, *Anselm and Luther on the Atonement: Was It 'Necessary'?* (San Francisco: Mellen Research University Press, 1992), 6; Althaus, 202–23.
27 Luther, *Works*, 42:8–13.
28 Luther, *Works*, 51:19; 31:128–9, 351–2. See also Dietmar Lage, *Martin Luther's Christology and Ethics* (New York: Edwin Mellen Press, 1990), 75ff; Bengt R. Hoffmann, *Luther and the Mystics* (Minneapolis: Augsburg Publishing House, 1976), 15–16. There is a deep connection in Luther to mysticism

through the themes of humiliation, suffering, the hiddenness of God, and faith as union with Christ.

29 Luther, *Works*, 31:53.
30 Luther, *Works*, 31:44.
31 Luther, *Works*, 35:370–1.
32 Luther, *Works*, 33:64; 42:50; 44:23, 28; 25:383.
33 Luther, *Works*, 21:340.
34 Luther, *Works*, 31:129.
35 Luther, *Works*, 44:28–30.
36 Luther, *Works*, 35:242, 369; 14:84; 31:348–50.
37 Luther, *Works*, 35:370–1.
38 Luther, *Works*, 31:350; 44:241–2; 35:370; 25:382. See also Loewenich, *Martin Luther*, 95.
39 Luther, *Works*, 31:366–71.
40 Luther, *Works*, 31:57–8.
41 Luther, *Works*, 42:107–8.
42 Luther, *Werke*, 1:128–9.
43 Luther, *Werke*, 7:784ff; Luther, *Works*, 42:183–6; 44:28. See also Walther von Loewenich, *Luther's Theology of the Cross*, trans. Herbert J.A. Bouman (Minneapolis: Augsburg Publishing house, 1976), 134–9; McGrath, *Luther's Theology*, 169–75.
44 Luther, *Works*, 31:39; 33:203.
45 Luther, *Works*, 30:110.
46 Luther, *Works*, 42:48–9, 71–4.
47 Holl, 28. This word was coined by the German mystics, who influenced the young Luther. Simone Weil's term 'decreation' is synonymous. See further in section 3.4.2 below.
48 George Grant, 'Two Theological Languages,' in *Two Theological Languages by George Grant and Other Essays in Honour of His Work*, ed. Wayne Whillier (Queenston: Edwin Mellen Press, 1990), 7–15.
49 George Grant, 'Philosophy and Religion,' in *The Great Ideas Today 1961* (Chicago: Encyclopaedia Britannica, 1961), 370.
50 This is true of all twentieth-century Protestant theologians who have defined or been influenced by neo-orthodox theology, and it is certainly true of Barth, Brunner, and Niebuhr, whom Grant mentions.
51 George Grant, 'Acceptance and Rebellion' [1956], home, n. pag.
52 'Lutheran' here is taken to be an adherence to Luther rather than to Lutheran Protestantism as a whole.
53 George Grant, 'Addendum,' in *Two Theological Languages by George Grant*, 17.

3: Philosophy in the Mass Age

1 George Grant, *Selected Letters*, ed. William Christian (Toronto: University of Toronto Press, 1996), 181, 182.
2 George Grant, 'The Modern World' [1953], home, n. pag.
3 George Grant, 'The Minds of Men in the Atomic Age,' in *Texts of Addresses Delivered at the Twenty-Fourth Annual Couchiching Conference* (Toronto: Canadian Institute on Public Affairs and Canadian Broadcasting Federation, 1955), 39–45.
4 George Grant, 'An Ethic of Community,' in *Social Purpose in Canada*, ed. Michael Oliver (Toronto: University of Toronto Press, 1961), 3–26; see also *Philosophy in the Mass Age* (Toronto: Copp Clark, 1959), 4.
5 George Grant, 'The Uses of Freedom – a Word and Our World,' *Queen's Quarterly* 62, no. 4 (1956): 515–27.
6 A.S.P. Woodhouse, *Puritanism and Liberty* (London: J.M. Dent, 1938), 13–100.
7 Max Weber, *The Protestant Ethic and the Spirit of Capitalism*, trans. T. Parsons (London: George Allen & Unwin, 1930), 103, 119.
8 Grant, 'The Uses of Freedom,' 518.
9 Simone Weil, *Intimations of Christianity among the Ancient Greeks* (1957; London: Ark Paperbacks, 1987), 184.
10 Simone Weil, *Oppression and Liberty*, trans. Arthur Wills (London: Routledge & Kegan Paul, 1958), 83.
11 Weil, *Oppression*, 108–22.
12 Simone Weil, *The Notebooks of Simone Weil*, trans. Arthur Wills, 2 vols (London: Routledge & Kegan Paul, 1956), 596 and 552; also cited in *Gravity and Grace*, trans. Emma Craufurd (London: Routledge & Kegan Paul, 1952), 155.
13 Simone Weil, *La Source grecque* (Paris: Librairie Gallimard, 1953), 11–42; *Intimations*, 24–55; *First and Last Notebooks*, trans. Richard Rees (London: Oxford University Press, 1970), 14.
14 Weil, *Intimations*, 35.
15 Weil, *Intimations*, 54.
16 Simone Weil, *Waiting for God*, trans. Emma Craufurd (London: Collins, 1951), 76–93; *On Science, Necessity and the Love of God*, trans. and ed. Richard Rees (London: Oxford University Press, 1968), 170–98.
17 Simone Weil, *Attente de Die* (Paris: La Colombe, 1950), 124ff; *Notebooks*, 3; *Les Cahiers Simone Weil*, 3 vols (Paris: Librairie Plon, 1952–5), 1:94–6.
18 Weil, *Waiting for God*, 77.
19 Weil, *On Science*, 175; *Notebooks*, 603, 235.
20 Weil, *On Science*, 172–4.

21 Weil, *On Science*, 175.
22 George Grant, 'Plato and Popper,' *Canadian Journal of Economics and Political Science* 20, no. 2 (1954): 185–94; 'Philosophy and Adult Education,' *Food for Thought* 14, no. 1 (1953): 4–5.
23 George Grant, 'Jean-Paul Sartre,' in *Architects of Modern Thought* (Toronto: Canadian Broadcasting Corporation, 1955), 65; 'Philosophy and Religion,' in *The Great Ideas Today 1961* (Chicago: Encyclopaedia Britannica, 1961), 358–9.
24 Grant, 'Jean-Paul Sartre,' 71–2; 'Acceptance and Rebellion' [1956], home, n. pag.
25 Grant, 'Jean-Paul Sartre,' 74.
26 George Grant, 'Philosophy,' in *Royal Commission Studies: A Selection of Essays Prepared for the Royal Commission on National Development in the Arts, Letters and Sciences* (Ottawa: Edmond Cloutier, Printer to the King, 1951), 122; 'Speech on Education at Teacher's Institute' [1954], home, n. pag.
27 Fulton Anderson, Introduction, *Philosophy in Canada: A Symposium*, ed. John A. Irving (Toronto: University of Toronto Press, 1952), 3–4. See also *William Christian, George Grant: A Biography* (Toronto: University of Toronto Press, 1994), 154.
28 Grant, *Letters*, 175.
29 George Grant, 'In Pursuit of an Illusion: A Commentary on Bertrand Russell,' *Dalhousie Review* 32, no. 2 (1952): 103.
30 Grant, 'Plato and Popper,' 185, 187.
31 Grant, 'Plato and Popper,' 194.
32 Grant, 'The Minds of Men,' 43–5.
33 Grant, 'Philosophy,' 126; 'Canadian Universities,' rev. of *Henry Marshal Tory*, by E.A. Corbett, *Canadian Forum* 34, no. 403 (1954): 112–13.
34 Grant, 'Acceptance and Rebellion.' See also G.F. Hegel, *Philosophy of History*, trans. J. Sibree (London: Colonial Press, 1900), 412–57.
35 Grant, 'The Uses of Freedom,' 518ff.
36 Grant, 'The Uses of Freedom,' 522.
37 Grant, 'The Uses of Freedom,' 525.
38 George Grant, 'Conceptions of Health,' in *Psychiatry and Responsibility*, ed. Helmut Schoeck and James W. Wiggins (Princeton: D. Van Nostrand, 1962), 117, 118.
39 George Grant, 'Carl Justav Jung,' in *Architects of Modern Thought*, Fifth and Sixth Series, Twelve Talks for CBC Radio (Toronto: Canadian Broadcasting Corporation, 1962), 64–74.
40 Grant, 'Conceptions,' 130.

41 Grant, 'Conceptions,' 134; 'Adult Education in the Expanding Economy,' *Food for Thought* 15, no. 1 (1954): 10.

42 Grant, *Letters*, 194; comments on Hegel from Notebooks 1, 4 [1956–8], home, n. pag.

43 Grant, 'Acceptance and Rebellion.'

44 Grant, 'Philosophy,' 56.

45 Grant, 'Philosophy,' 68–72.

46 Grant, 'Philosophy,' 119.

47 Grant, 'Philosophy,' 119–33.

48 George Grant, 'What Is Philosophy' [1954], home, n. pag. In the later 1950s, Michael Foster's book *Mystery and Philosophy* (London: SCM Press, 1957) became important to Grant in relating mystery to Greek philosophy and biblical religion. See especially 31–50, 87–94.

49 Grant, 'What Is Philosophy.'

50 George Grant, 'The Teaching Profession in an Expanding Economy' [1955], home, n. pag.

51 Grant, 'Acceptance and Rebellion,' 425.

52 The good and God are interchangeable terms for Weil, Plato, and Grant.

53 Weil, *Notebooks*, 230, 266.

54 Weil, *Intimations*, 74; *Notebooks*, 505, 542; *The Need for Roots: Prelude to a Declaration of Duties towards Mankind*, trans. A.F. Wills (Boston: The Beacon Press, 1952), 262; *Selected Essays, 1934–1943*, trans. R. Rees (London: Oxford University Press, 1962), 35–54.

55 Weil, *Waiting for God*, 34, 114; *Notebooks*, 436; *The Need for Roots*, 262.

56 Weil, *Intimations*, 184; *Waiting for God*, 118.

57 Weil, *Intimations*,185ff; *Notebooks*, 254; *The Need for Roots*, 288.

58 Weil, *Waiting for God*, 87.

59 Weil, *Intimations*, 3.

60 Weil, *Waiting for God*, 113–34; *Intimations*, 184–94.

61 Weil, *The Need for Roots*, 288.

62 Weil, *Waiting for God*, 98ff.

63 Weil, *Intimations*, 175; *Selected Essays*, 27.

64 Weil, *Waiting for God*, 33, 66–76; Simone Petrement, *Simone Weil: A Life*, trans. R. Rosenthal (New York: Pantheon Books, 1976), 243–7.

65 Weil, *Waiting for God*, 96–7, 100.

66 Weil, *Intimations*, 86–7; *First and Last Notebooks*, 130.

67 Weil, *Notebooks*, 233, 258; *Gravity and Grace*, 132–4.

68 Weil, *Waiting for God*, 144.

69 Weil, *Gravity and Grace*, 104; *Notebooks*, 432.

70 Weil, *Gravity and Grace*, 29; *Notebooks*, 193; *Selected Essays*, 27.

71 Weil, *Gravity and Grace*, 28; *Notebooks*, 342.
72 Weil, *Notebooks*, 463.
73 Weil, *First and Last Notebooks*, 152.
74 Weil, *Waiting for God*, 84–6.
75 Weil, *Gravity and Grace*, 23; *Notebooks*, 342.
76 Weil, *On Science*, 184.
77 Weil, *Gravity and Grace*, 24; *Notebooks*, 343.
78 Weil, *Gravity and Grace*, 10.
79 Weil, *Waiting for God*, 51.
80 Hebrews 11:1; Isaiah 45:15; *Notebooks*, 149, 195, 219; *First and Last Notebooks*, 161; *Intimations*, 198–9; *Gravity and Grace*, 16–17.
81 Weil, *On Science*, 196–7. See also *Waiting for God*, 20; *Intimations*, 3, 5.
82 Weil, *On Science*, 154–9; *Intimations*, 198–9.
83 Weil, *Waiting for God*, 35, 55; *Notebooks*, 255.
84 Weil, *Gravity and Grace*, 116; *Notebooks*, 240.
85 Weil, *First and Last Notebooks*, 262–3; *Intimations*, 1–8.
86 Weil, *Gravity and Grace*, 150. See also *Oppression and Liberty*, 78, 143.
87 Weil, *Gravity and Grace*, 151; *Notebooks*, 466–7; *First and Last Notebooks*, 17.
88 George Grant, notes on Simone Weil's *Notebooks* [1958–60], home, n. pag; notes on Simone Weil in Notebook 1 [1956–7], home, n. pag.
89 George Grant, 'Some Comments on Weil and the Neurotic and the Alienated' [early 1960s], home, n. pag.
90 George Grant 'The Rite of Holy Communion,' sermon at McMaster University, Hamilton [early 1960's], home, n. pag.
91 Grant, 'The Rite.' See also '*Qui Tollit*,' sermon at McMaster University, Hamilton [early 1960s], home, n. pag; 'Conversation between Pilate and Jesus,' sermon at McMaster University, Hamilton [early 1960s], home, n. pag.
92 Grant, 'Acceptance and Rebellion.'
93 Grant, 'Acceptance and Rebellion.'
94 Grant, *Letters*, 178.
95 George Grant, 'Good Friday,' *United Church Observer* 14, no. 3 (1952): 3. See also Sheila Grant, 'George Grant and the Theology of the Cross,' in *George Grant and the Subversion of Modernity: Art, Philosophy, Politics, Religion, and Education*, ed. Arthur Davis (Toronto: University of Toronto Press, 1996), 248–9.
96 George Grant, lecture notes on philosophy and theology [1959], home, n. pag.
97 Grant, lecture notes on philosophy and theology.
98 Grant, lecture notes on philosophy and theology.

99 George Grant, 'Fyodor Dostoevsky,' in *Architects of Modern Thought*, Third and Fourth Series, Twelve Talks for CBC Radio (Toronto: Canadian Broadcasting Corporation, 1959), 76–7, 83.
100 George Grant, 'Faith and the Multiversity,' *The Compass: A Provincial Review* 4 (1978): 4.
101 Grant, 'The Modern World'; 'The Minds of Men,' 45.
102 Grant, 'An Ethic of Community,' 16–20.
103 Grant, 'An Ethic of Community,' 26.
104 George Grant, 'The Paradox of Democratic Education,' *The Bulletin* 35, no. 6 (1955): 275.
105 Grant, 'The Paradox,' 279.
106 Grant, 'Adult Education,' 9.
107 Grant, 'Philosophy and Adult Education,' 6–8.
108 Grant, *Philosophy in the Mass Age*, 1.
109 Grant, *Philosophy in the Mass Age*, 11–13.
110 Grant, *Philosophy in the Mass Age*, 20.
111 Grant, *Philosophy in the Mass Age*, 29.
112 Grant, *Philosophy in the Mass Age*, 39.
113 What Grant has in mind here is the Western interpretation of Christianity, although he will make the distinction between Western and Eastern interpretations more explicit in the 1960s.
114 Grant, *Philosophy in the Mass Age*, 46.
115 Grant, *Philosophy in the Mass Age*, 76.
116 Grant, *Philosophy in the Mass Age*, 82–90.
117 Grant, *Philosophy in the Mass Age*, 91–7.
118 Grant, *Philosophy in the Mass Age*, 111.
119 Joan O'Donovan, in *By Loving Our Own: George Grant and the Legacy of 'Lament for a Nation,'* ed. Peter Emberley (Ottawa: Carleton University Press, 1990), 137.
120 George Grant, Introduction, *Philosophy in the Mass Age* (Toronto: University of Toronto Press, 1966), 117–22.
121 This is O'Donovan's term in *George Grant and the Twilight of Justice* (Toronto: University of Toronto Press, 1984).

4: Intimations of Deprivation

1 George Grant, Introduction, *Philosophy in the Mass Age* (Toronto: University of Toronto Press, 1966), 117–22.
2 George Grant, rev. of *The Technological Society*, by Jacques Ellul, *Canadian Dimension* 3, nos. 3–4 (1966): 60.

3 Jacques Ellul, *The Technological Society*, trans. J. Wilkinson (New York: Random House, 1964), xxv.
4 Ellul, 429.
5 Ellul, 28–60.
6 Grant, in *George Grant in Process: Essays and Conversations*, ed. Larry Schmidt (Toronto: Anansi, 1978), 145–7; rev. of *The Technological Society*, 60.
7 Leo Strauss, *What Is Political Philosophy and Other Studies* (Glencoe, IL: Free Press of Glencoe, 1959), 11–20.
8 Strauss, *What Is Political Philosophy*, 27–39. See also, *Thoughts on Machiavelli* (Glencoe, IL: Free Press of Glencoe, 1958), 11.
9 Strauss, *What Is Political Philosophy*, 44, 170–220; *Thoughts on Machiavelli*, 174–273.
10 Strauss, *What Is Political Philosophy*, 50–2; *Natural Right and History* (Chicago: University of Chicago Press, 1963), 252–91.
11 Strauss, *Thoughts on Machiavelli*, 294–9.
12 George Grant, 'Tyranny and Wisdom,' in *Technology and Empire: Perspectives on North America* (Toronto: Anansi, 1969), 82ff.
13 Grant, 'Tyranny and Wisdom,' 103.
14 Grant, 'Tyranny and Wisdom,' 105–9.
15 Strauss, *Natural Right and History*, 150–62; Grant, in *George Grant in Process*, 64–5; Zdravko Planinc, 'Paradox and Polyphony in Grant's Critique of Modernity,' in *George Grant and the Future of Canada* (Calgary: University of Calgary Press, 1992), 34.
16 Philip Sherrard, *The Greek East and the Latin West: A Study in the Christian Tradition* (London: Oxford University Press, 1959), v–vi.
17 Sherrard, 5–20.
18 Sherrard, 73–110.
19 George Grant, *Selected Letters*, ed. William Christian (Toronto: University of Toronto Press, 1996), 201–3.
20 George Grant, 'Philosophy and Religion,' in *The Great Ideas Today 1961* (Chicago: Encyclopaedia Britannica, 1961); William Christian, *George Grant: A Biography* (Toronto: University of Toronto Press, 1994), 208–9.
21 Grant, *Letters*, 207–8.
22 Grant, 'What Kind of Life Is the Best Life?' *Hamilton Spectator*, 19 March 1966, p. 16; 'The Clever Young Are Just Filled with Questions,' *Hamilton Spectator*, 26 March 1966, p. 16.
23 George Grant, 'The Academic Study of Religion in Canada,' in *Scholarship in Canada, 1967: Achievement and Outlook*, ed. R.H. Hubbard (Toronto: University of Toronto Press, 1968), 59.
24 Grant, 'Academic Study,' 61.

25 George Grant, 'Religion and the State,' in *Technology and Empire*, 57.

26 Grant, rev. of *The Predicament of Democratic Man*, by Edmond Cahn, *University of Toronto Law Journal* 15, no. 4 (1964): 461–3.

27 George Grant, 'The University Curriculum,' in *Technology and Empire*, 113.

28 Grant, 'The University Curriculum,' 122.

29 Grant, 'The University Curriculum,' 131.

30 Grant, 'The University Curriculum,' 133.

31 Grant, *Technology and Empire*, 44.

32 George Grant, 'Value and Technology,' in *Conference Proceedings: Welfare Services in a Changing Technology* (Ottawa: Canadian Conference on Social Welfare, 1964), 28, 29.

33 George Grant, rev. of *Christianity and Revolution: The Lesson of Cuba*, by Leslie Dewart, *Canadian Forum* 43, no. 518 (1964): 282.

34 Grant, rev. of *Christianity and Revolution*, 283.

35 For example, see Grant, *Letters*, 220, 229.

36 George Grant, rev. of *The Secular City*, by Harvey Cox, *The United Church Observer* 28, no. 9 (1966): 16.

37 Grant, rev. of *The Secular City*, 17.

38 Grant, rev. of *The Secular City*, 26.

39 Douglas John Hall, *Thinking the Faith: Christian Theology in a North American Context* (Minneapolis: Augsburg Press, 1989), 349–67.

40 Grant, *Letters*, 243; Christian, *Biography*, 245.

41 George Perlin, *The Tory Syndrome* (Montreal: McGill-Queen's University Press, 1980), 63–72.

42 George Grant, *Lament for a Nation: The Defeat of Canadian Nationalism* (Toronto: McClelland and Stewart, 1965), 4.

43 In David Cayley, *The Moving Image of Eternity* (Toronto: CBC, 1986), 2; *Letters*, 214–15; 'Diefenbaker: A Democrat in Theory and Soul,' *Globe and Mail*, 23 Aug. 1979, p. 7.

44 Grant, *Letters*, 222.

45 Grant, *Lament*, 3.

46 Grant, *Lament*, 5–6.

47 Grant, *Lament*, 54.

48 Grant, *Lament*, 89.

49 Grant, *Lament*, 89–90.

50 Grant, *Lament*, 94.

51 Carl Berger, *The Sense of Power: Studies in the Canadian Ideas of Imperialism 1867–1914* (Toronto: University of Toronto Press, 1970), 265.

52 Ramsey Cook, 'Loyalism, Technology and Canada's Fate,' *Journal of Canadian Studies* 5 (1970): 50–60; R.K. Crook, 'Modernization and Nostalgia:

A Note on the Sociology of Pessimism,' *Queen's Quarterly* 73 (1966): 269–84.

53 Arthur Kroker, *Technology and the Canadian Mind: Innes / McLuhan / Grant* (Montreal: New World Perspectives, 1984), 26.

54 Gad Horowitz, 'Red Tory' [1965], home, 260 [publication source unknown].

55 Horowitz, 'RedTory'; Mel Hurtig, 'One Last Chance: The Legacy of *Lament for a Nation*,' in *By Loving Our Own: George Grant and the Legacy of 'Lament for A Nation*,' ed. Peter Emberley (Ottawa: Carleton University Press, 1990), 44–9; W.L. Morton, 'The Possibility of a Philosophy of Conservatism,' *Journal of Canadian Studies* 5 (1970): 3–14.

56 Cayley, *The Moving Image*, 3; Christian, *Biography*, 254–5.

57 George Grant, 'An interview with George Grant,' with Larry Schmidt, *Grail* 1 (1985): 36; *Letters*, 244, 247.

58 George Grant, 'Introduction,' *Lament for a Nation: The Defeat of Canadian Nationalism*, The Carleton Library, no. 50 (1970; rpt. Ottawa: Carleton University Press, 1991), xii.

59 Grant, *Lament*, 97.

60 George Grant, 'From Roosevelt to LBJ,' in *The New Romans: Candid Canadian Opinions of the U.S.*, ed. A.W. Purdy (Edmonton: M.G. Hurtig; New York: St Martin's Press, 1968), 41.

61 Grant, *Letters*, 240.

62 George Grant, 'The Value of Protest' [1966], home, n. pag.

63 George Grant, 'Critique of the New Left,' *Our Generation* 3, no. 4 to 4, no. 1 (1966): 47.

64 Grant, 'Critique of the New Left,' 50–1.

65 George Grant, 'Comments on the Great Society from the Thirty-fifth Annual Couchiching Conference,' in *Great Societies and Quiet Revolutions*, ed. John Irwin (Toronto: Canadian Broadcasting Corporation, 1967), 71.

66 Grant, 'Comments on the Great Society,' 75.

67 George Grant, 'Canadian Fate and Imperialism,' in *Technology and Empire*, 63.

68 Grant, 'Canadian Fate,' 70–1.

69 Christian, *Biography*, 251.

70 Grant, 'Canadian Fate,' 78.

71 George Grant, 'Simone Weil: An Introduction' [1963], home, n. pag.

72 George Grant, 'Religion' [1967], home, n. pag.

73 George Grant, 'Horowitz and Grant Talk,' *Canadian Dimension* 6, no. 6 (Dec. 1969–Jan. 1970): 19.

74 On the importance of limits for a theology of the cross, see Douglas J. Hall,

Lighten Our Darkness: Towards an Indigenous Theology of the Cross (Philadelphia: Westminster Press, 1976), 213ff.
75 Grant, *Letters*, 230.
76 Grant, *Letters*, 232.
77 George Grant, 'In Defence of North America,' in *Technology and Empire*, 20.
78 Grant, 'In Defence,' 35.
79 Grant, 'In Defence,' 36.
80 Grant, 'A Platitude,' in *Technology and Empire*, 137.
81 Grant, 'A Platitude,' 143.
82 Grant, *Letters*, 283; Sheila Grant, 'George Grant and the Theology of the Cross,' in *George Grant and the Subversion of Modernity: Art, Philosophy, Politics, Religion, and Education*, ed. Arthur Davis (Toronto: University of Toronto Press, 1996), 256.
83 Reinhold Niebuhr, *Justice and Mercy* (Louisville, KY: Westminster / John Knox Press, 1974), i.
84 The elements of the hiddenness of beauty or love, on the one hand, and the purity of love expressed positively, on the other, are revealed most fully in the crucified Christ.
85 Philip J. Hanson, 'George Grant: A Negative Theologian on Technology,' *Research on Technology and Philosophy* 1 (1987): 307–8; Frank K. Flinn, 'George Grant's Three Languages,' *Chesterton Review* 11, no. 2 (1985): 159.
86 Dennis Duffy, 'Ancestral Journeys: Travels with George Grant,' with French summary, *Journal of Canadian Studies* 22, no. 3 (1987): 97.
87 David R. and Edwin B. Heaven, 'Some Influences of Simone Weil on George Grant's Silence,' in *George Grant in Process: Essays and Conversations*, ed. Larry Schmidt (Toronto: Anansi, 1978), 68–77; E. Mandel, 'George Grant: Language, Nation, the Silence of God,' *Canadian Literature* 83 (1979): 172–3.

5: Faith and Justice in the Technological Era

1 George Grant, *Time As History*, Massey Lectures, ninth series (Toronto: Canadian Broadcasting Corporation, 1969); Martin Heidegger, *An Introduction to Metaphysics*, trans. R. Manheim (New Haven: Yale University Press, 1959), 38, 84.
2 Grant, *Time As History*, 10–13.
3 Grant, *Time As History*, 21–2.
4 Grant, *Time As History*, 29–30; Friedrich Nietzsche, 'The Gay Science,' in *The Portable Nietzsche*, ed. and trans. W. Kaufmann (New York: Penguin Books, 1954), 95.

5 Friedrich Nietzsche, *Beyond Good and Evil*, trans. R.J. Hollingdale (Middlesex: Penguin Books, 1973), 14.
6 Friedrich Nietzsche, *Thus Spoke Zarathustra*, trans. R.J. Hollingdale (Middlesex: Penguin Books, 1961), 84–5, 136, 139, 214.
7 Grant, *Time As History*, 29; Nietzsche, *The Portable Nietzsche*, 95–6; Martin Heidegger, 'The Word of Nietzsche: "God Is Dead,"' in *Question concerning Technology and Other Essays*, trans. William Lovitt (New York: Garland Publishing Inc., 1977), 59–60.
8 Friedrich Nietzsche, *On the Genealogy of Morals*, trans. W. Kaufmann and R.J. Hollingdale (New York: Vintage Books, 1969), 96,163.
9 Grant, *Time As History*, 33–5.
10 Nietzsche, *Thus Spoke Zarathustra*, 42, 109; *On the Genealogy of Morals*, 96.
11 Grant, *Time As History*, 36–43; Nietzsche, *Beyond Good and Evil*, 71; *Thus Spoke Zarathustra*, 216, 237.
12 Grant, *Time As History*, 46.
13 Nietzsche, *On the Genealogy of Morals*, 92.
14 Grant, *Time As History*, 52.
15 George Grant, 'Revolution and Tradition,' in *Tradition and Revolution*, ed. L. Rubinoff (Toronto: Macmillan in association with York University, 1971), 82.
16 Grant, 'Revolution and Tradition,' 94–5.
17 William Christian, 'George Grant's Nietzsche,' in *Time As History*, by George Grant (Toronto: University of Toronto Press, 1995), xix–xxxi.
18 Nietzsche, *Thus Spoke Zarathustra*, 124–5; *Beyond Good and Evil*, 13, 58, 71, 106–7; *On the Genealogy of Morals*, 54; *The Will to Power*, trans. W. Kaufmann (New York: Vintage Books, 1968), 55.
19 Christian, 'George Grant's Nietzsche,' xxix–xxxi.
20 Martin Heidegger, *Nietzsche*, trans. David F. Krell, 4 vols (San Francisco: Harper Collins Publishers, 1991).
21 *George Grant in Process: Essays and Conversations*, ed. Larry Schmidt (Toronto: Anansi, 1978), 67; George Grant, rev. of *Nietzsche's View of Socrates*, by Werner J. Dannhauser, *American Political Science Review* 71, no. 3 (1977): 1127–9.
22 Ronald Beiner, 'George Grant, Nietzsche, and the Problem of a Post-Christian Theism,' in *George Grant and the Subversion of Modernity: Art, Philosophy, Politics, Religion, and Education*, ed. Arthur Davis (Toronto: University of Toronto Press, 1996), 110.
23 David Cayley, *George Grant in Conversation* (Toronto: Anansi, 1995), 90; *The Moving Image of Eternity* (Toronto: CBC, 1986), 16. See also 'The Beautiful Itself,' lecture on Plato's Symposium [1970s], home, n. pag; 'Confronting

Heidegger's Nietzsche' [1970s–'80s], home, n. pag. Heidegger confirms and supports this Nietzschean perspective. See his *Nietzsche*, 1:151–209.

24 George Grant, rev. of *Science, God and Nature in Victorian Canada*, by Carl Berger, *Saturday Night* 99, no. 3 (1984): 66; *George Grant in Process*, 145; Heidegger, *Nietzsche*, 3:137–49.

25 George Grant, 'Nietzsche and the Ancients,' in *Technology and Justice* (Toronto: Anansi, 1986), 91; *George Grant in Process*, 145.

26 George Grant, 'Justice and Technology,' in *Theology and Technology: Essays in Christian Analysis and Exegesis*, ed. C. Mitcham and J. Grote (Lanham, MD: University Press of America, 1984), 243–4; Plato, *Gorgias*, trans. W.C. Helmbold (Indianapolis: Bobbs-Merrill Educational Publishing, 1952); Heidegger, *Nietzsche*, 4:168–73.

27 George Grant, 'George Grant and Religion: A Conversation Prepared and Edited by William Christian,' *Journal of Canadian Studies* 26, no. 1 (Spring 1991): 53.

28 George Grant, 'Notes on Good and Technique' [1976], home, n. pag.

29 Laurence Lampert, 'Zarathustra and George Grant: Two Teachers,' *Dalhousie Review* 58 (1978): 456.

30 George Grant, *Selected Letters*, ed. William Christian (Toronto: University of Toronto Press, 1996), 363.

31 Louis-Ferdinand Céline, *Castle to Castle*, trans. R. Manheim (New York: Delacorte Press, 1968); *North*, trans. R. Manheim (New York: Delacorte Press, 1972); *Rigadoon*, trans. R. Manheim (New York: Delacorte Press, 1974). Grant's most developed expression of appreciation for Céline's work is a lengthy essay which he never had published during his lifetime. It was published posthumously in a recent collection of essays on his thought under the title 'Céline's Trilogy' (*George Grant and the Subversion of Modernity*, 13–52).

32 Grant, 'Céline's Trilogy,' 16; Céline, Interview, in *Castle to Castle*, v; *Rigadoon*, 257.

33 George Grant, 'Céline: Art and Politics,' *Queen's Quarterly* 90, no.3 (1983): 806, 812.

34 Grant, 'Céline's Trilogy,' 14, 25.

35 Céline, Interview, in *Castle to Castle*, xii.

36 Grant, 'Céline's Trilogy,' 43.

37 Grant, 'Céline's Trilogy,' 51–2; *Letters*, 378.

38 George Grant, '"The computer does not impose on us the ways it should be used,"' in *Beyond Industrial Growth*, ed. Abraham Rotstein (Toronto: University of Toronto Press, 1976), 128.

39 George Grant, 'Knowing and Making,' *Transactions of the Royal Society of*

Canada, ser. 4, 12 (1975): 63; Cayley, *George Grant in Conversation*, 133–4. See also Heidegger, *Question concerning Technology*, 3–35.

40 Grant, 'Knowing and Making,' 61, 65–7.
41 Grant, '"The computer,"' 118, 119.
42 Grant, '"The computer,"' 129–30.
43 George Grant, 'Thinking about Technology,' in *Technology and Justice*, 11, 18–34. See also Heidegger, *An Introduction to Metaphysics*, 37.
44 Grant, '"The Computer,"' 128,130.
45 Cayley, *George Grant in Conversation*, 379.
46 Grant, *Letters*, 285, 296.
47 George Grant, *English-Speaking Justice* (Toronto: Anansi, 1974), 5–12.
48 John Rawls, *A Theory of Justice* (Cambridge: Harvard University Press, 1971).
49 Grant, *English-Speaking Justice*, 13–23; Rawls, 118ff, 136–42.
50 Grant, *English-Speaking Justice*, 32.
51 Grant, *English-Speaking Justice*, 34–47.
52 Grant, *English-Speaking Justice*, 48–63.
53 Grant, *English-Speaking Justice*, 69.
54 George Grant, 'Abortion and Rights,' in *Technology and Justice*, 117–30.
55 Grant, *English-Speaking Justice*, 77–80; 'The Language of Euthanasia,' in *Technology and Justice*, 109–12.
56 Grant, 'Abortion and Rights,' 119.
57 George Grant, 'The Case against Abortion' *Today Magazine*, 3 Oct. 1981, pp. 12–13; Cayley, *George Grant in Conversation*, 156; *The Moving Image*, 2.
58 Grant, 'Abortion and Rights,' 128–9.
59 George Grant, 'Commentary Script on Abortion' [1988], home, n. pag.
60 George and Sheila Grant, 'Sacrifice and the Sanctity of Life,' in *New Life: Addressing Change in the Church*, ed. K.M. Haslett et al. (Toronto: Anglican Book Centre, 1989), 83–4. See also 'Kill the Retarded? Cause for Despair,' *Globe and Mail*, 30 July 1977, n. pag.
61 Grant, 'The Language of Euthanasia,' 112–15.
62 'Liberal' and 'Conservative' have little to do with official political party policy.
63 William Christian, *George Grant: A Biography* (Toronto: University of Toronto Press, 1994), 288–9; George Grant, 'Nationalism and Rationality,' in *Power Corrupted: The October Crisis and the Repression of Quebec*, ed. Abraham Rotstein (Toronto: New Press, 1971), 51–5; 'Inconsistency Ruled in Canada's 70s,' *Globe and Mail*, 31 Dec. 1979, p. 7; dinner speech presented on 28 June 1977 in Toronto, in *Grant and Lamontagne on National Unity* (Toronto: Cemasco Management Ltd, for Constellation Life Assurance Company of Canada, 1977), 5–9.

64 George Grant, 'Lament for a Nation Revisited: An Interview with George Grant,' with Monica V. Halil, *International Insights: A Dalhousie Journal on International Affairs* 4, no. 1 (1988): 7; rev. of *If You Love This Country: Facts and Feelings on Free Trade*, ed. L. Lapierre, *Books in Canada* 17, no. 1 (1988): 19; 'Diefenbaker: A Democrat in Theory and Soul,' *Globe and Mail*, 23 Aug. 1979, p. 7; rev. of *Benjamin Disraeli: The Early Letters, Volumes I and II*, ed. J.A.W. Gunn et al., *Globe and Mail*, 8 May 1982, p. E15.

65 George Grant, 'Ideology in Modern Empires,' in *Perspectives of Empire: Essays Presented to Gerald S. Graham*, ed. J.E. Flint and G. Williams (London: Longman; New York: Barnes and Noble, 1973), 191, 196–7.

66 George Grant, 'An Interview with George Grant,' with Larry Schmidt, *Grail* 1 (1985): 39–40; 'Lament for a Nation Revisited,' 8.

67 George Grant, 'The Battle between Teaching and Research,' *Globe and Mail*, 28 April 1980, p. 7; 'Research in the Humanities,' in *Technology and Justice*, 97–102.

68 George Grant, rev. of *The Gladstone Diaries, Volumes III and IV*, ed. M.R.D. Foot and H.C.G. Matthew, *Globe and Mail*, 20 Sept. 1975, p. 35; letter under the caption 'St. John's Visions,' *Globe and Mail*, 3 Dec. 1983; p. 7; 'The Beautiful Itself.'

69 George Grant, 'Notebook for Class on Simone Weil' [1976], home, n. pag; 'Justice and Technology,' 244.

70 George Grant, 'The Beautiful and the Good,' lecture notes on Plato from Notebook E [1970s], home, n. pag.

71 Grant, 'The Beautiful and the Good'; 'The Beautiful Itself.'

72 Grant, 'Justice and Technology,' 244.

73 George Grant, 'Acceptance and Rebellion' [1956–7], home, n. pag.

74 Grant, 'Justice and Technology,' 237.

75 George Grant, 'Addendum,' in *Two Theological Languages by George Grant and Other Essays in Honour of His Work*, ed. Wayne Whillier (Queenston: Edwin Mellen Press, 1990), 16.

76 Peter Self, 'George Grant: Unique Canadian Philosopher,' *Queen's Quarterly* 98, no. 1 (1991): 37.

77 Grant, *Two Theological Languages*, 19.

78 Grant, 'Notebook for Class on Simone Weil.'

79 Grant, 'George Grant and Religion,' 58.

80 George Grant, rev. of *The First Torturer's Trial 1975*, by Amnesty International, *Globe and Mail*, 11 June 1977, p. 41; 'Dennis Lee – Poetry and Philosophy,' in *Tasks of Passion: Dennis Lee in Mid-Career*, ed. K. Mulhallen et al. (Toronto: Descant, 1982), 234.

81 Here Grant has in mind classical Protestantism as expressed in the

Reformation and particularly the theology of the cross as formulated by Luther.

82 Grant, *Letters*, 352; Cayley, *George Grant in Conversation*, 176.

83 George Grant, 'In Defence of Simone Weil,' in *Best Canadian Essays 1989*, ed. D. Fetherling (Saskatoon: Fifth House Publishers, 1989), 167–72; 'Notebook for Class on Simone Weil.'

84 Grant, 'Notebook for Class on Simone Weil.'

85 George Grant, 'Five Lectures on Christianity,' from Notebook A [1976], home, n. pag; lecture notes from course on revelation theology (Augustine) 4F6 [1973–4], home, n. pag. See also Sheila Grant, 'George Grant and the Theology of the Cross,' in *George Grant and the Subversion of Modernity*, 247.

86 Grant, 'Five Lectures,' 8–10; 'Interview,' with Larry Schmidt, 47; 'Notebook for Class on Simone Weil'; 'In Defence of Simone Weil,' 168; Cayley, *The Moving Image*, 26; *George Grant in Process*, 102–3.

87 Grant, 'Interview,' with Larry Schmidt, 42; 'Notebook for Class on Simone Weil'; Cayley, *The Moving Image*, 25.

88 Grant, 'The Beautiful Itself'; 'Notebook for Class on Simone Weil.'

89 George Grant, 'Obedience,' *The Idler* 29 (1990): 25; Cayley, *George Grant in Conversation*, 177.

90 Cayley, *George Grant in Conversation*, 177; Grant, 'Obedience,' 28; 'Notes on Good and Technique.'

91 Grant, 'George Grant and Religion,' 56; 'Five Lectures.'

92 Grant, 'Notebook for Class on Simone Weil.'

93 Grant, 'Five Lectures'; 'Notebook for Class on Simone Weil.'

94 Grant, 'Notebook for Class on Simone Weil.'

95 Grant, *Letters*, 361; 'Notebook for Class on Simone Weil.'

96 George Grant, 'Jelte Kuipers – an Appreciation,' *The Silhouette* [McMaster University], 2 Oct. 1970, p. 6.

97 Grant, 'George Grant and Religion,' 42.

98 Grant, 'Faith and the Multiversity,' in *Technology and Justice*, 38; Simone Weil, *Gravity and Grace*, trans. Emma Craufurd (London: Routledge & Kegan Paul, 1952), 116; *The Notebooks of Simone Weil*, trans. Arthur Wills (London: Routledge & Kegan Paul, 1956), 240.

99 Grant, 'Faith and the Multiversity,' 3; *George Grant in Process*, 107.

100 Grant, *Technology and Justice*, 42.

101 Grant, *Technology and Justice*, 44.

102 Grant, *Technology and Justice*, 46–9.

103 Grant, *Technology and Justice*, 54.

104 Grant, *Technology and Justice*, 55.

105 Grant, *Technology and Justice*, 55–60.
106 Grant, *Technology and Justice*, 69.
107 Grant, *Technology and Justice*, 70.
108 Grant, *Technology and Justice*, 75.
109 Douglas John Hall, *Thinking the Faith: Christian Theology in a North American Context* (Minneapolis: Augsburg, 1989), 349–67.
110 Grant, *Technology and Justice*, 76–7.

Conclusion

1 David Cayley, 'George Grant 1918–1988,' *Books in Canada*, Nov. 1988, n. pag.
2 See Barry Cooper, 'George Grant and the Revival of Political Philosophy,' in *By Loving Our Own: George Grant and the Legacy of 'Lament for a Nation,'* ed. Peter Emberley (Ottawa: Carleton University Press, 1990), 117–18; Zdravko Planinc, 'Paradox and Polyphony in Grant's Critique of Modernity,' in *George Grant and the Future of Canada*, ed. Yusuf K. Umar (Calgary: University of Calgary Press, 1992), 17–45. See also Schmidt's counter criticism in *George Grant and the Subversion of Modernity: Art, Philosophy, Politics, Religion, and Education*, ed. Arthur Davis (Toronto: University of Toronto Press, 1996), 265, 276.
3 For example, Bruce Ward, in *Two Theological Languages by George Grant and Other Essays in Honour of His Work*, ed. Wayne Whillier (Queenston: Edwin Mellen Press, 1990), 102.
4 Bernard Zylstra and Zdravko Planinc make this criticism of Grant. See Bernard Zylstra, 'Philosophy, Revelation and Modernity: Crossroads in the Thought of George Grant,' in *George Grant in Process: Essays and Conversations*, ed. Larry Schmidt (Toronto: Anansi, 1978), 148–56; Planinc, *George Grant and the Future of Canada*, 17–45.
5 Douglas John Hall, *Lighten Our Darkness: Towards an Indigenous Theology of the Cross* (Philadelphia: Westminster Press, 1976), 204, 213, 220; 'Toward an Indigenous Theology of the Cross,' in *Theology and Technology: Essays in Christian Analysis and Exegesis*, ed. C. Mitcham and J. Grote (Lanham, MD: University Press of America, 1984), 259, 262, 265.
6 Hall, in *George Grant in Process*, 126–7. See also *Confessing the Faith: Christian Theology in a North American Context* (Minneapolis: Fortress Press, 1996).
7 Hall, *Confessing the Faith*, 453–69.
8 Grant, *Two Theological Languages*, 6–17; *Selected Letters*, ed. William Christian (Toronto: University of Toronto Press, 1996), 209.

9 Tillich's Platonism is well documented throughout his writing. Barth also has great respect for the tradition of Athens, although it is clearly subservient to the truth of the tradition of Jerusalem in his thought. Niebuhr, on his part, is more directly critical of the tradition of Athens. See Reinhold Niebuhr, *The Nature and Destiny of Man: A Christian Interpretation, Volume I. Human Nature* (New York: Charles Scribner's Sons, 1941), 4–12; and *Faith and History: A Comparison of Christian and Modern Views of History* (New York: Charles Scribner's Sons, 1949), 55–69. See also Hall, *Confessing the Faith*, 483–97.

10 Plato, *Great Dialogues of Plato*, trans. W.H.D. Rouse (New York: New American Library, 1956), 312ff.

11 Emmanuel Levinas, 'Simone Weil against the Bible,' in *Difficult Freedom: Essays on Judaism*, trans. Sean Hand (London: The Athlone Press, 1990), 133–41.

Index

pioneers, pioneering 58, 71, 111, 172, 207

Plato 4, 13, 25, 27, 31, 50, 52, 72–4, 78, 82, 84, 86–90, 92, 101, 104, 108–9, 113–14, 119, 123, 125, 133–7, 146, 149–50, 160, 168, 170–2, 176–7, 179–82, 185, 189, 192–5, 202, 207, 219–25, 228, 230, 232–5, 237, 239–40, 244, 246–7, 249–50

Popper, Karl 72–4

positivism 72, 140

pragmatism 13, 72–5

prayer 59, 71, 77

predestination (or election) 39, 59–60

Presbyterianism 8, 11, 27–8

progress (belief in, doctrine/religion of) 7, 10, 13–15, 18, 20–1, 24, 28–31, 48, 56, 65, 68, 79, 82–3, 87, 107, 111, 113–17, 120, 123, 126, 130, 132, 133, 141–4, 146, 148–9, 151, 154–9, 164–6, 173, 183–7, 189–91, 198, 206, 208, 213, 217, 248

Protestantism 7, 10, 23–4, 50–2, 59–61, 72, 75–7, 80, 103, 111, 117, 146–7, 150, 160, 168, 170, 172–5, 177, 179, 207, 240, 247–50, 271n81

providence: divine 7, 10, 13, 18, 22, 28, 49, 59–60, 62, 65, 82–3, 88–9, 101, 103, 115–17, 120, 123, 133, 146, 149, 155–6, 159, 169, 224, 229–30, 235, 240, 245, 248; particular 59–60, 229

Psalms 33

psychotherapy 78–80

purification (spiritual or divine) 38, 84, 95, 103, 167–8, 178, 222, 227, 241

Puritanism 9, 23, 28, 59–61, 76, 108, 116–17, 133, 172, 177, 220. See also Calvinism

Pythagoreans 90

Quebec 154, 214–15

Queen's University 8, 11–13, 75

rational theology 23–5, 28, 50–3, 69, 87. See also natural theology

Rawls, John 204–6

reason 23–5, 34–7, 50, 53, 72, 77, 79, 82, 86–7, 109, 113–14, 123, 127, 132, 135–7, 149, 169, 171, 174, 177–8, 199, 205, 216, 219–20, 222, 224–5; instrumental or technical 73, 75, 110, 112, 114, 126, 173, 193, 205, 222

Reformation 33, 47, 75–6, 81, 83, 87, 108, 115, 172, 223, 226, 271n81

repentance 19, 29–30, 79, 133, 227

restraint(s) 8, 10, 21, 29–30, 138, 147–8, 154, 158, 163, 167–8, 170, 172, 174, 184–5, 188, 208, 210, 236

resurrection 41, 104, 137, 176, 228

revelation (divine) 24–8, 34, 37, 39, 40–2, 48, 52–3, 67, 78, 88–9, 92–4, 96, 98, 100, 104–5, 127, 132, 134, 136–7, 140, 143–4, 146, 149, 169, 172, 174–5, 177–9, 189, 195, 202, 219, 221–2, 225, 228, 230–1, 234–8, 240, 247, 251

Rhodes Scholarship 13

rights (human or individual) 194, 204–6, 208–12, 218–20

Roman Catholicism 116, 146, 168, 240

Rome 88, 102, 110, 117, 134–5, 228

Rousseau, Jean-Jacques 128–9, 133, 148, 206, 208

Russell, Bertrand 72–3

Russia 15, 19

saint(s) 101, 152, 159, 171, 179, 190, 197, 221–2, 234, 246

sanctity 35, 43, 100, 221–2, 228

Sanders, E.P. 216

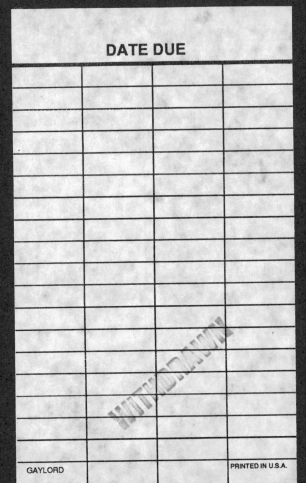